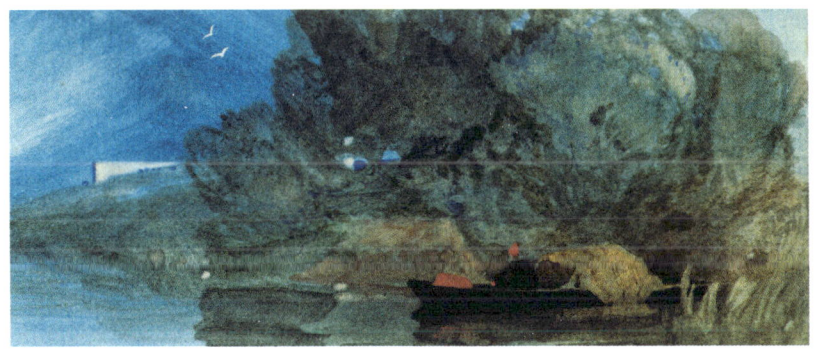

IMPRESSIONS IN WATERCOLOUR

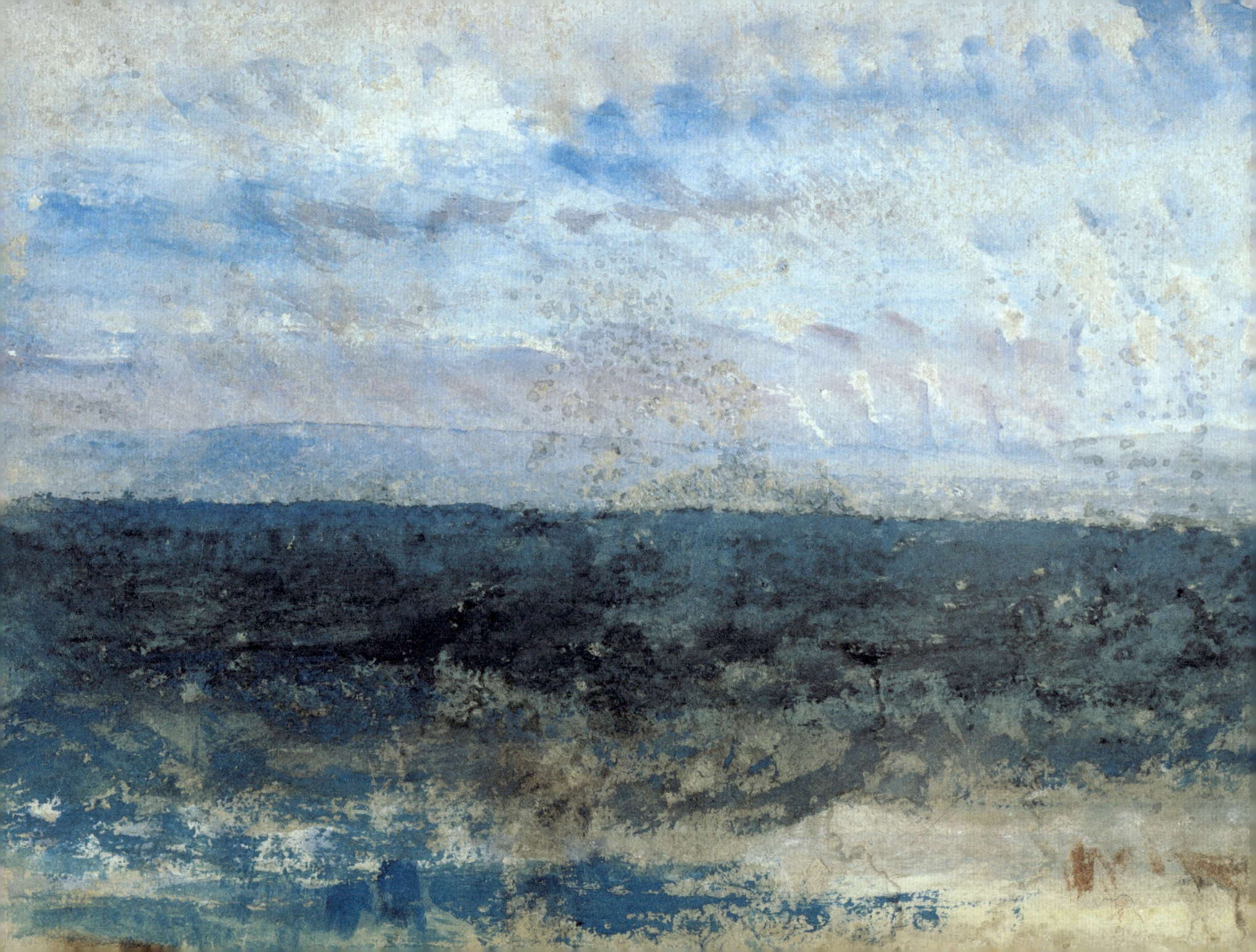

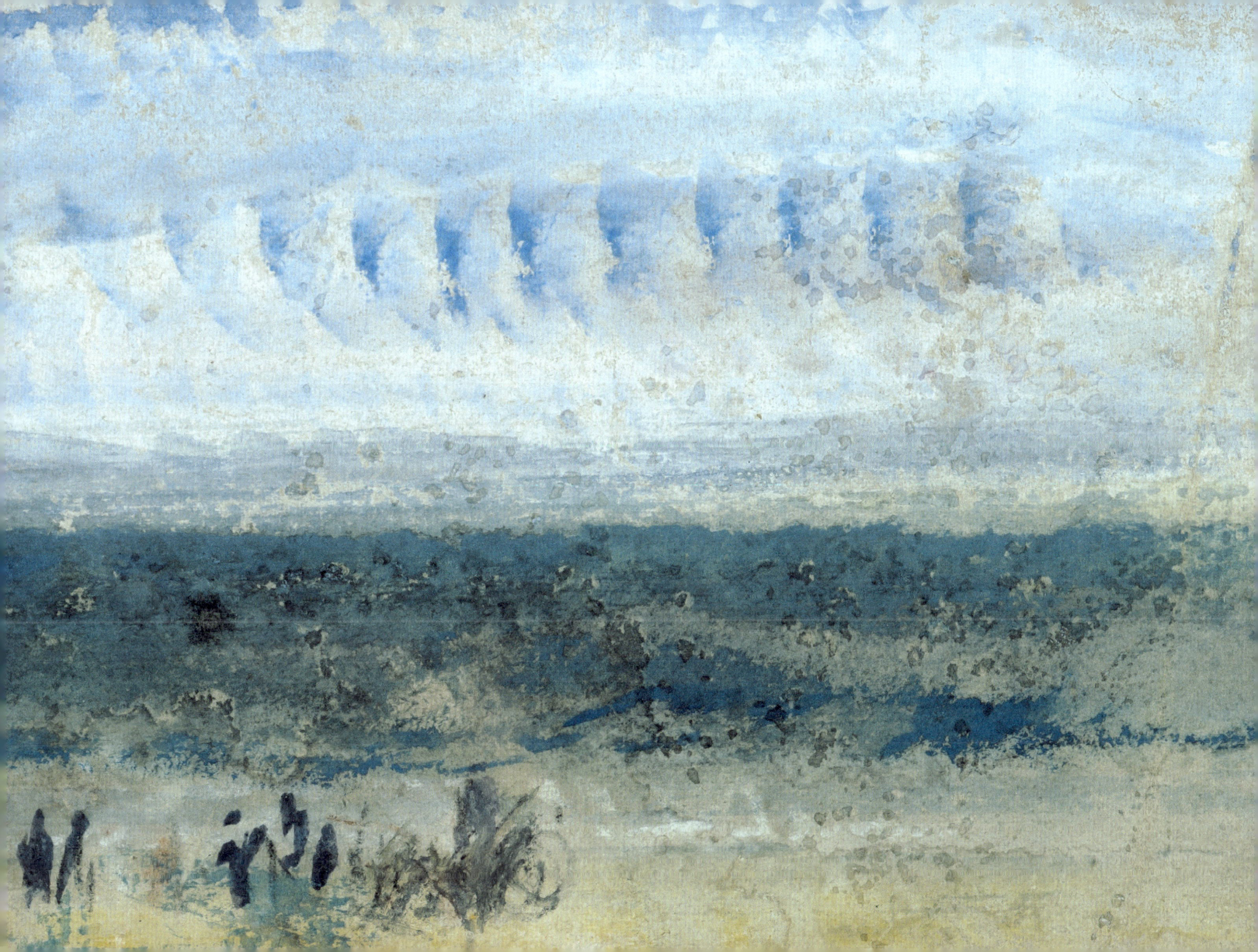

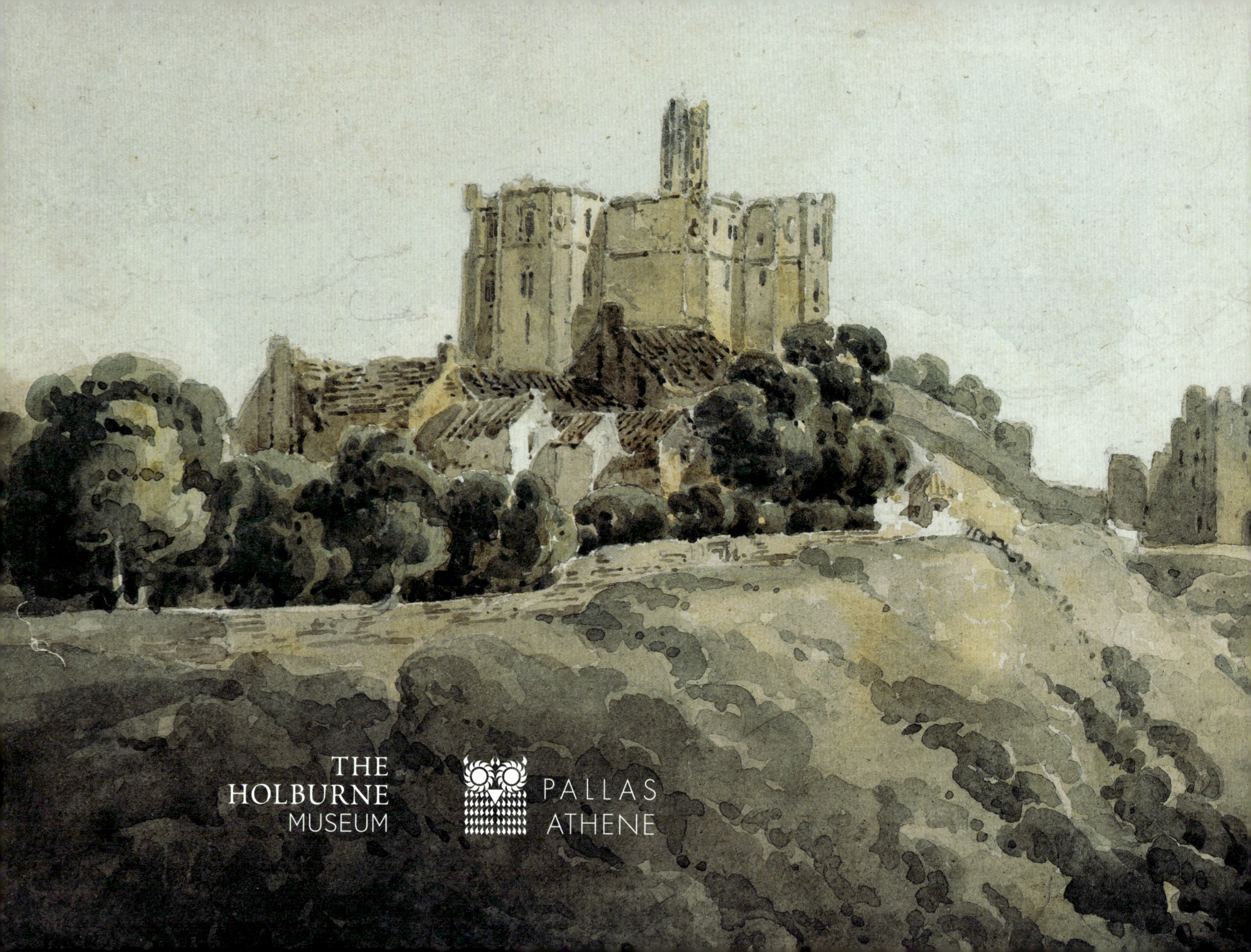

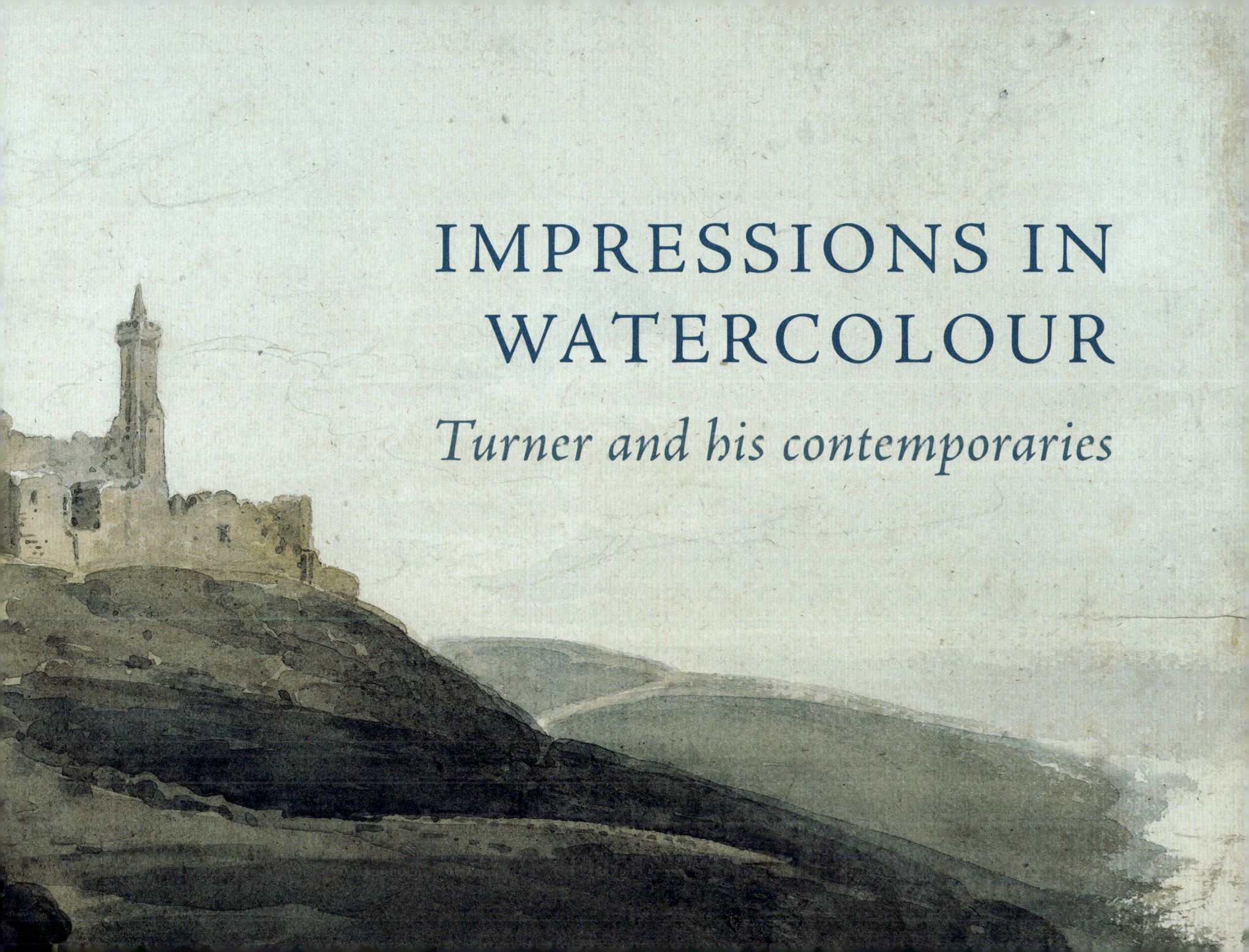

IMPRESSIONS IN WATERCOLOUR

Turner and his contemporaries

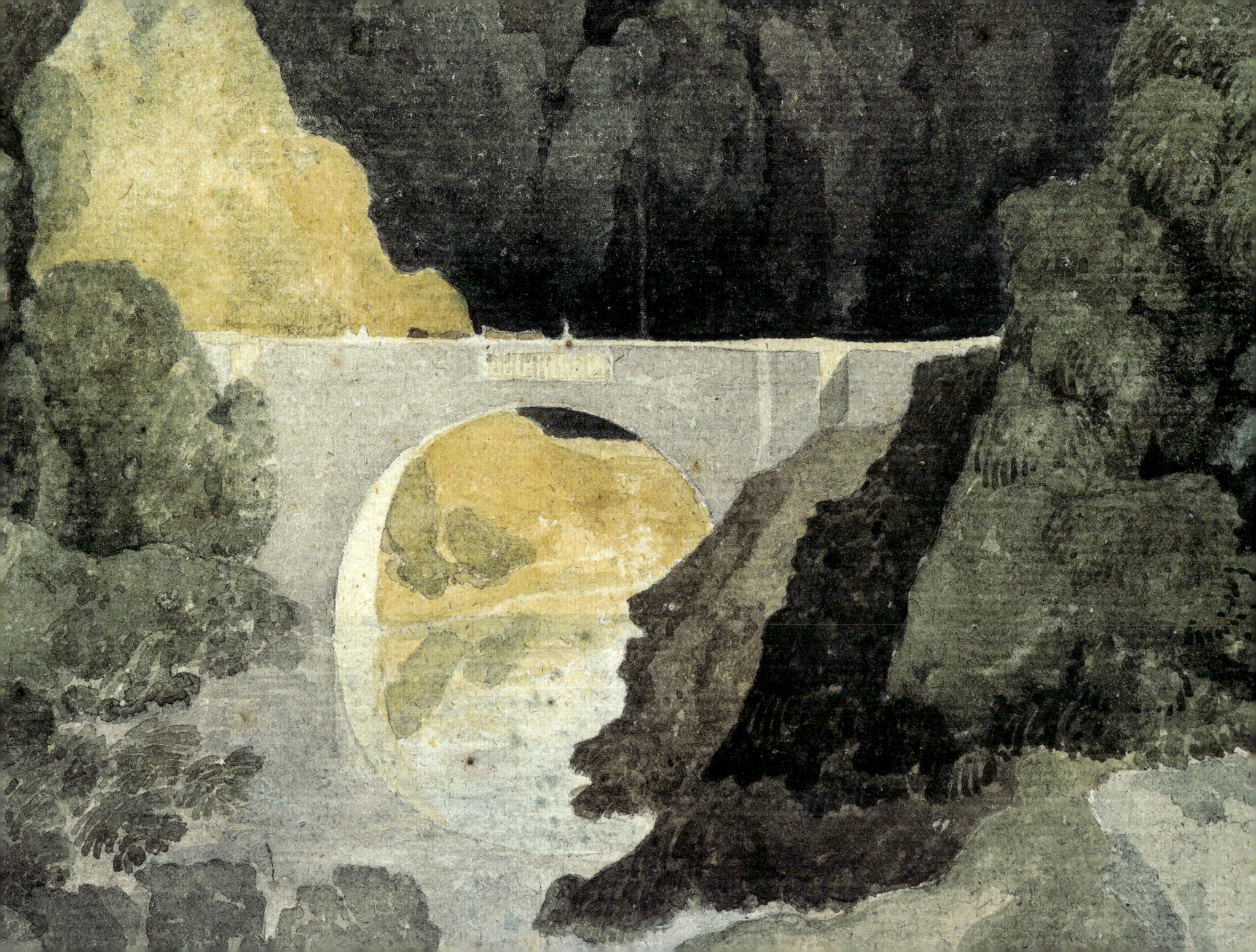

Director's Foreword

Chris Stephens

I HAVE BEEN IN LOVE with the work of John Sell Cotman ever since my first term at university where, amongst the small selection of postcards on my new girlfriend's shelf, was his *Crambe Beck Bridge*. Ignorant of the artist, I could not believe the work had been made in 1805; it seemed so modern in its stark, simple clarity. As a modernist by instinct, my understanding of artistic progress was fundamentally challenged by that one work made during the reign of George III. One can't help but wonder whether Hickman Bacon might have shared similar thoughts. Buying English watercolours during the 1890s and 1900s, he assembled an extraordinary collection in which a significant number of works seem to betray taste formed in the wake of the innovations of the Impressionists and their followers. Nowhere is that more evident than in the extraordinary sequence of seascapes by Turner which are so sublime in their simple beauty.

I am delighted that, when I started a conversation with my old friend and colleague Ian Warrell about how the Holburne might mark J. M. W. Turner's 250th anniversary, he suggested we seek to exhibit a selection from the Hickman Bacon Collection. I am grateful to Ian for that idea and for fulfilling the difficult task of selecting around sixty works from a collection of hundreds. No one could be better qualified to do so. I am, of course, also deeply thankful to the current guardians of the Hickman Bacon Collection who did not hesitate to agree their support for our proposal. As well as Ian, I must thank Timothy Wilcox for his contribution to this publication and Alexander Fyjis-Walker at Pallas Athene for its design and production. At the Holburne, I am especially grateful to Nina Harrison-Leins and Eleanor Hutchison for sensitively managing both exhibition and catalogue. We are delighted that the exhibition will also be seen at the Towner in Eastbourne, and I must thank Joe Hill and Sara Cooper for their generous cooperation.

At once Modern and Romantic, the works in this book demonstrate the deep continuities that underlie a history that sometimes seems to be made up of a sequence of revolutions. Just as the artists of the Romantic period found security in nature and landscape at a time of seismic change, so we might find something reassuringly constant in these images of nature made with such unimaginable skill and sensitivity.

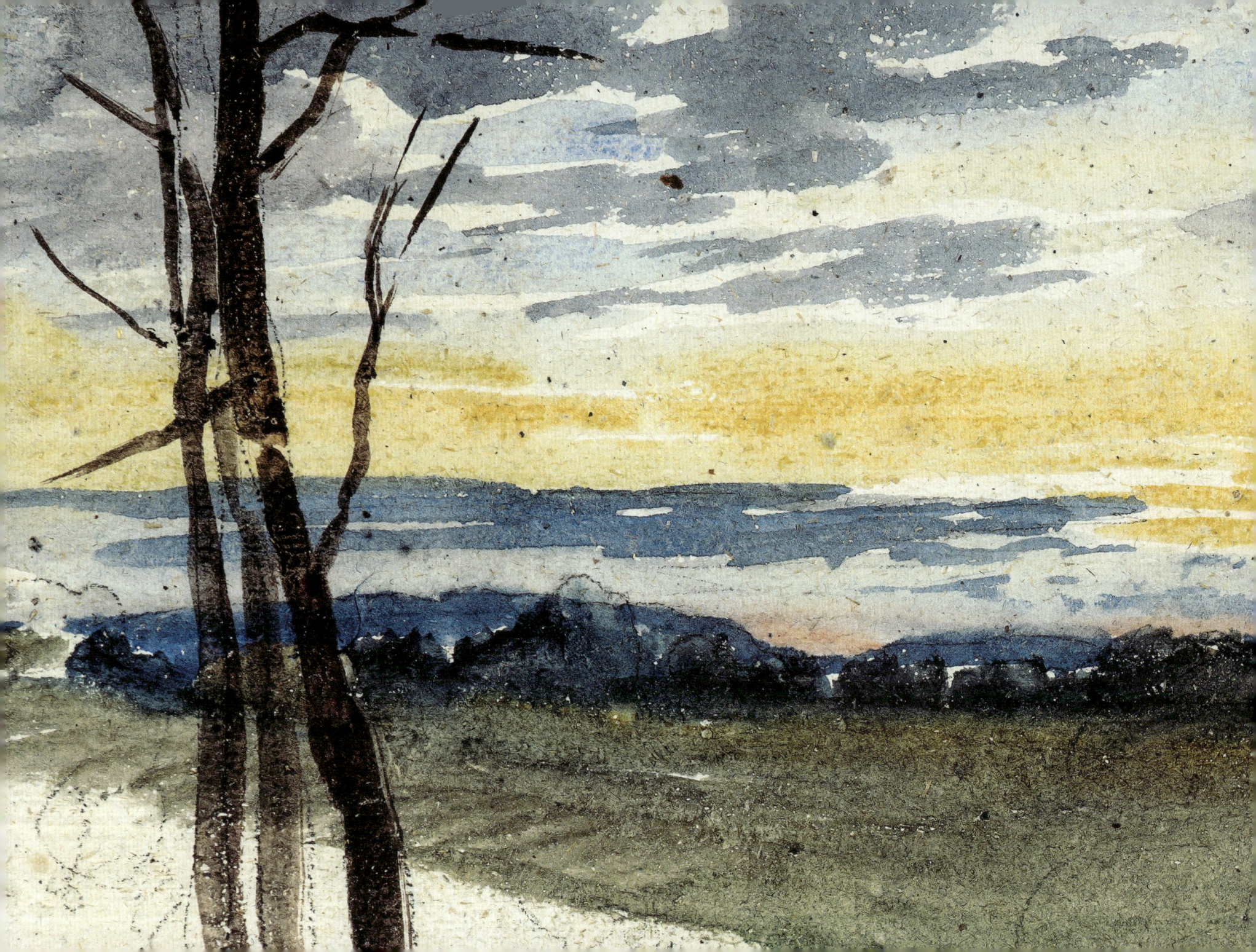

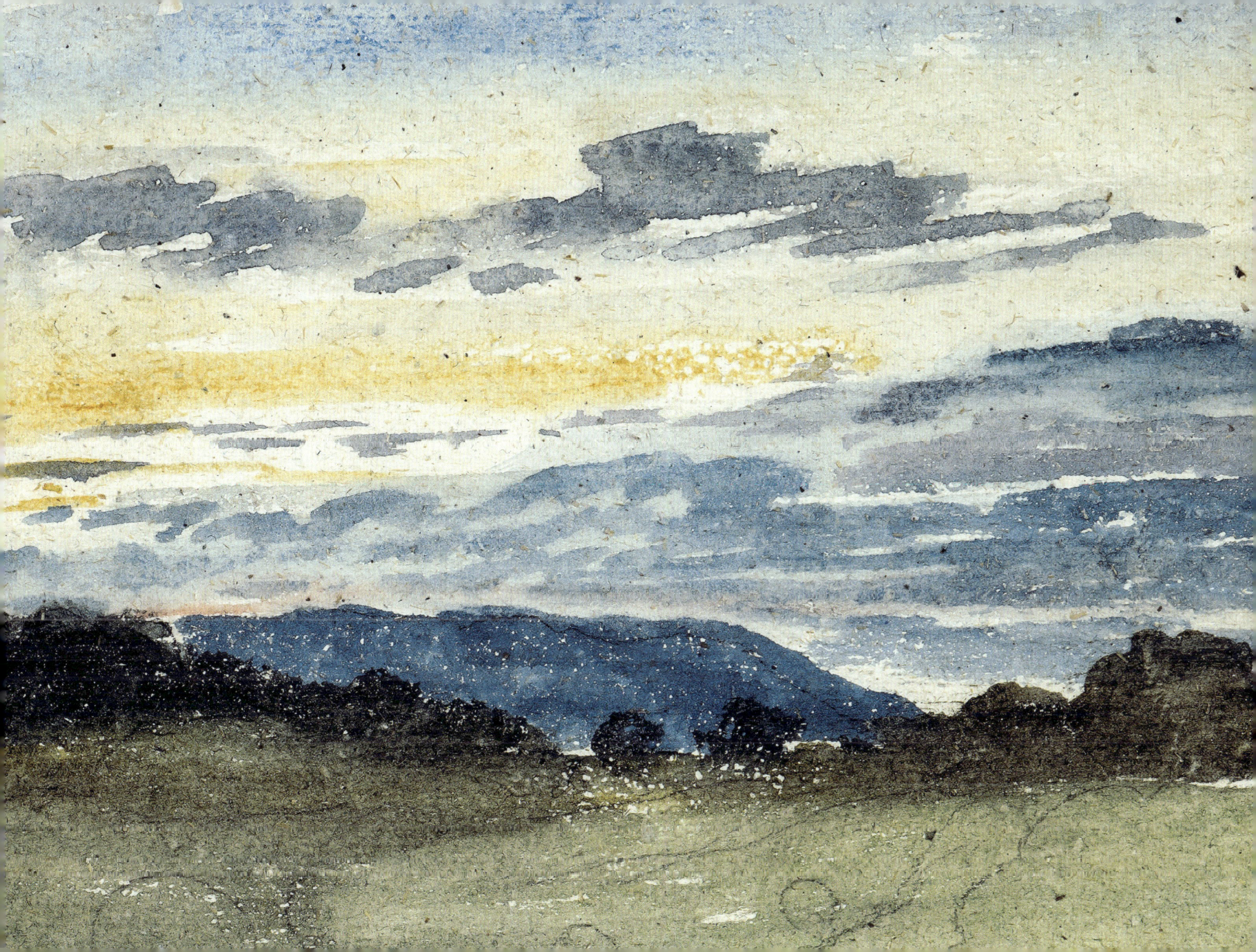

Nature Raw or Cooked: Approaches to Sketching in British Landscape Watercolours

Ian Warrell

IN THE HISTORY OF BRITISH ART the practice of sketching in watercolours has its origins several centuries ago.[1] But it was in the period between the late eighteenth and the middle of the nineteenth centuries, at the moment when landscape as a genre acquired a new appeal and gravitas, that sketching became a widely established process in itself. For that generation, and those that followed, the act of travelling and recording nature in both its delicate specificity and its sublime grandeur acquired the status of a mission. The exciting burst of creativity in the medium of watercolour unleashed in these years was quickly claimed as a national achievement. Many accounts even proposed that watercolour painting was a uniquely British invention.[2]

As late as the mid-1930s it was possible for the satirist Pont (the professional name of Graham Laidler) to include 'The Gift for Water-Colours' among his series of clichéd tendencies that defined The British Character (fig. 1), along with a 'Keen interest in the Weather', 'Enthusiasm for Gardening', 'Horsiness', and the 'Importance of Tea'. Pont's image coincidentally anticipates Nikolaus Pevsner's claims in his 1955 Reith lectures on 'The Englishness of English Art' of the nation's reverence for watercolours as a trait unmatched anywhere else.[3] But Pont's caricature also provides a useful summary of how established perceptions of the traditions of British watercolour had by then ossified to suggest its limitations. Here the artist exhibits a narrow preoccupation with a picturesque setting; there is the possibility that the practitioner is an amateur artist, coupled, furthermore, with the not-so-subtle implication in the age of thrusting modernity that here was an art form in which women might prevail. Affectionate mockery this may be, but it diminishes and strips away the fervour and limitless potential that was inherent at the beginning of the nineteenth century when the artists featured in this book were at work.

Back in the early 1800s it was only in recent decades that watercolours had been framed for exhibition. But watercolour artists increasingly resented the way their creations were relegated to peripheral spaces at the Royal

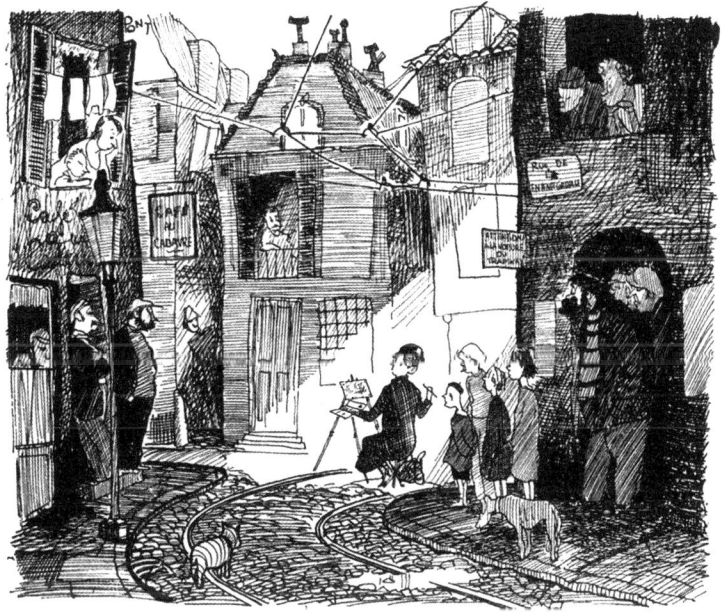

Fig. 1 Pont (Graham Laidler; 1908-1940)
The British Character: The Gift for Water-Colours, 1936

Academy of Arts, then the host of the principal annual London exhibition in which reputations could be made and sales achieved. As in other aspects of British life, the art world was undoubtedly affected by the prevailing desire for change. Although the country was still at war with France, new forms of industrial innovation were spreading, while the population itself shifted away from its traditional rural basis into predominantly urban settings, thereby creating new audiences for art. Competing artistic societies and exhibition venues soon began to appear in response to the swelling numbers of painters in watercolour, and the increasing demand for their work. The deceptive simplicity of the process tempted countless amateurs – female and male – to seek to acquire this accomplishment through tuition from a phalanx of drawing teachers. Meanwhile, improvements in the equipment necessary for painting in watercolour, such as a variety of papers specifically made for this function, and hard cakes of pigment, contributed to watercolour's popularity, and gradually facilitated a greater portability to its essential materials.[4] Prevented from undertaking foreign travels by the ongoing conflicts until peace ensued after Waterloo in 1815, artists championed their native scenery, producing images imbued with patriotic pride that could also be engraved for the burgeoning print market.

A clear marker of the new status of watercolour was the establishment of the Society of Painters in Water-

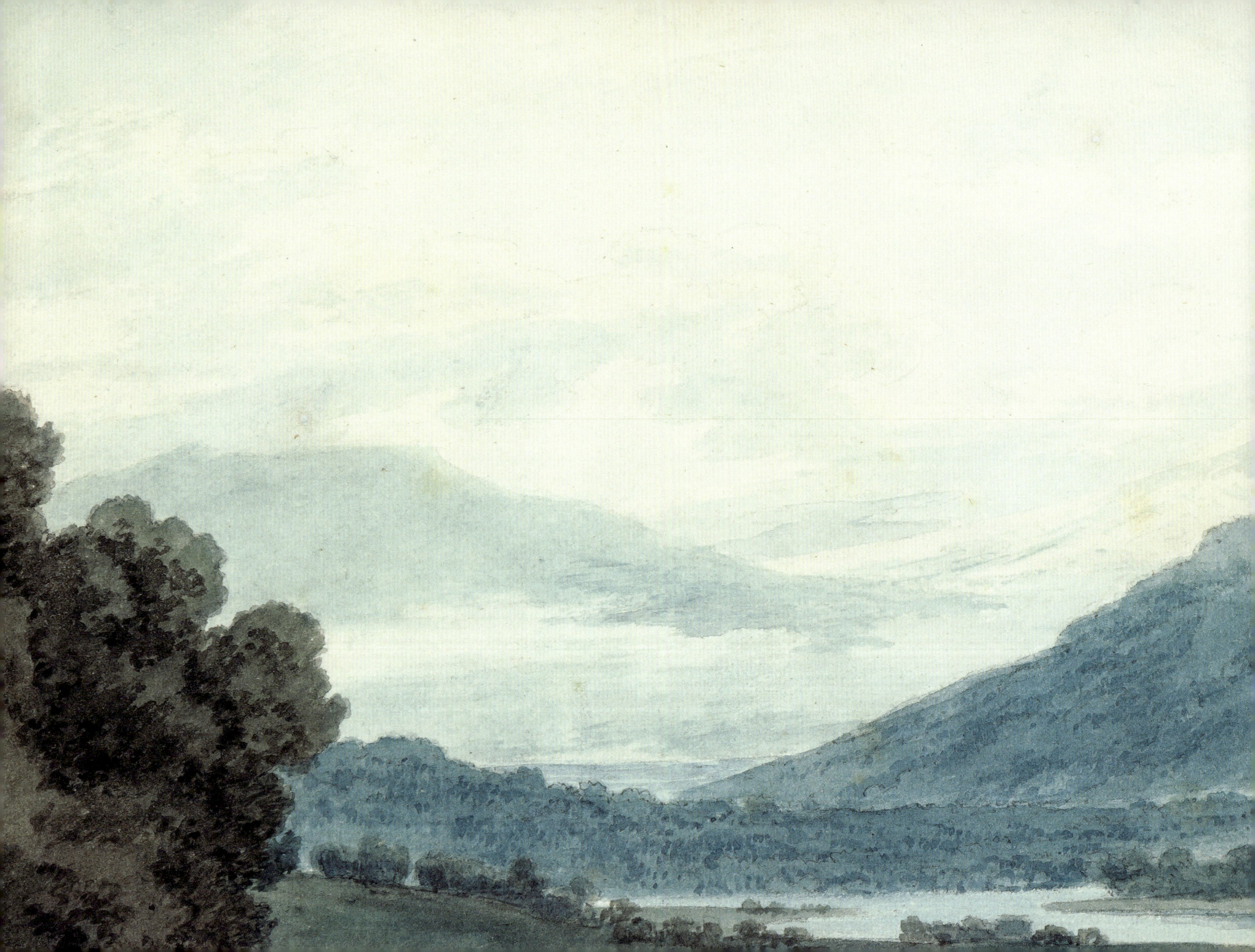

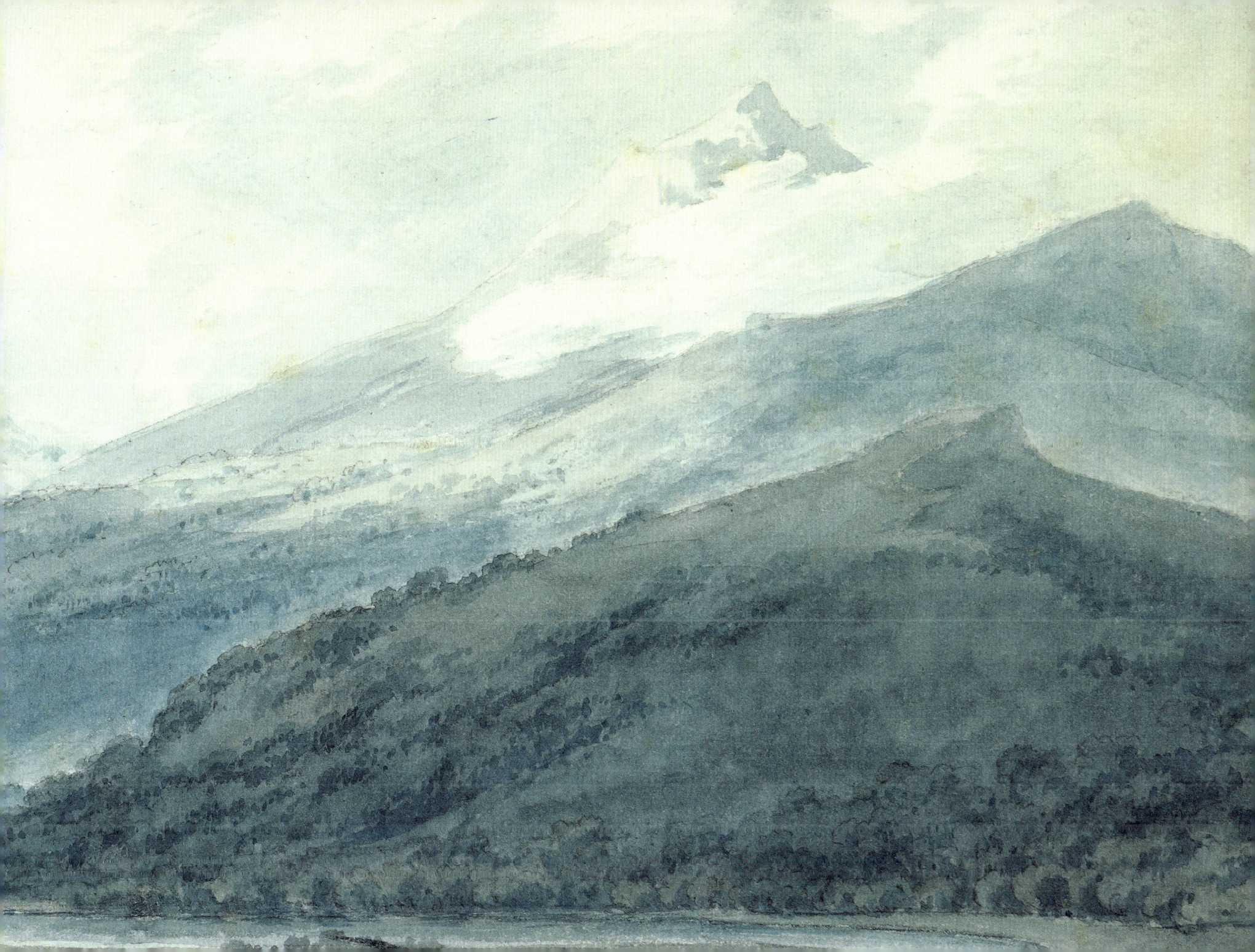

Colours in November 1804, which thereafter staged annual exhibitions in central London, becoming the first of many venues in which watercolours were promoted. (After the founding of a rival institution in 1832, it was referred to as the Old Water-Colour Society.[5]) Here the emphasis was almost exclusively on landscape subjects, with an exception made for the still lifes of Anne Byrne, the society's first woman member.[6] One of the chief founders of the society was William Frederick Wells (1762–1836), himself an artist and a close friend of J. M. W. Turner (1775–1851).[7] Turner had already contributed substantially to the transformation of perceptions of landscape subject matter in general, and of the expressive possibilities of watercolour in particular. As a result, he had begun to dominate the Royal Academy exhibitions (both with his watercolours and oils), and rapidly achieved the extraordinary distinction of gaining full membership of the Academy at the age of only twenty-seven, in 1802.[8] Although he was unable to exhibit with the new watercolour society because the Academy's rules prevented him from exhibiting elsewhere, the vigour and novelty he had achieved served as an impetus

for his peers and their own dedication to extending the range of landscape imagery.

Like others of his generation, Turner had deployed simple washes of grey and blue for his first works (no. 2). But he and his sometime collaborator Thomas Girtin (1775–1802) learned from earlier topographical draughtsmen, most notably from Paul Sandby (1730–1809), how to enrich the scenes they recorded with local incident and colour. A still more potent influence on them were the watercolour views of Switzerland and Italy by John Robert Cozens (1752–1797), richly permeated with atmospheric nuances, which were later described by John Constable (1776–1837) as 'all poetry'.[9] Working from Cozens's outline transcriptions of his own compositions, Girtin and Turner advanced their respective skills by creating versions of his images, with the former transferring the structure of a design before Turner embellished it with overlapping layers of watercolour.[10]

Cozens offered an idealised version of reality, completed away from his motifs. Working from pencil sketches made on the spot, he relied on his recollections of lighting and atmospheric conditions, or notations of these effects. For other artists, such as Francis Towne, an insistence on the factual veracity of observed specifics was often claimed, even when they revised their images or added colours subsequently.[11] But more normally it was standard academic practice to accumulate sketches – of details as well as general vistas – which could be blended and improved imaginatively in the studio. John Varley (1778–1842), the author of a contemporary *Treatise on the Principles of Landscape Drawing* (1816–21), summed up the process neatly by making a culinary metaphor: 'Nature needs cooking'.[12]

That academic sentiment certainly predominated right up to the mid-nineteenth century, but alongside it was an increasing appreciation for the informal, first-hand observations preserved in artists' watercolour sketches. During this period there was often what art historian Greg Smith has discerned as a new 'ambiguity' in the status of these sketches, as collectors began to prize these preliminary studies.[13] However, unfinished works were explicitly prohibited from being exhibited at the Society of Painters in Water-Colours in 1823.[14] Yet the standard process of studying with a drawing master inevitably familiarised students and connoisseurs with the intimacy and unfiltered freshness present in the primary researches of landscape painters, thus arguably generating the beginnings of a different æsthetic.

Looking back from the twenty-first century perspective, it is often the experimental, the unusual focus, or the apparently unresolved spontaneity of these sketches in watercolours that speak most directly to our sensibility, even as we admire the techniques and craft of the more complete works. Such features leap across time, despite being rooted in the æsthetic choices of the Romantic era.

In the present book, and the exhibition it accompanies, the majority of the works were created in the first instance essentially as a fundamental response by the artists for their own benefit. Sometimes they may have consciously had a specific purpose in mind for works that could be developed more fully back in the studio. But when looking at them it is not always possible to tell their function solely from their aesthetic appearance. Indeed, where colour is used it may not always have been applied on site, either to save time, or because it was not practical, despite the improved portability of watercolour materials.[15]

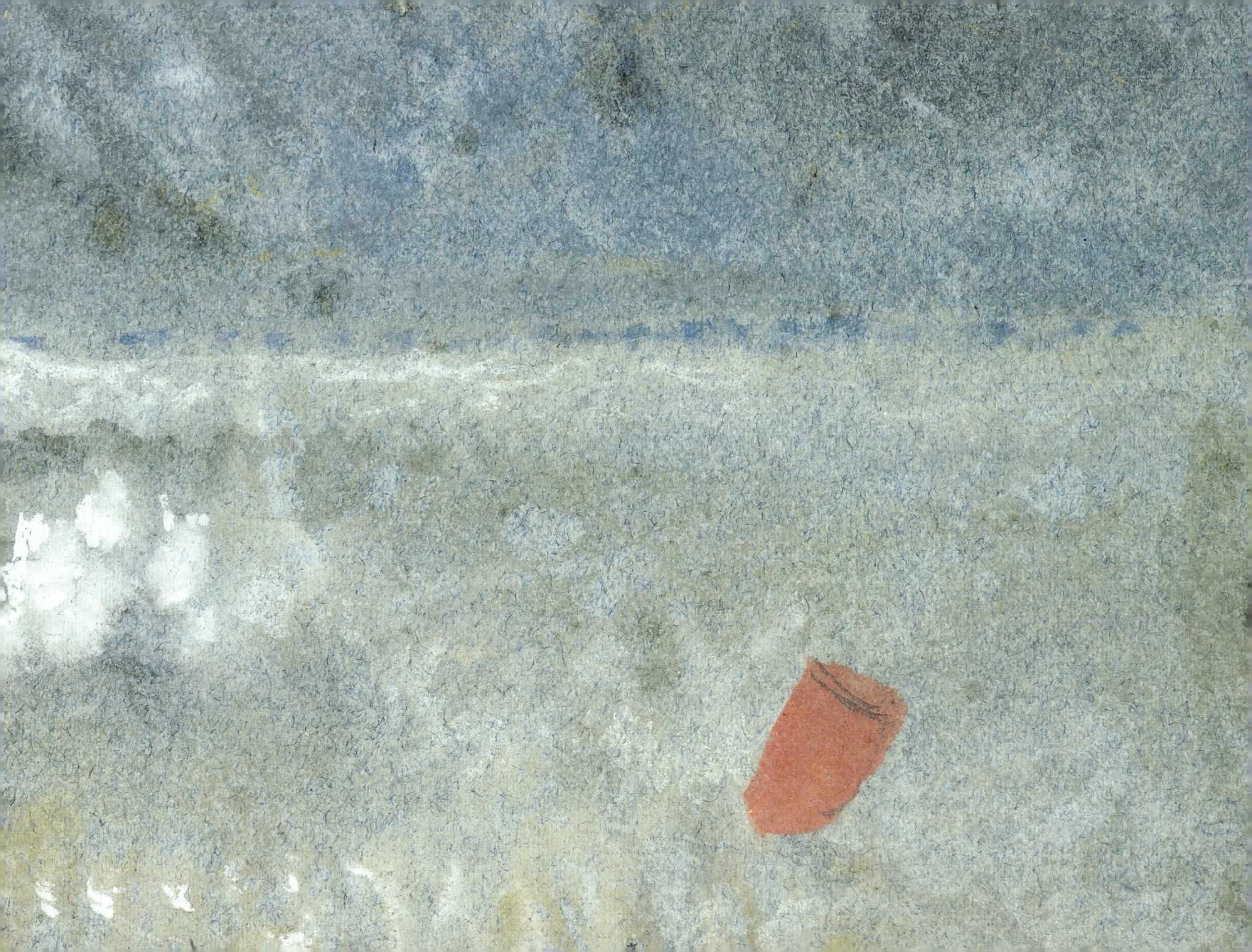

The bold direction pursued by Girtin in his travel sketches, for example, and the more resolved watercolours based on them, was initially thought by contemporaries more daring than Turner's style. Working outside the Royal Academy schools, he found steady gainful employment making topographical views, and, like Turner, was soon sharing his skills by teaching amateur artists.[16] His aspirations for watercolour as an art form were just as ambitious as Turner's, leading him to establish the Sketching Society in 1799, a short-lived, but influential series of convivial gatherings at which the assembled artists competed to illustrate a designated effect, theme or poetic source. As a master of broad effect as well as local detail, Girtin embarked on two panoramic projects, the first resulting in the *Eidometropolis*, a huge 360-degree recreation of the view over London from the southern end of Blackfriars Bridge.[17]

Even before that was complete and opened to the public in 1802, Girtin had travelled to Paris to compile useful expansive views of the French capital, suddenly accessible to British visitors during the Peace of Amiens. As well as creating a set of twenty *Picturesque Views in Paris and its Environs*, Girtin painted some scenes on the spot that were afterwards scaled up to serve as sets for one of Thomas Dibdin's pantomime productions at the Theatre Royal Covent Garden.[18] This may include his remarkable *View of the Rue St Denis*, with its precise, but deftly shaded, deep perspective, and its curious absence of figures (fig. 2).

While Girtin's essentially functional sketches of London and Paris were also æsthetically appealing, Turner's approach was somewhat more minimal. Like many of his peers, he was also in Paris in 1802, but he pressed on south to the Alps, making quick rudimentary sketches in small notebooks.[19] Since the mid-1790s he had permitted potential patrons to look at his sketchbooks and select scenes they wanted him to paint.[20] However, on his Alpine tour, and in Scotland a year earlier, he produced batches of large compositions that occupy a more intermediate status than the perfunctory records of place. Working on larger sheets prepared with a grey wash, he outlined his subject in graphite, supplementing these basics with a few dull earthy tones to suggest the interplay of masses and textures (no. 8). Once he was back in London, the

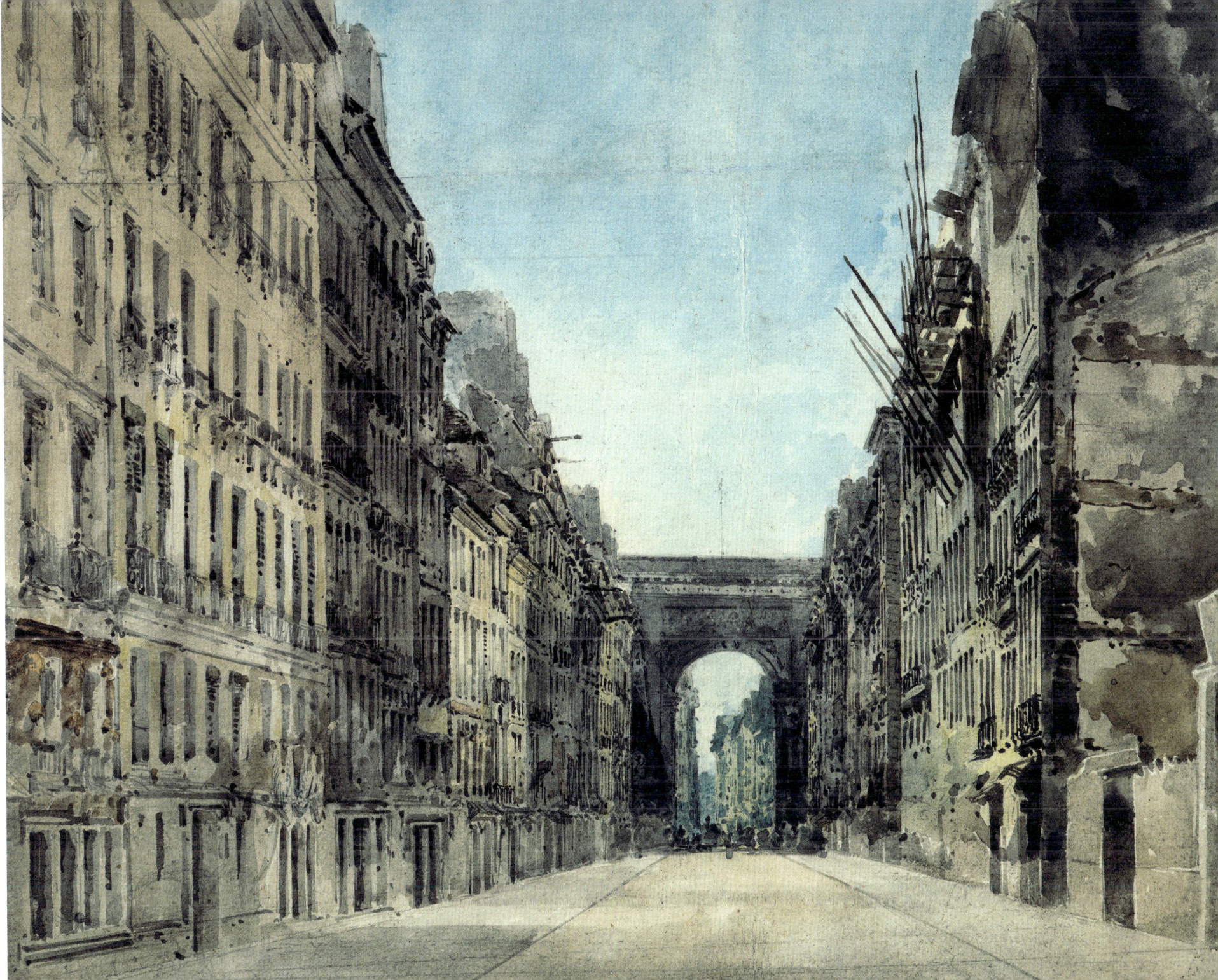

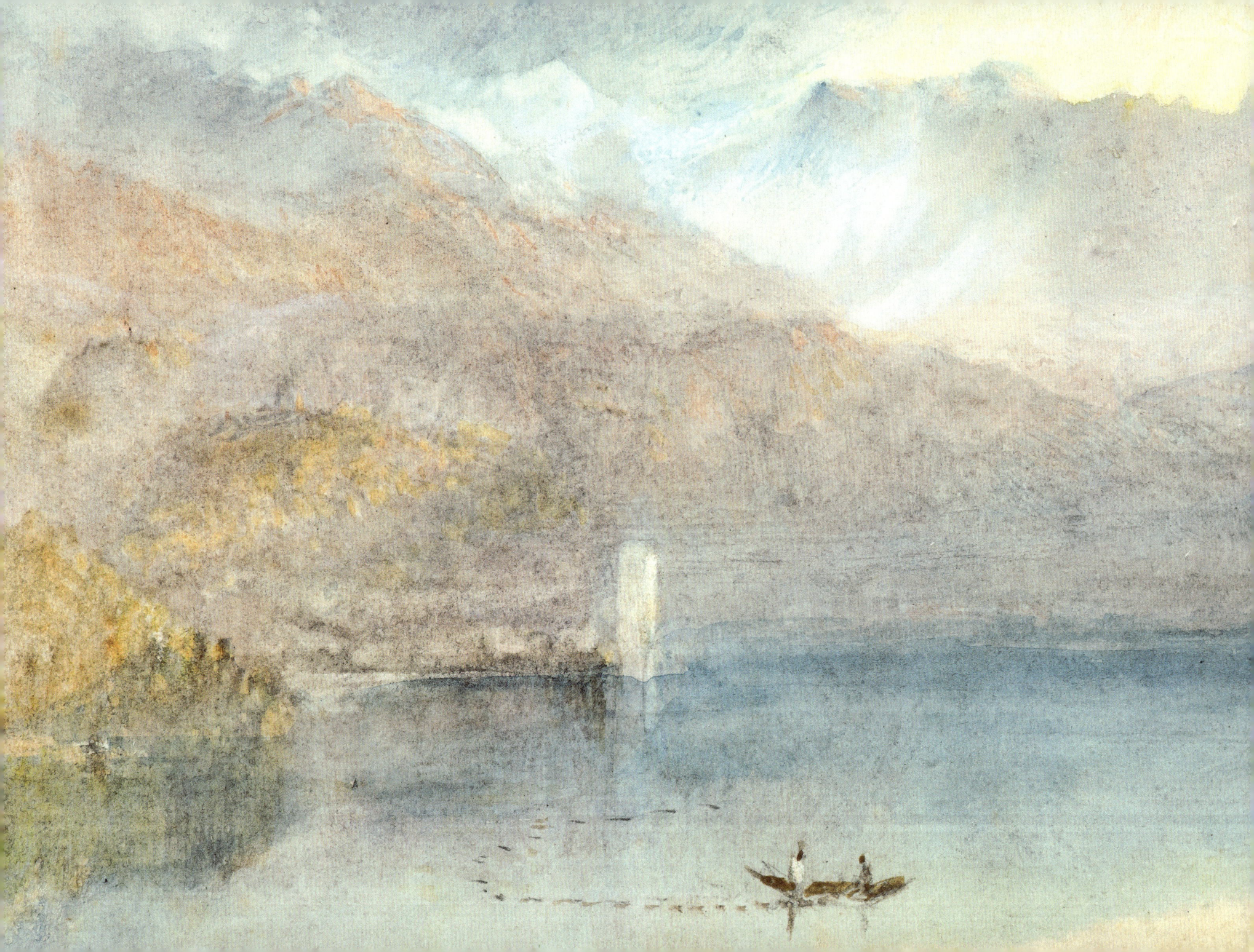

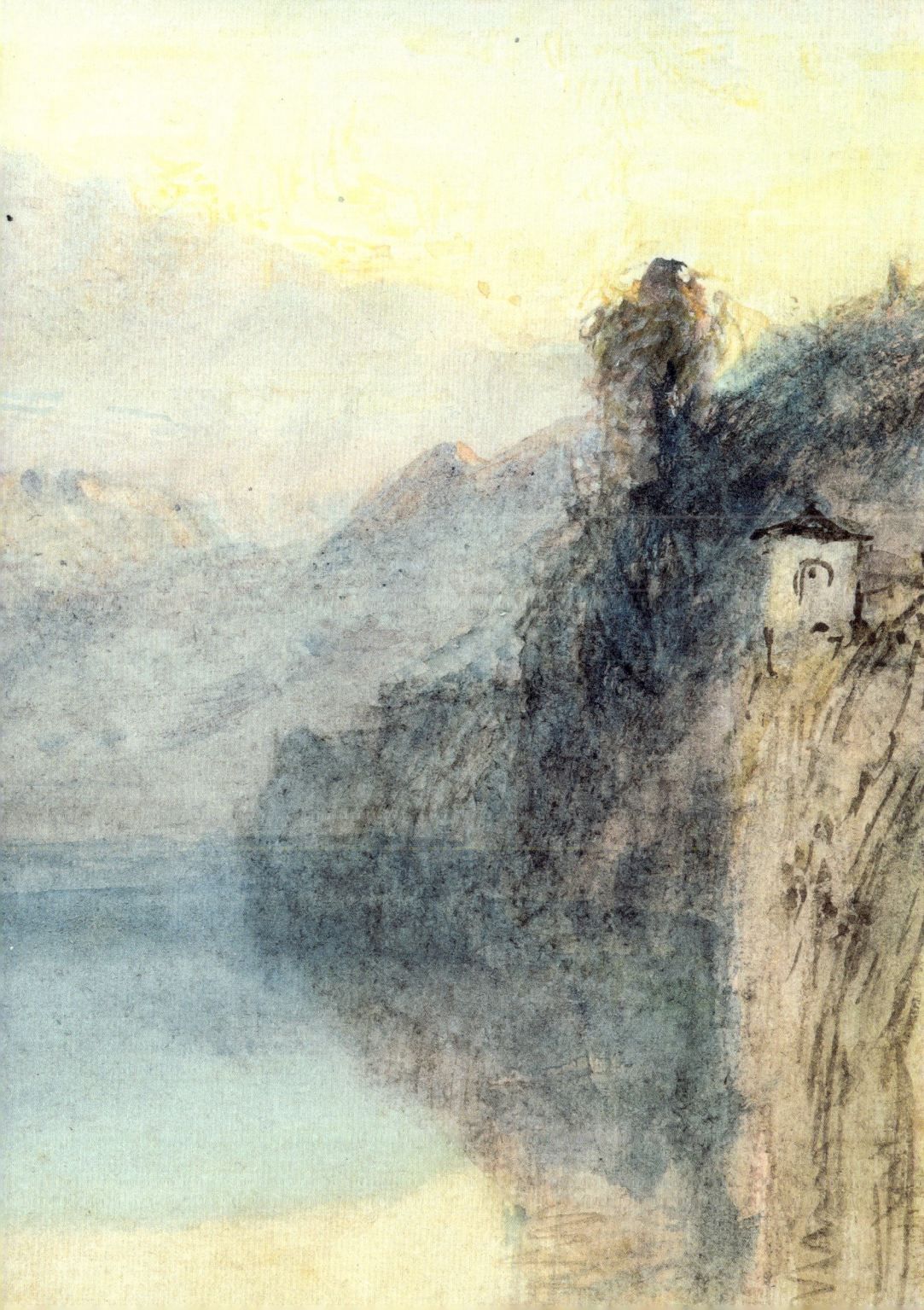

experience of the Alps in these works inspired some of his finest and most inventive watercolours during the next two decades, chiefly for his patron Walter Fawkes. When displayed together in a momentous exhibition at Fawkes' home in 1819 they caused the art press to acclaim Turner as an 'astonishing magician', and to identify him as the leading force in British watercolour painting.[21]

Meanwhile, beyond London, the momentum behind landscape and watercolour painting had led to the founding of the Norwich Society of Artists in 1803, and its first exhibition two years later.[22] The chief instigator in this case was John Crome (1768–1821), another artist who, like most of the artists featured here, came from a humble background, and was dependent for his living on acting as a drawing master.[23] While his pictures in oil and watercolour drew deeply on the examples of seventeenth-century Dutch masters, such as Jacob van Ruisdael and Rembrandt, Crome approached the natural world with the same keen realism as contemporaries such as Constable.[24] Some viewers even associated him with Turner's foray in that direction, describing their apparently artless manner as a kind of 'scribbling of painting',

21

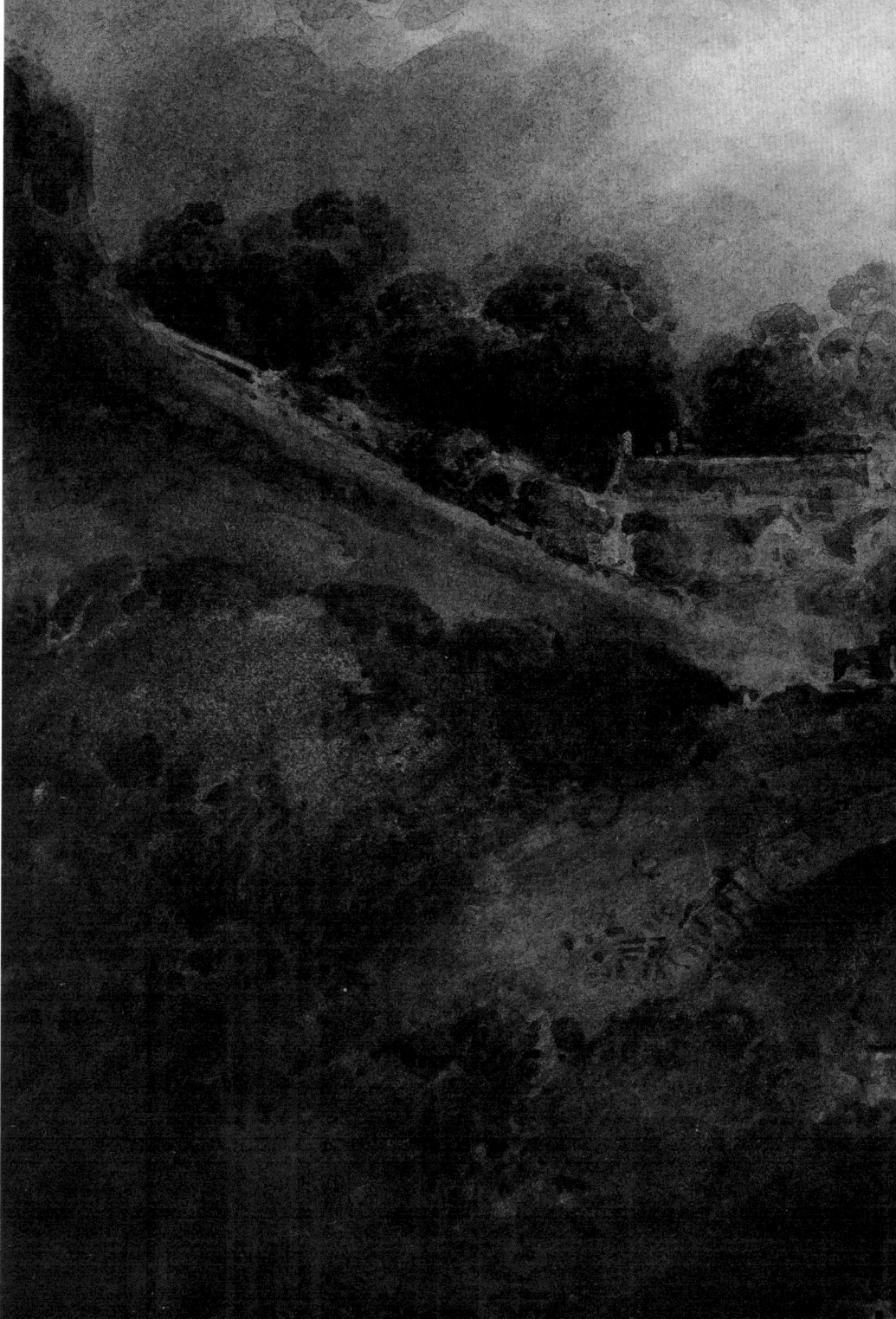

and proposed that both needed 'a little more finishing'.[25] Perhaps they would have felt the same about Crome's deceptively simple picture, *A Blasted Oak* (no. 14), of a couple of years or so later, which retains the crisp acuity of a sketch from nature, though its scale indicates it is more likely to have been an exhibition piece.[26]

 Another notable Norfolk artist, who worked in watercolours and eventually also in oils, was John Sell Cotman (1782–1842). After moving to London in 1798 he became an associate of Girtin at the Sketching Society, where he also encountered the French artist François Louis Thomas Francia (1772–1839). The spell of Turner's images proved captivating, causing Cotman to study and copy the older artist's exhibited works and the mezzotints issued as *Liber Studiorum*, which adumbrated his ambitions for recognition of the diversity of landscape types.[27] Despite succumbing to what has been described as the 'self-inflicted handicap' of Turner's influence,[28] Cotman nevertheless evolved a unique and radically different style of image making, moving away from brooding, Turneresque dark images, with rubbed or scratched-out highlights (nos. 9-12, and detail here). Instead his

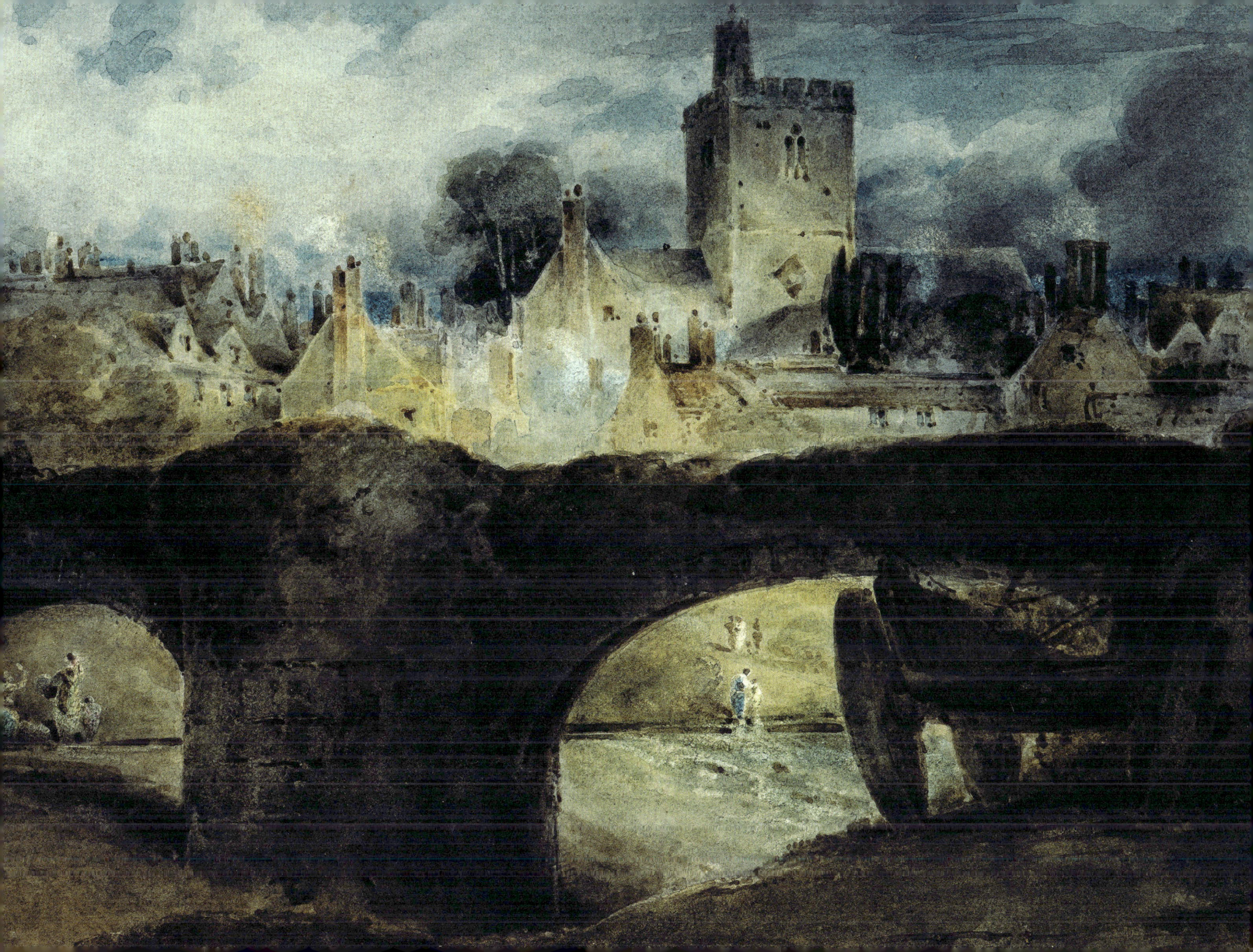

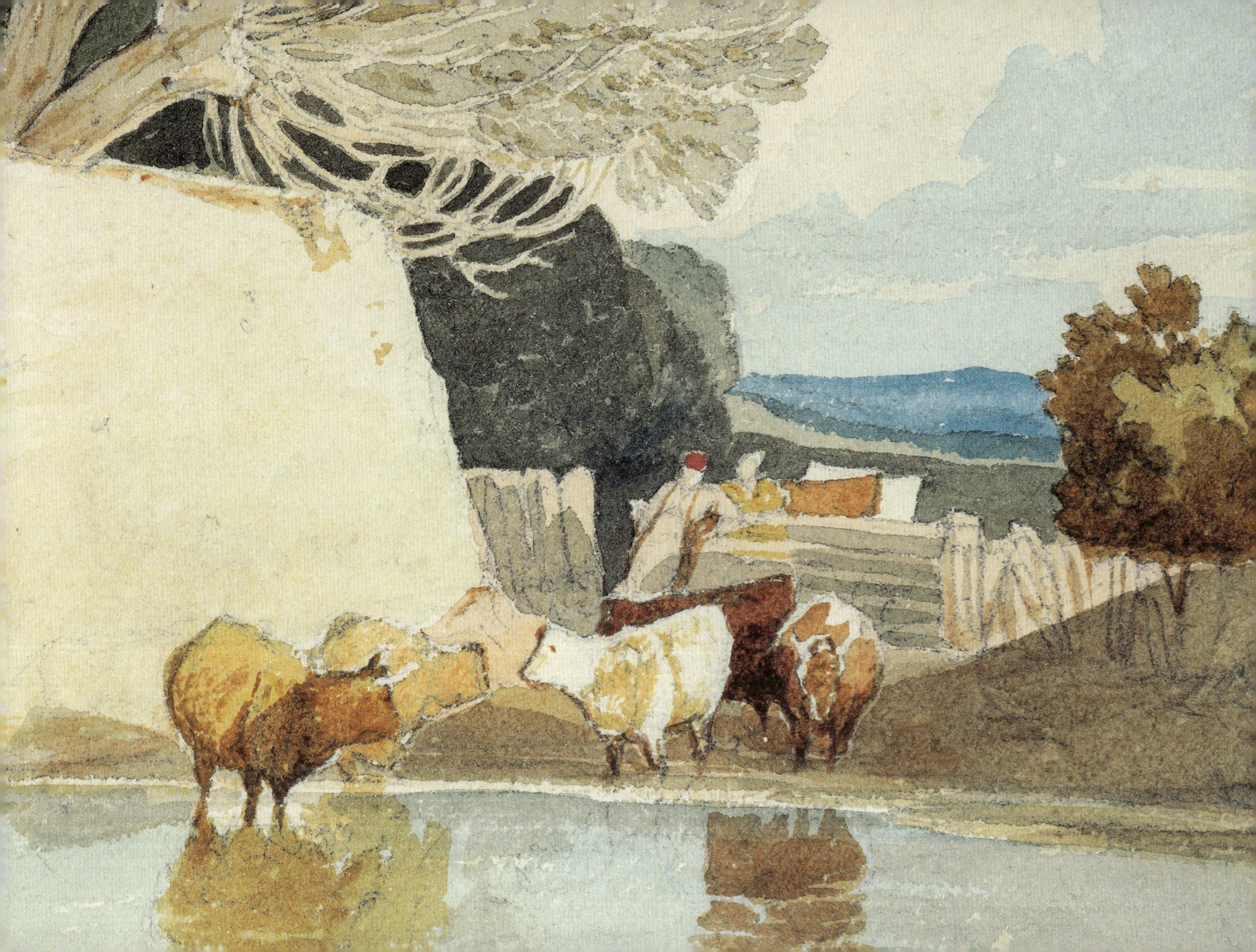

distinctive works are conceived structurally, and built up with discrete planes of pure wash that cause the eye to move across the sheet rhythmically. He enjoyed a decisive advance around 1805, while working as a drawing teacher for the Cholmeley family at Brandsby Hall in Yorkshire, producing there some of his most memorable studies of nature – almost like snapshots – of random fragments observed along the banks of the River Greta.[29] Remarkably he managed to retain the poised economy of sketches such as *Trees near the River Greta* (no. 15, and detail overleaf) in some of the finished watercolours he exhibited subsequently, introducing a blunt rawness that challenged contemporary expectations. This is epitomised in one of Cotman's most celebrated studio watercolours, *The Ploughed Field* (fig. 3). Yet it has recently been suggested that the apparently frank naturalism of this image perhaps resonates with allusions to Robert Bloomfield's once popular poem *The Farmer's Boy* (1800).[30]

Regrettably Cotman's innovative approach did not secure him significant patronage, and so after 1806 he retreated from the competitive London art world, moving back to Norwich, where his teaching practice

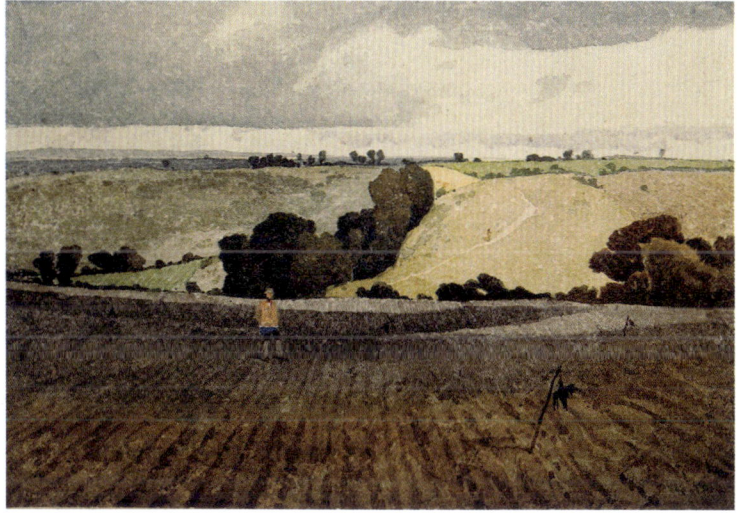

Fig. 3. John Sell Cotman, The Ploughed Field, c. 1805-6
watercolour over pencil on wove paper, 22.8 x 35 cm, Leeds Art Gallery

was crucial to the development there of an independent school of painting.[31] Nevertheless he remained attuned to cosmopolitan developments, not least the more vibrant, prismatic palette Turner had adopted by the 1820s (fig. 4, p. 28). Turner is known to have been quick to exploit new pigments, notoriously chrome yellows, but Cotman too seems to have supplemented his tonal range by

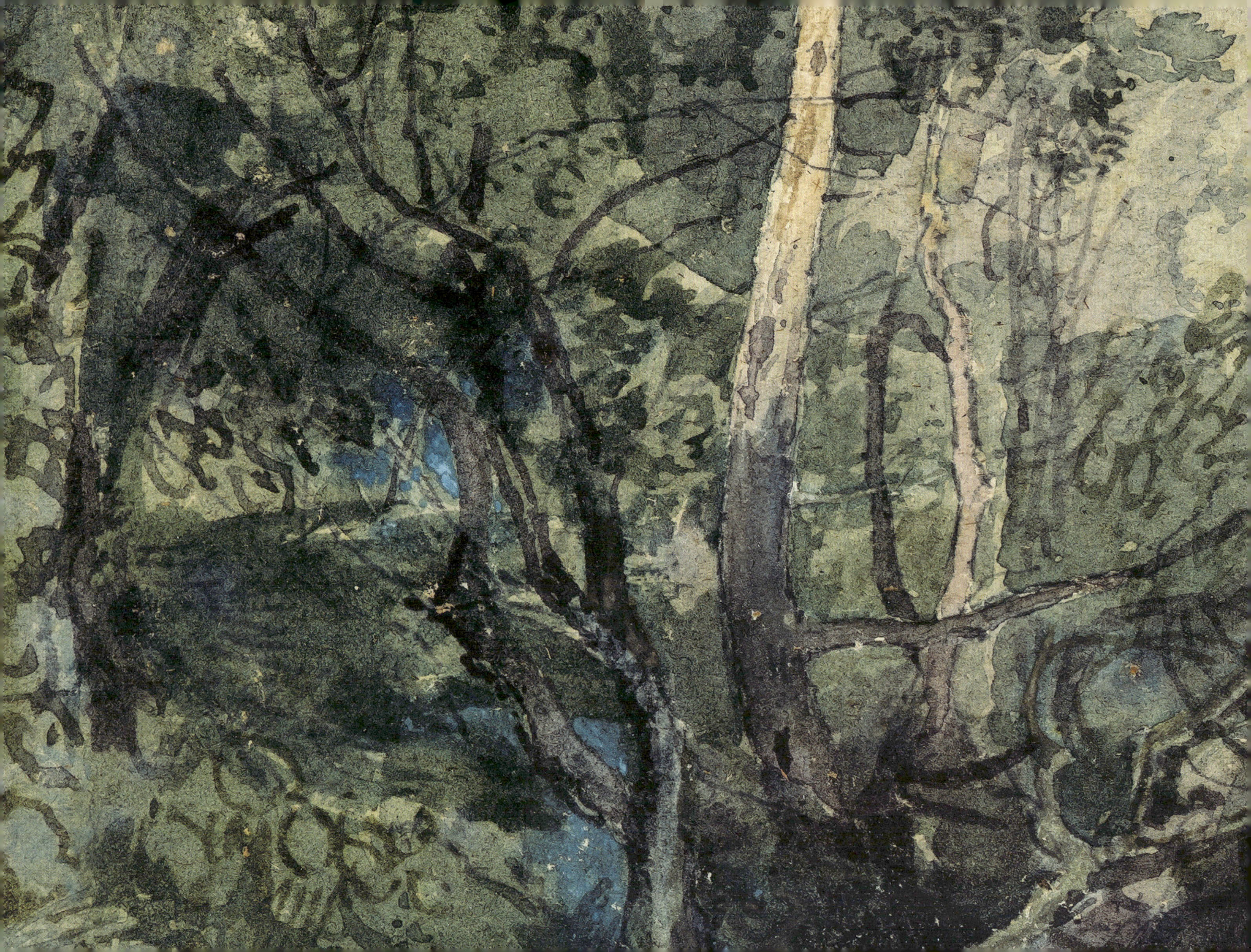

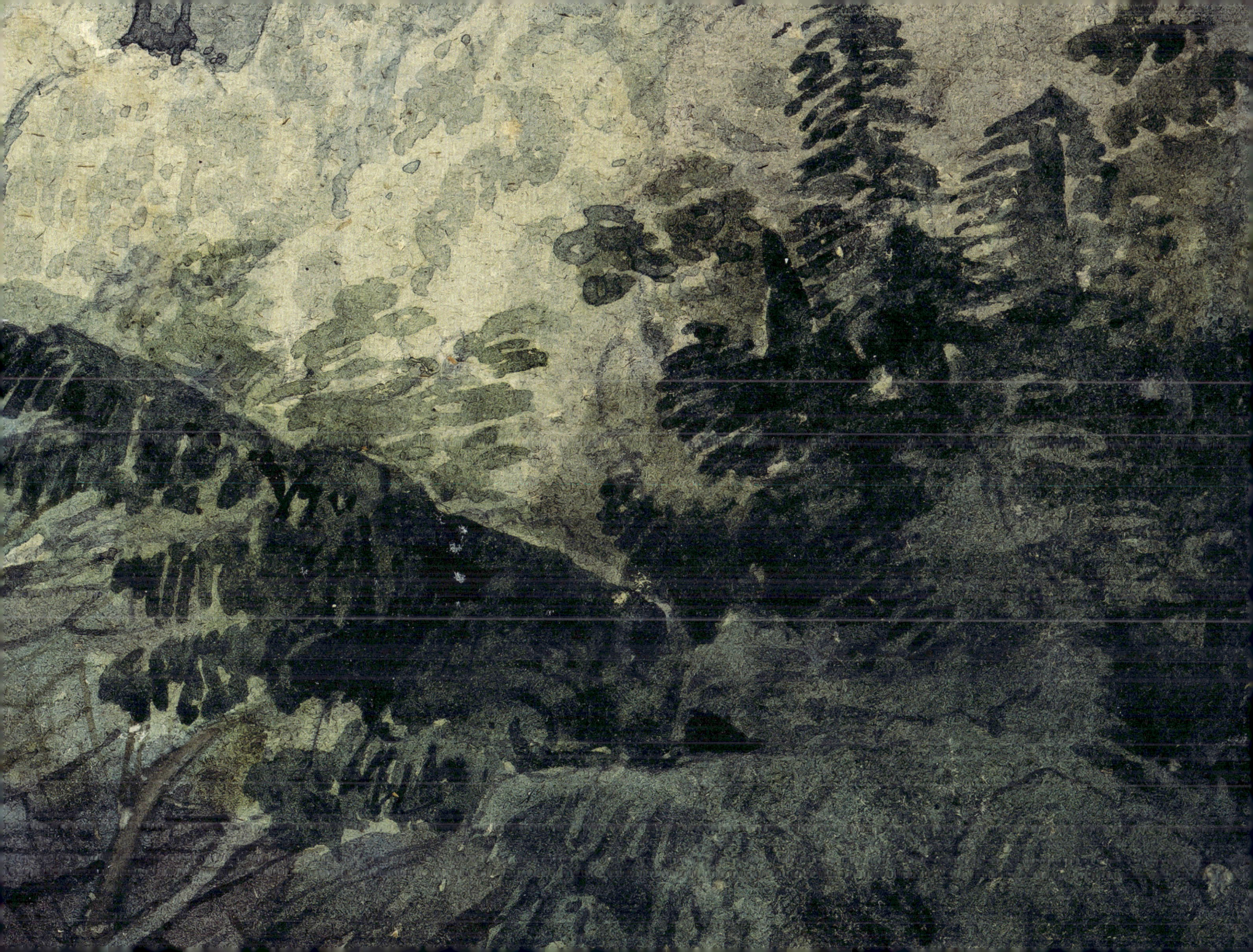

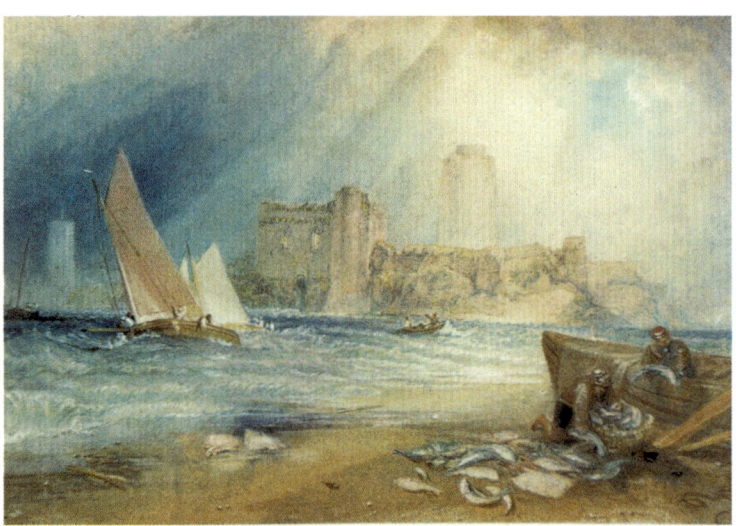

Fig. 4 J. M. W. Turner, Pembroke Castle, c. 1829-30 (from *Picturesque Views in England and Wales*)
watercolour on paper, 29.8 x 42.6 cm, Holburne Museum, Bath

deploying a new synthetic ultramarine from the later 1820s, which (sometimes strengthened with a thickening agent, possibly flour) provided luxurious blue contrasts and deeper perspectives (nos. 61-62).[32]

By this date Cotman was not alone in putting to one side the intense scrutiny of picturesque details

that had also been pursued between circa 1800 and circa 1815 by countless artists, including Henry Edridge (1768–1821), David Cox (1783–1859) and Peter De Wint (1784–1849), not just in watercolours but also in the parallel activity of plein air sketching in oils.[33] The focus of what has been called the 'decade of English Naturalism' began to dilate to encompass a more experimental approach to the representation of landscape, in which the materiality of painting was as present as the subject itself.[34] Paradoxically, a vital figure in this shift was John Varley, mentioned above. Although he famously encouraged a cumulative approach to the creation of landscape images, through the judicious addition of imaginative elements to the information gathered on location, he actively encouraged pupils and presumably also Cox and De Wint to pursue the primary response of sketching directly from nature to achieve more faithful representations.[35]

The Birmingham artist David Cox was one of the most prolific contributors to the watercolour exhibitions during this period.[36] Through his *Treatise on Landscape Painting and Effect in Water Colours* (1813–14), he made a lasting contribution to the development of

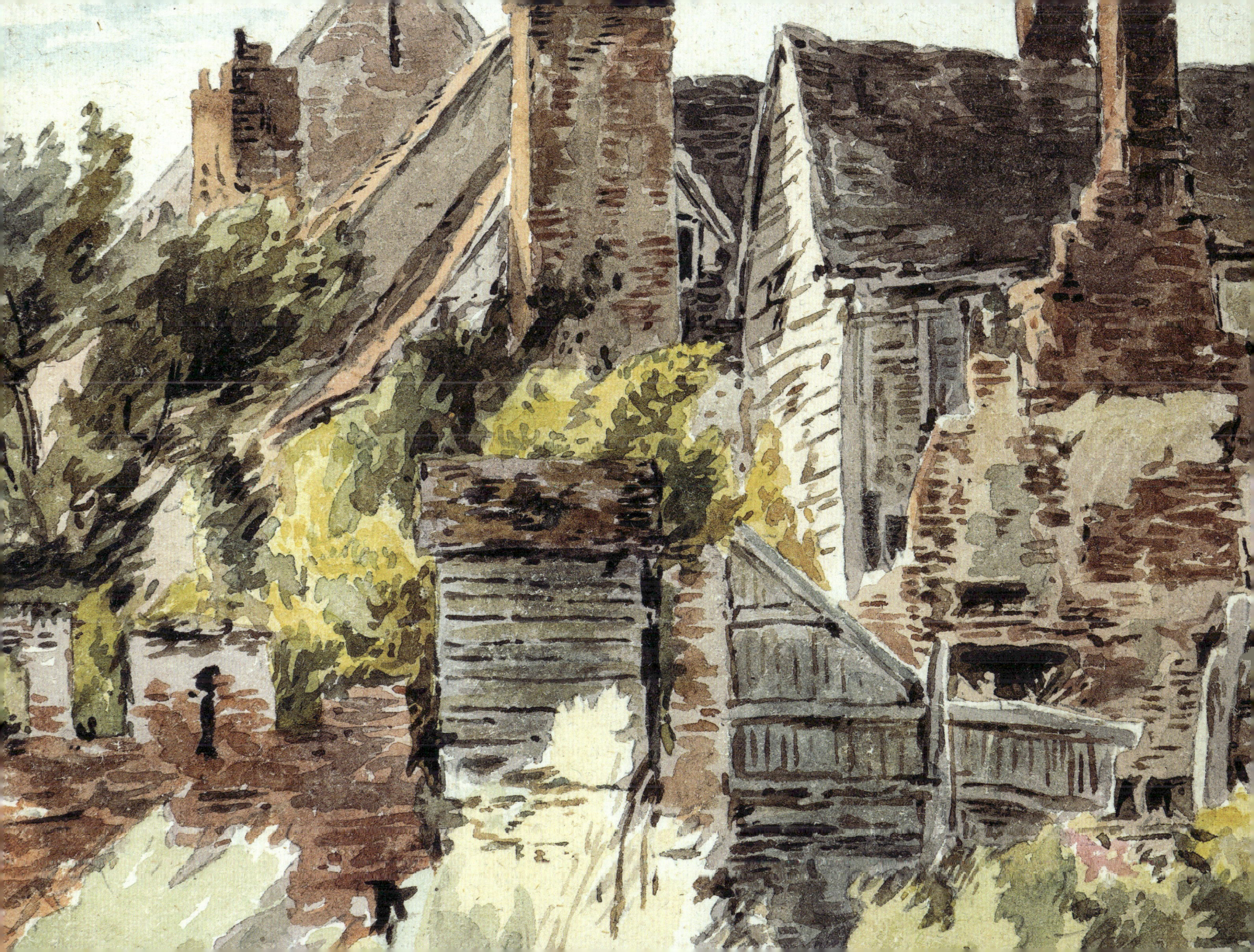

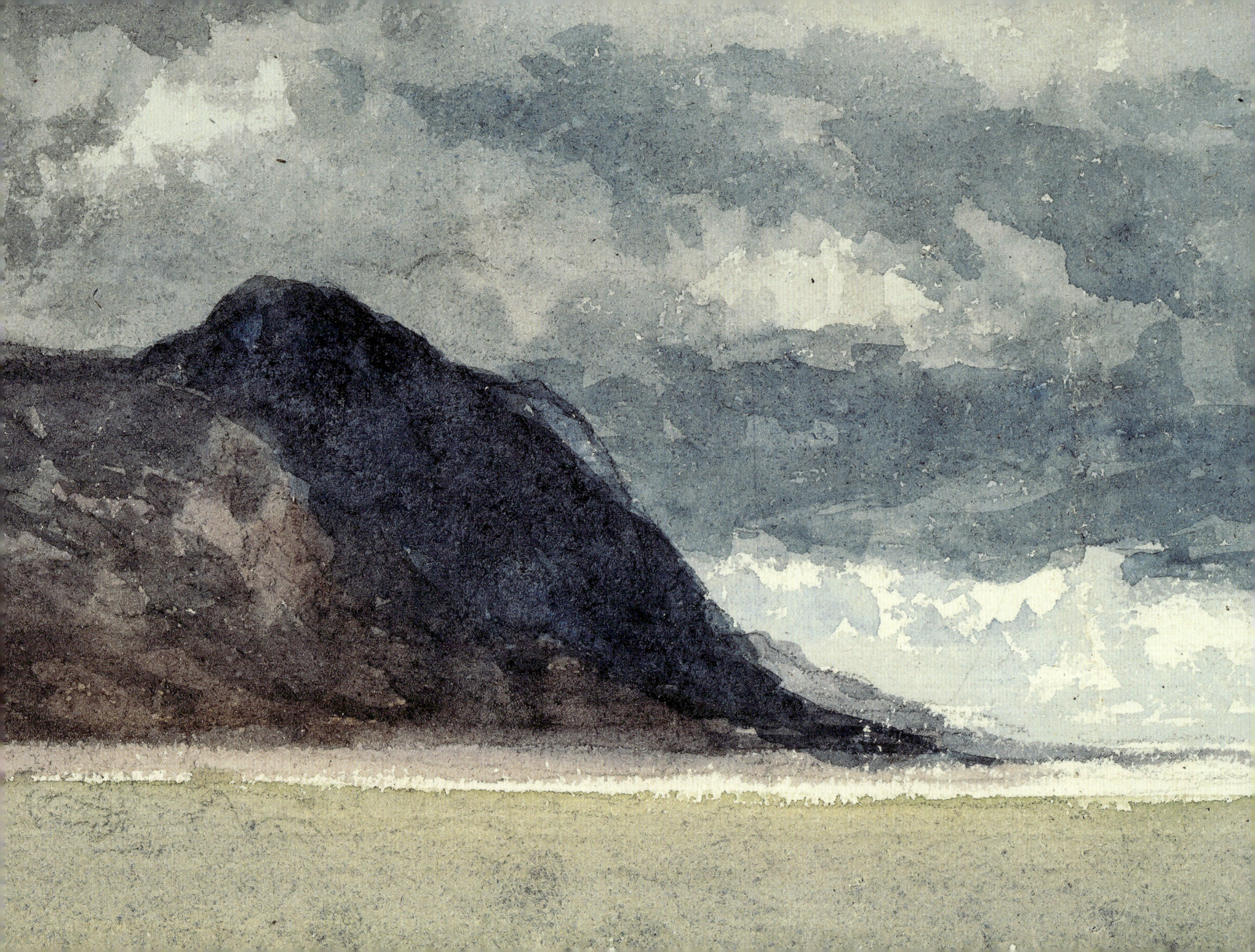

watercolour in the nineteenth century. His range of subjects reflected his extensive travels around Britain, and especially his repeated visits to North Wales. Though not as intrepid as Turner, he also crossed the Channel on three occasions to visit northern Europe (1826, 1829, 1832), sketching during the second of these in Paris from a carriage after he injured his ankle. The extra stability and privacy this provided possibly encouraged him to work in colour over his pencil outlines. But more generally, and especially in his later work he trusted much to memory. He famously claimed that it suited his purposes to turn his back on the scene he had studied and to set down only the key essentials he could remember (fig. 5).[37] This is clearly at odds with claims that his views of the blustery Welsh and north-west coast anticipate the French Impressionists, at least in terms of the process of setting down an 'impression'. In his mature works Cox followed the example of Turner's watercolours for the *Picturesque Views in England and Wales* (1825–39) of slackening the precision of his handling, which slightly diminished the earlier visual distinction between sketches and finished watercolours.

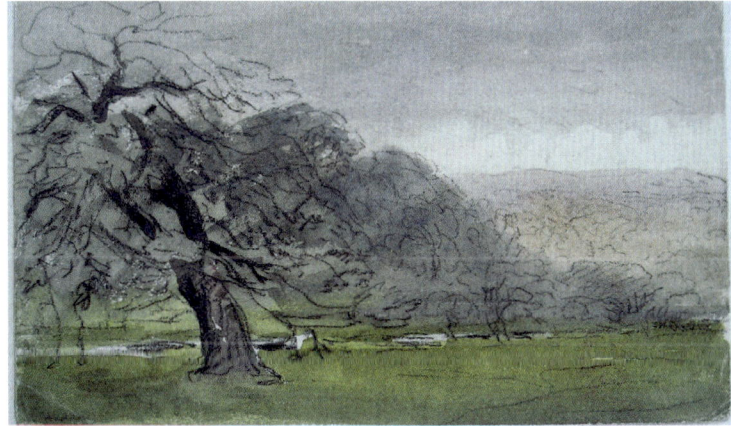

Fig 5 David Cox, Trees by a Stream, c. 1845, black chalk and watercolour on paper, 17.6 x 27.8 cm, private collection

Both Cox and Peter De Wint were very particular about the types of paper they used for their watercolours, possibly in response to advice from Varley. Both generally eschewed James Whatman's smooth and highly sized papers that Turner and Cotman often selected in favour of more noticeably textured sheets, particularly the heavier 'cartridge' paper made by Thomas Creswick.[38] For each artist the traces recording the movement of the wet paint became a striking feature of their sketches.

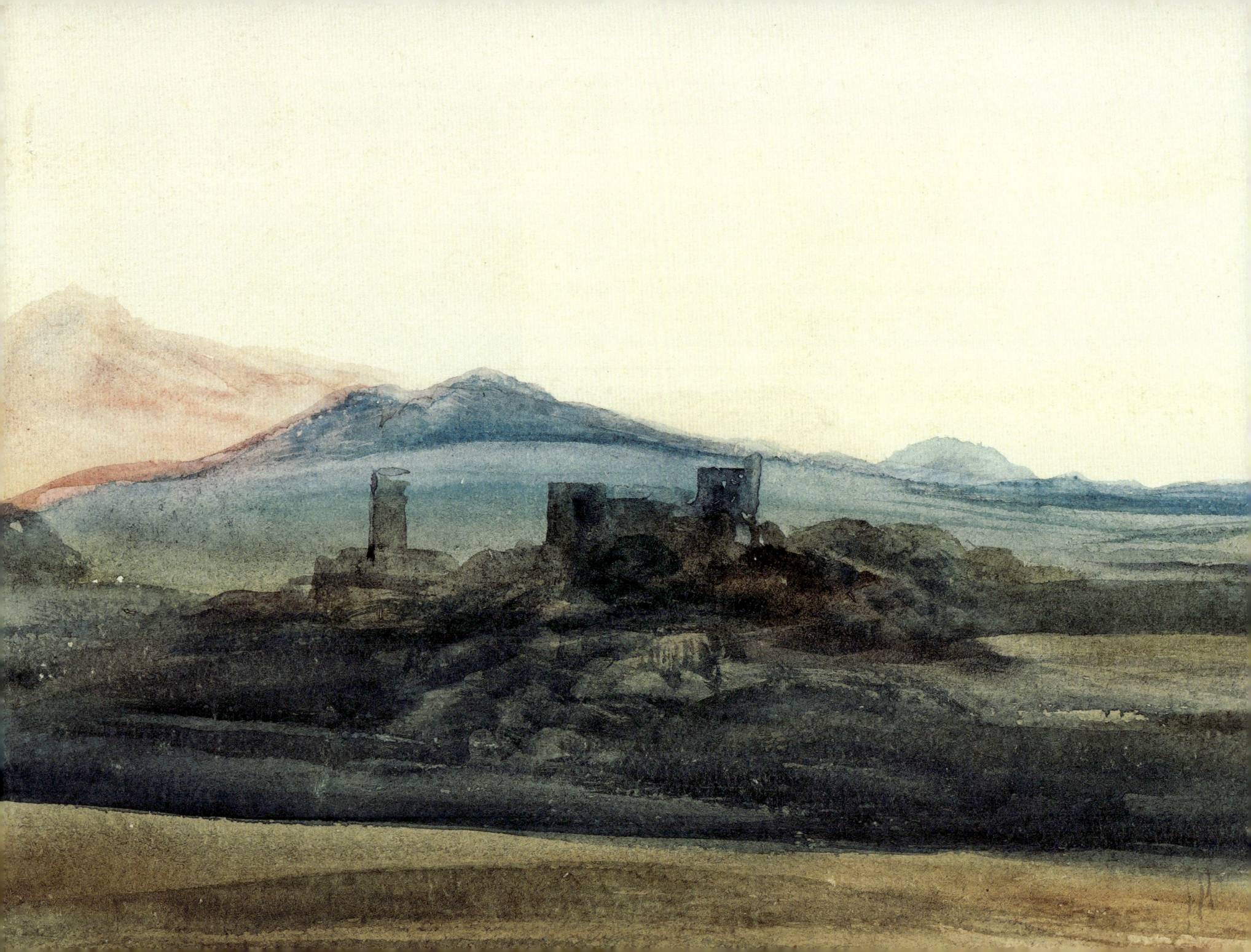

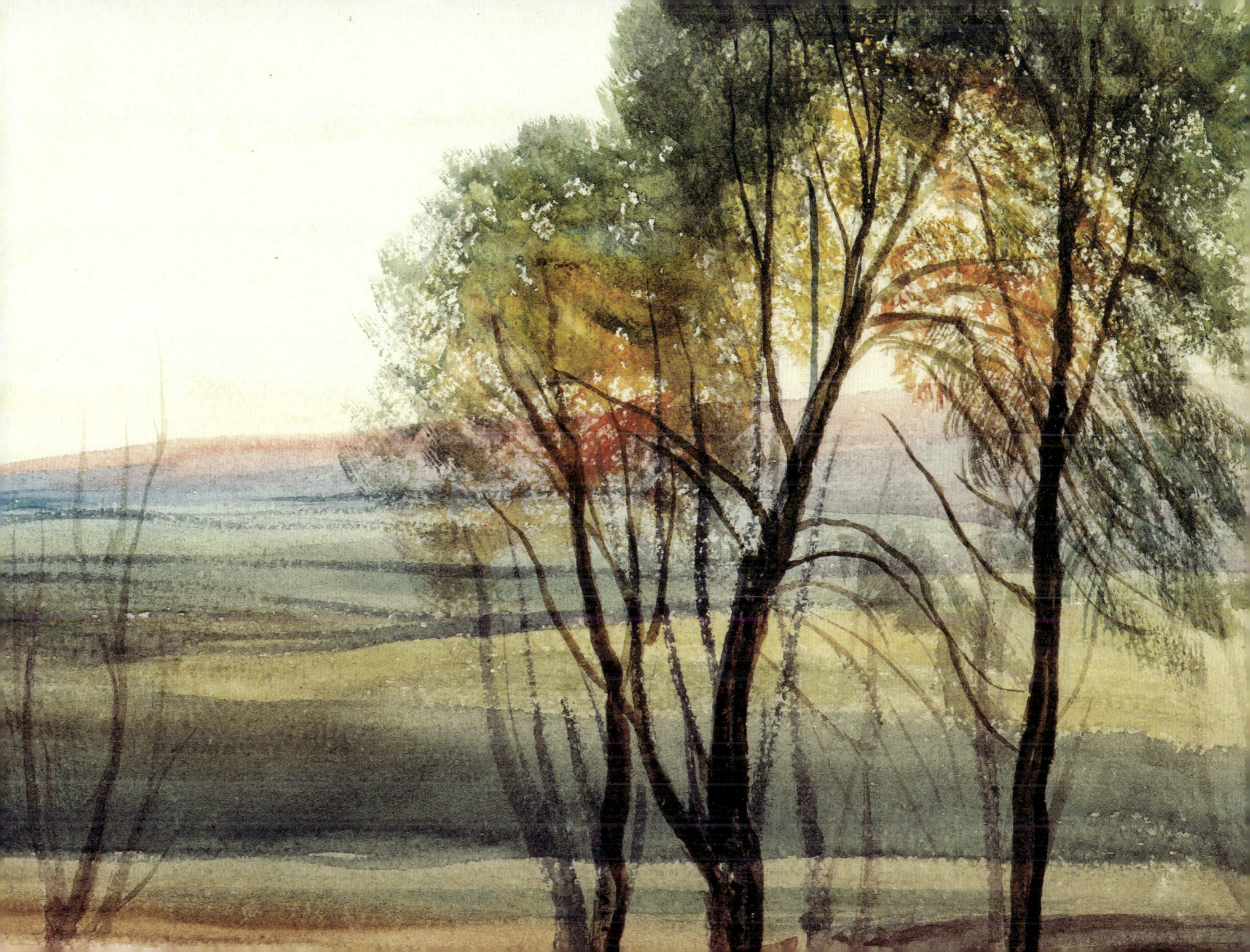

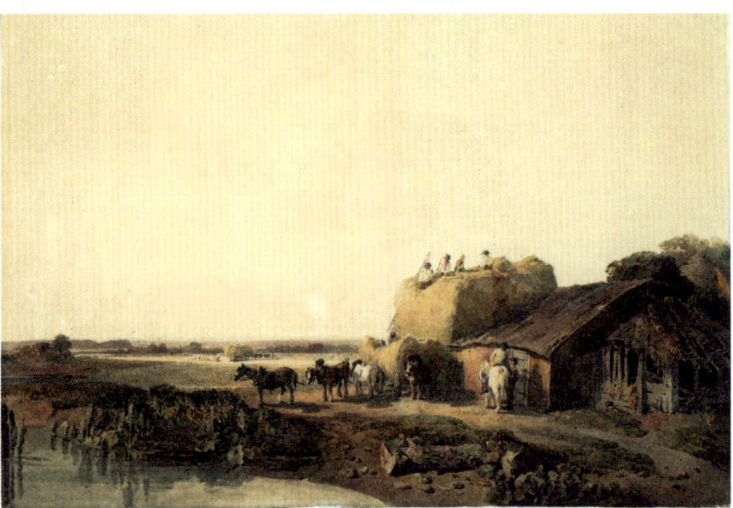

Fig. 6 Peter De Wint, The Farmyard, c. 1820
watercolour, 53.4 x 78.1 cm, Birmingham Museums

De Wint was an inveterate sketcher and truly embraced the spontaneity and partial nature of recording his observations informally.[39] His training benefited, like that of Girtin and Turner before him, from exposure to the collection of drawings assembled by Dr. Thomas Monro.[40] But more essential to the shape of his career was the experience of sketching along the river and in the fields around his wife's hometown of Lincoln (fig. 6). The *plein air* sketches he made – both in watercolour and oil – exude confidence and pleasure in the process of painting, and seem to have been known to admirers such as the poet John Clare.[41] De Wint was fortuitous in acquiring notable patrons across Britain, whose homes he was able to visit, including the Earl of Lonsdale at Lowther Castle (no. 47). The topographical focus of his work in the 1820s and 30s coincided with a period of intense competition for views of this kind, and many of the sketches De Wint made speculatively in the hopes of gaining commissions remained chastely unplundered in his portfolios.[42] These later sketches often possess a timeless simplicity, using striking colour combinations with a lightness of touch that is quite distinct from his more laboured and (unfortunately) overexposed exhibited works.

Like Cox, De Wint visited France in the later 1820s, making this single foreign excursion in 1828. But the frenzied market for engraved depictions of new unfamiliar places induced him to develop finished watercolours from other artists' sketches of Italy and Southern

France for book projects.[43] This was, of course, a market crowned by Turner's skilfully crafted illustrations, not only of the rivers Loire and Seine published in the *Turner's Annual Tour* volumes between 1833 and 1835, but also of more distant places that were similarly dependent on first-hand sketches by amateur draughtsmen.[44]

More crucially, the inter-relationship between Turner's art and his travels was a fundamental driver of his ceaseless creativity. Even as he approached his seventh decade, he was embarking on new sets of delicately resolved watercolour views based on his travels along the Rhine and, more particularly, in Switzerland (fig. 7).[45] The genesis of these works returned to his adolescent experience of gaining affirmation from his patrons for their choice of specific subjects to develop, based on their selection from his travel sketches. Despite his supposed reticence about letting anyone see his working methods, Turner seems here to have relished the participation of his collectors in the process of transforming his colour sketches into larger, more intricately nuanced, finished versions.

Most of these sketches remained in his own collection, and thereafter became part of his bequest to

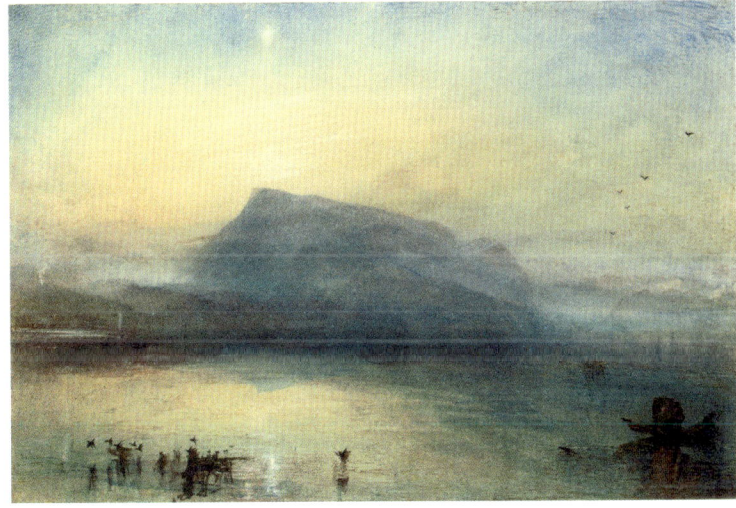

Fig. 7 J. M. W. Turner The Blue Rigi, Lake of Lucerne, Sunrise, 1842 watercolour, gouache, pen and brown ink, heightened with white chalk and with scratching out on paper, 29.7 x 45 cm, Tate

the nation (now at Tate Britain).[46] But his last years were divided between his studio in central London and more furtive arrangements with Mrs Sophia Booth. She had been his landlady at Margate, her lodgings offering both an expansive view over the sea, along with her domestic companionship. As well as working on projects such as

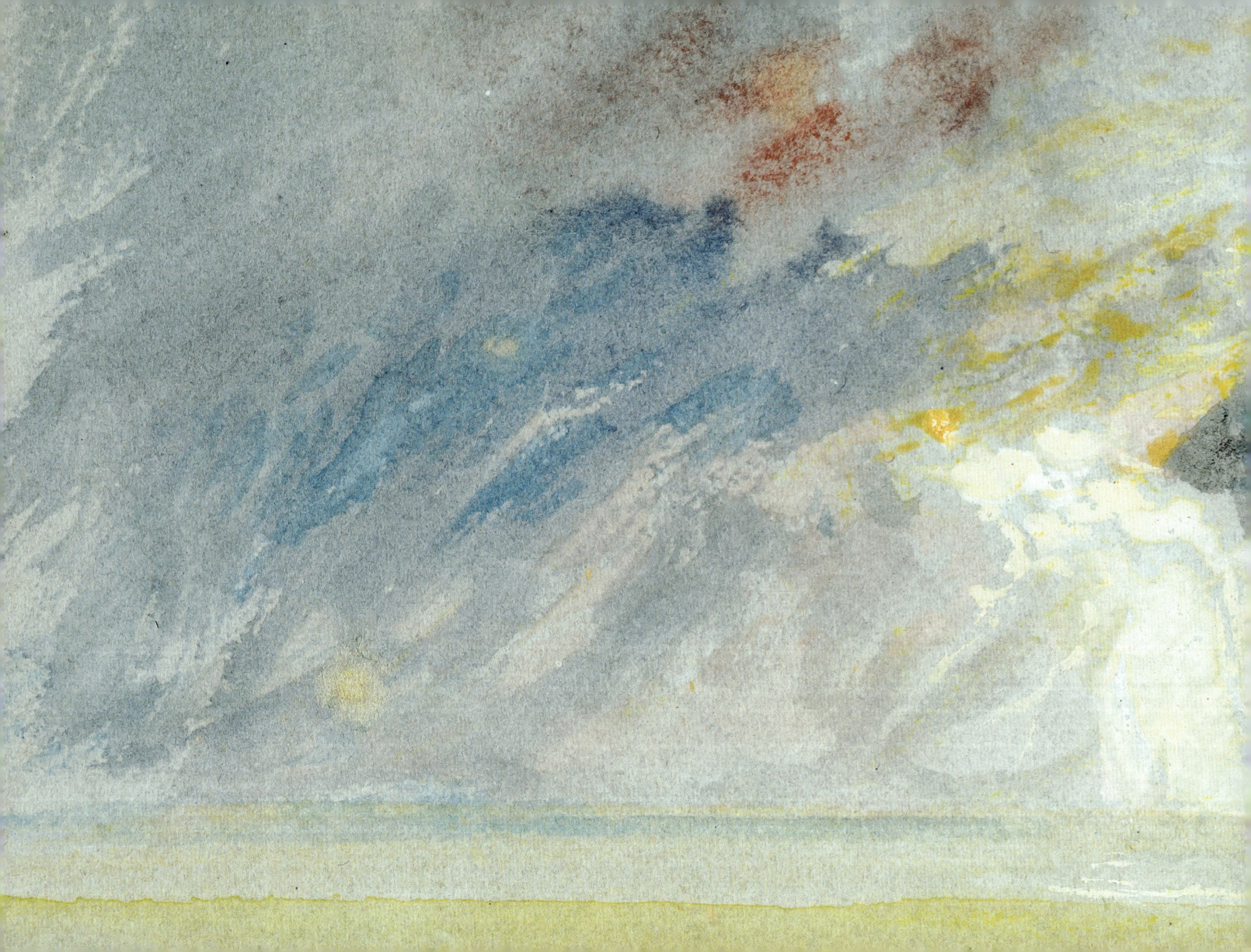

the Swiss watercolours in her home, he produced there numerous colour studies of effects of light, clouds or waves; a means of giving substance to his claim that the variety of light over the Isle of Thanet gave it the loveliest skies in all Europe.[47] If he sometimes found an outlet for these researches in the paintings he exhibited during the 1840s, that was secondary to the act of watching and recording his impressions in itself, which was purely a personal response. Did he anticipate that these exercises would themselves be posthumously considered as art works? We can never know, yet it appears when making provision for the contents of his studio he intended that both finished and unfinished works should be preserved for display, so that students might understand his processes, thereby indicating his captivation with the mysterious alchemy he delighted in as part of his studio practice.

After Turner's death in 1851 it was only a little over a decade before the sketches that remained in Mrs Booth's property at Margate (as well as her later home at Chelsea) started to come onto the market at Christie's.[48] This was a new development that necessitated the auction house to reassure potential buyers of the authenticity of such unconventional examples of the artist's handiwork. But sales of sketches in the dispersal of artists' studios such as this constitute an important factor in the shift towards a wider acceptance of the unvarnished, primary experience of engaging directly with nature that took on such importance in the second half of the nineteenth century. Coincidentally, in 1862, the Old Water-Colour Society had introduced a separate winter exhibition specifically dedicated to studies, which further legitimized the sketching æsthetic.[49]

Almost all the artists included here would have had an awareness of photography in their later years, but the cumbersome equipment needed to capture an image meant that the kind of decisive snapshot, possible even in watercolour, was still decades away. The precise beauties preserved in the miraculous early calotypes and daguerreotypes certainly offered a new æsthetic (fig. 8).[50] However, this new form of realism did not yet challenge the watercolour sketcher's ability to transcribe fleeting instants of atmosphere or light, as well as motion and gestures. Nevertheless, the arrival of this new technology ultimately meant something was lost. It would

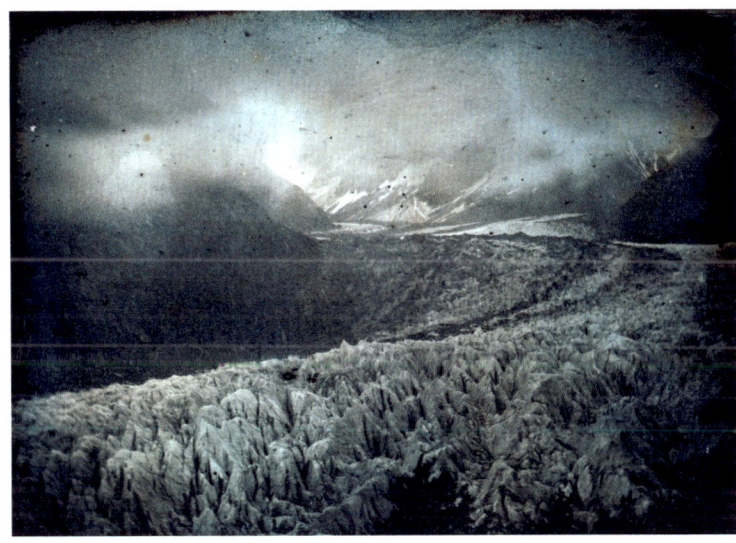

Fig. 8 The Mer de Glace, daguerrotype by John Ruskin and John Hobbs, 1844
Whitehouse Collection, The Ruskin, Lancaster University

offer apparently objective images against which the more subjective response of eye and hand could be measured and would struggle to compete. By contrast, looking at the very individual ways in which the handful of artists gathered here viewed the world provides a way back to seeing with more innocent eyes.

For previous selections from the Hickman Bacon collection, see: Eric Shanes, *British Watercolours from The Hickman Bacon Collection*, Tokyo 1990; Eric Shanes, *The Golden Age of Watercolours: the Hickman Bacon Collection*, London 2001; Timothy Wilcox, *Turner and his Contemporaries: the Hickman Bacon Watercolour Collection*, Kendal 2012.

Both this essay and the captions for individual works are indebted to the recent research on the Hickman Bacon collection undertaken by Timothy Wilcox. I am grateful to him for sharing this rich unpublished source of information.

1. The literature on the history of watercolour is vast, but useful recent surveys are as follows: Scott Wilcox, *British Watercolours. Drawings of the 18th and 19th Centuries from the Yale Center for British Art*, New Haven 1985; Andrew Wilton and Anne Lyles, *The Great Age of British Watercolours 1750-1880*, London 1993; Charles Nugent, *From View to Vision. British Watercolours from Sandby to Turner in the Whitworth Art Gallery*, Manchester 1993; Jane Munro, *British Landscape Watercolours 1750-1850*, Cambridge 1994; Alison Smith (ed), *Watercolour*, London 2011; Katherine Coombs, *British Watercolours 1750-1950*, London 2012; Jane Munro (ed), *Watercolour. Elements of Nature*, Cambridge 2015; Kim Sloan (ed), *Places of the Mind, British Watercolour Landscapes 1850-1950*, London 2017. For a French view of the subject, see Marie-Pierre Sale, *Watercolor: A History*, Paris 2023.

2 See William Henry Pyne, 'The Rise and Progress of Water-Colour Painting in England', parts I-IX, *Somerset House Weekly Miscellany of the Arts*, London, 8 November 1823-3 January 1824

3 See Timothy Wilcox, 'Questions of Identity: the Place of Watercolour in British Art', in Colin Harrison (ed), *Great British Drawings*, Oxford 2015, pp. 29-41

4 The paper historian Peter Bower has written widely on many of the artists featured here, but see especially, *Turner's Papers: A Study of the Manufacture, Selection and Use of his Drawing Papers*, London 1990 and 1999. For the pigments and other materials used in this period, see Joyce Townsend, *Turner's Painting Techniques*, London 1993; Joyce H. Townsend and Tony Smibert, *Tate Watercolour*

Manual Lessons from the Great Masters, London 2014; and most recently Joyce H. Townsend, *How Turner Painted. Materials and Techniques*, London 2019

5 See, Greg Smith, 'Watercolourists and Watercolours at the Royal Academy, 1780-1836', in David H. Solkin (ed), *Art on the Line. The Royal Academy Exhibitions at Somerset House 1780-1836*, New Haven and London 2001, pp. 189-200; Simon Fenwick, *Two Hundred Years of the Royal Watercolour Society*, Bristol 2004; Tim Wilcox and Charles Nugent, *The Triumph of Watercolour: The early years of the Royal Watercolour Society, 1805-55*, London 2005

6 Fenwick, *op. cit.*, p. 22

7 See Evelyn Joll, Martin Butlin and Luke Herrmann (eds), *The Oxford Companion to J. M. W. Turner*, Oxford 2001. For recent studies focusing on Turner's watercolours, see: Eric Shanes (ed), *Turner. The Great Watercolours*, London 2000; Nicola Moorby and Ian Warrell (eds), *How to Paint like Turner*, London 2010; Nicholas R. Bell (ed), *Conversations with Turner: The Watercolours*, Mystic 2019

8 See Eric Shanes, *Young Mr Turner. The First Forty Years, 1775-1815*, New Haven and London 2016

9 See Kim Sloan, *Alexander and John Robert Cozens. The Poetry of Landscape*, New Haven and London 1986, pp. 132

10 See the account given by Turner on 12 November 1798: Kenneth Garlick and Angus Macintyre (eds), *The Diary of Joseph Farington*, New Haven and London, 1979, III, pp. 1089-90. For a recent analysis of Turner's statement, see Greg Smith, 'Section 2: Thomas Monro and John Henderson: Making Creative Copies, 1794-98', on the Thomas Girtin website, hosted by the Paul Mellon Center

11 See Timothy Wilcox, *Francis Towne*, London 1997

12 R. and S. Redgrave, *A Century of Painters of the English School*, London 1866, I, p. 292

13 See Greg Smith, 'Turning "His Back to the Scene". The Watercolourist and the Ambiguities of the Landscape Sketch, 1770-1860', in *The Spooner Collection of British Watercolours at the Courtauld Institute Gallery*, Kendal 2006, pp. 17-36. The author is indebted to this article and personal communications with Greg Smith in the current essay

14 Coombs, *op. cit.*, p. 47

15 Turner complained that 'it would take up too much time to colour in the open air – he could made 15 or 16 pencil sketches to one coloured' (Letter from John Soane Jr, 15 November 1819). See A. J. Finberg, *The Life of J. M. W. Turner*, Oxford 1961, p. 262

16 Greg Smith (ed), *Thomas Girtin: The Art of Watercolour*, London 2002. See especially, Susan Morris, 'Families and Friends: A Network of Lady Pupils and Patrons', pp. 255-258

17 Ibid, pp. 189-193

18 Ibid p. 229, no. 178

19 David Hill, *Turner in the Alps. The Journey through France & Switzerland in 1802*, London 1992

20 Ian Warrell, *Turner's Sketchbooks*, London 2014, pp. 24-5

21 See Ian Warrell, '"The Wonder-Working artist": Contemporary Responses to Turner's Exhibited and Engraved Watercolours' in Eric Shanes (ed), *Turner. The Great Watercolours*, London 2000, pp. 37-39

22 Andrew Hemingway, *The Norwich School of Painters 1803-1833*, Oxford 1979; Andrew W. Moore, *The Norwich School of Artists*, Norwich 1985; David Blayney Brown, Andrew Hemingway and Anne Lyles, *Romantic Landscape. The Norwich School of Painters*, London 2000

23 Giorgia Bottinelli (ed), *A Passion for Landscape. Rediscovering John Crome*, Norwich 2021

24 See Michael Rosenthal, 'The "Natural Painture"', in *Constable. The Painter and his Landscape*, New Haven and London 1983, pp. 91-132

25 See Kathryn Cave (ed), *The Diary of Joseph Farington*, New Haven and London 1982, Vol. VII, p. 2748 (5 May 1806)

26 See Tim Wilcox, 'Charm without beauty: John Crome's watercolours and drawings', in Bottinelli, *op. cit.*, pp. 57-65

27 Andrew W. Moore, *John Sell Cotman 1782-1842*, Norwich 1982; Patrick Le Nouëne and Annette Haudiquet (eds), *Louis Francia*, Calais 1988; Gillian Forrester, *Turner's Drawing Book, The Liber Studiorum*, London 1995

Overleaf: Detail of Peter De Wint, Landscape with Church Tower (no. 48)

28 Timothy Wilcox, 'The Influence of Anxiety: John Sell Cotman and J. M. W. Turner', *Turner Society News*, 137, Spring 2022, p. 15

29 Andrew Hemingway, 'The Constituents of Romantic Genius: John Sell Cotman's Greta Drawings', in M. Rosenthal, C. Payne and S. Wilcox (eds), *Recent Essays in British Landscape 1750-1880*, New Haven and London 1997, pp. 183-203; David Hill, *Cotman in the North: Watercolours of Durham and Yorkshire*, New Haven and London 2005

30 See David Hill, 'Cotman, Bloomfield and The Ploughed Field', published 25 November 2018, on www.sublimesites.co, accessed January 202531 Miklos Rajnai and Marjorie Allthorpe-Guyton, *John Sell Cotman, Early Drawings in Norwich Castle Museum*, Norwich 1979; Miklos Rajnai (ed), *John Sell Cotman 1782-1842*, London 1982. See also David Hill's entries on www.cotmania.org, accessed January 2025

32 For Turner's adoption of new pigments, see Townsend, *op. cit.*, p. 41. Research into the materials used by Cotman and Crome was undertaken at the Hamilton Kerr Institute in 2011-13, but focused primarily on their work in oils. For discussion of Cotman's use of paste, see Anne Lyles in *Romantic Landscape. The Norwich School of Painters*, London 2000, p. 116

33 Robert Hoozee (ed), *British Vision. Observation and Imagination in British Art 1750-1950*, Ghent 2008; Michael Rosenthal and Anne Lyles, *Turner and Constable: Sketching from Nature*, London 2013

34 John Gage, *A Decade of English Naturalism 1810-1820*, Norwich 1969

35 See Anne Lyles, 'Naturalism' in *The Great Age of British Watercolours 1750-1880*, London 1993, pp. 134-5. I am grateful to Anne Lyles for further discussion on Varley

36 See Scott Wilcox (ed), *Sun, Wind and Rain. The Art of David Cox*, New Haven and London 2008

37 See Smith, *op. cit*, 2006, pp. 22-23

38 See Peter Bower, 'A Remarkable Understanding. David Cox's Use of Paper' in Wilcox, *op. cit*, 2008, pp. 97-111; and 'Peter DeWint and Thomas Creswick's Paper "Signed all over"', in John Lord (ed), *Peter De Wint 1784-1849. "For the common observer of life and nature"*, Aldershot and Burlington 2007

39 See David Scrase, *Drawings and Watercolours by Peter De Wint*, Cambridge 1979. John Lord, *op. cit.*, 2007, pp. 32-39

40 For the informal academy provided by Dr Thomas Monro, see the discussion mentioned under note 10 above

41 Leslie Parris, *Landscape in Britain, c. 1750-1850*, London 1973, pp. 109-10

42 Those in the Hickman Bacon are especially good examples. But see also *Peter De Wint 1784-1849. Colourist and Countryman*, London 2005

43 For example, De Wint's designs for John Hughes, *Views in the South of France*, 1825

44 Turner's designs made from Lt George White's sketches appeared in the latter's *Views in India chiefly among the Himalaya Mountains*, London and Paris 1836 (see Christie's, London, 6 July 2023, lot 8, 'Rocks at Colgong on the Ganges, Bihar')

45 See 'Turner's Late Finished Watercolours' in Ian Warrell, *Through Switzerland with Turner*, London 1995, pp. 149-155

46 See David Blaney Brown and Matthew Imms (eds), *J. M. W. Turner: Sketchbooks, Drawings and Watercolours*, https://www.tate.org.uk/art/research-publications/jmw-turner/, accessed January 2025

47 John Ruskin, *Fors Clavigera*, Letter 9 (September 1871), in E. T. Cook and Alexander Wedderburn, *Works of John Ruskin*, London 1907, XXVII, pp. 161-4. Some of the Margate subjects included here are given a wider context in Ian Warrell (ed), *Turner et la Couleur*, Paris and Aix-en-Provence 2026, pp. 149-183

48 Mrs Booth's collection appeared at Christie's on 25 March 1865. The contents of the sale are discussed in Imogen Holmes-Roe, *Turner. In Light and Shade*, Manchester 2025

49 Coombs, *op. cit.*, p. 47

50 See 'Revolutions in Landscape' in Dominique de Font-Réaulx, *Painting and Photography 1839-1914*, Paris 2012, pp. 109-140. For a useful, but too-often overlooked study of the connections between early photography and the traditional uses of sketches in the studio, see Ken Jacobson (ed), *Étude d'Après Nature: 19th century Photographs in Relation to Art*, Great Bardfield 1996

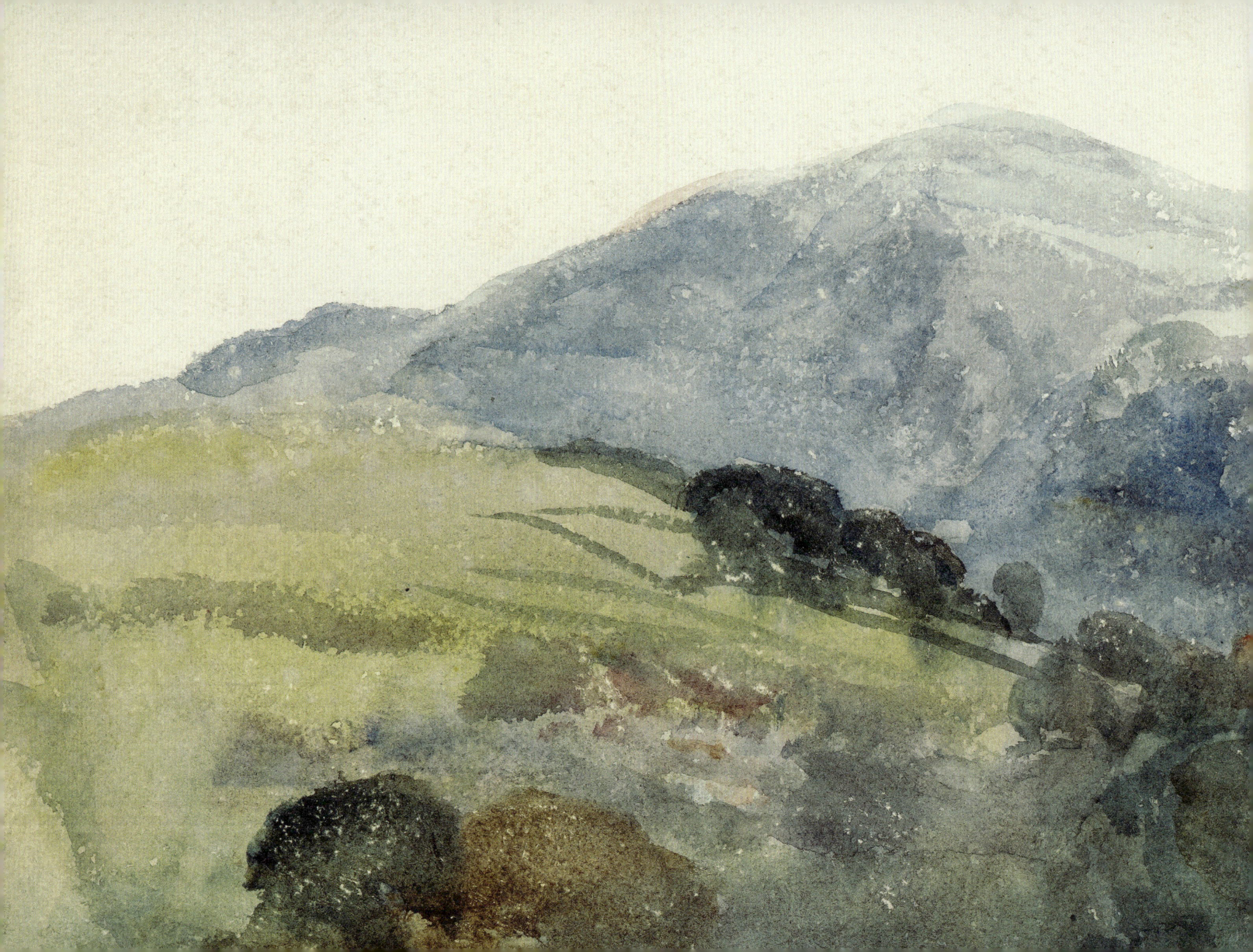

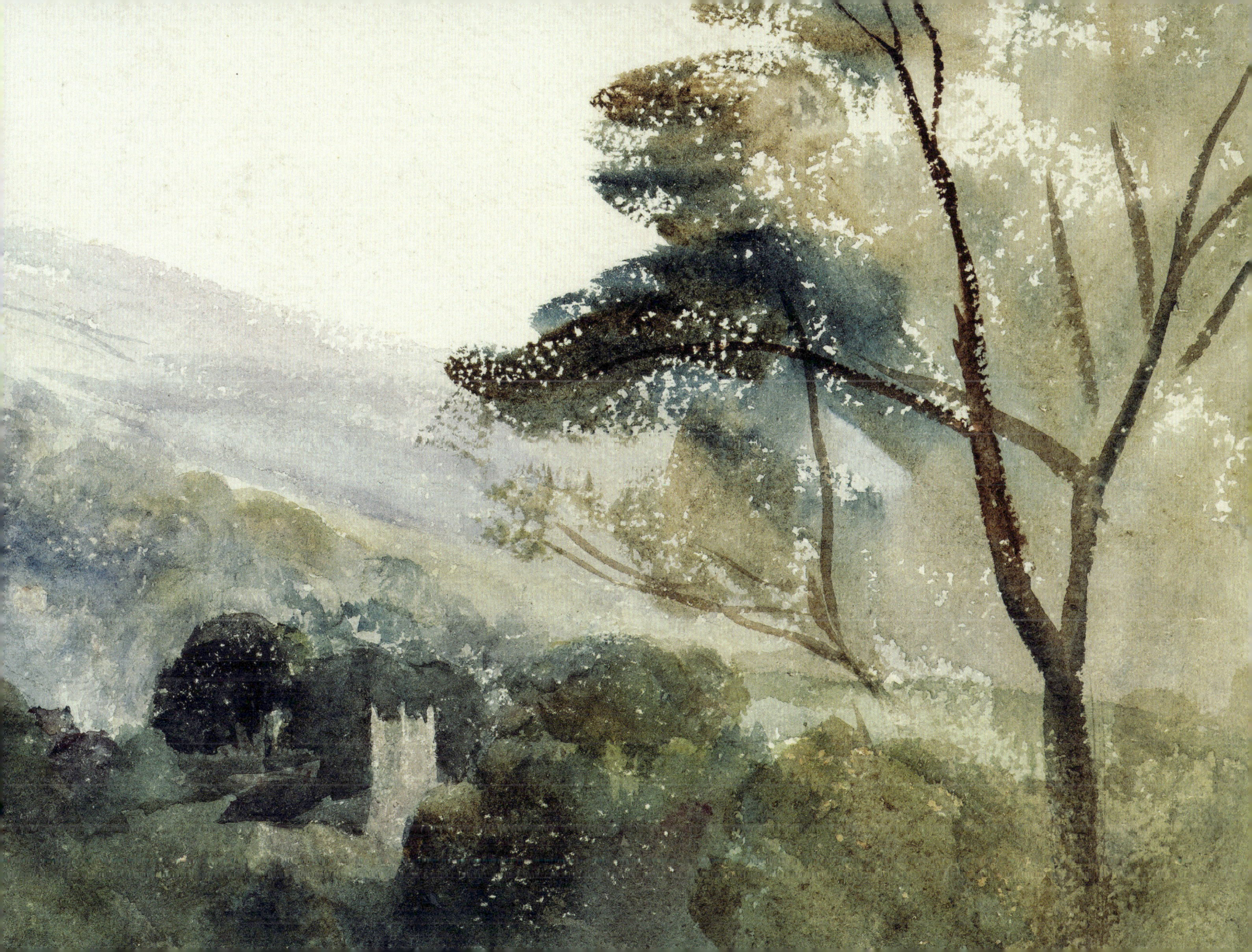

Perception, taste and judgement: Sir Hickman Bacon and his watercolour collection

Timothy Wilcox

THE COLLECTION OF ALMOST 500 English watercolours and drawings assembled by Sir Hickman Bacon (1855-1945) in less than twenty years around the turn of the last century is a truly remarkable achievement.

When Hickman Bacon inherited his baronetcy in 1872, at the age of only 17, there was no-one in his immediate family with any distinction in the field of the arts. Bacon had barely completed his five years at Eton. For a while, he lodged in the boarding house of the college's elderly drawing master, William Evans 'of Eton', but Bacon does not seem to have engaged in any artistic pursuits as a result. He enlisted in the Grenadier Guards, until concerns over his health led him to retire at the age of 23. He was advised to spend the winter months abroad, lest his weak constitution succumb to the spectre of tuberculosis. In fact, after a decade of warmth, sunshine and relaxation, he was found to be far stronger than ever expected, and he went on to live an extremely active life until the age of 90. He remained a bachelor, since the potential invalid was not considered as a prospect for the marriage market. How easy it would have been to dissipate his considerable wealth in self-indulgence; and how very much he did the entire opposite, devoting himself to innumerable good causes at local and national level.

Bacon was elected a member of the Society of Antiquaries in 1878, but it was not an interest in the remoter regions of British history which fired his intellectual passions. When he began collecting English watercolours, in the mid-1890s, the field was at the forefront of a thorough-going reassessment, amounting to a rediscovery of several generations of artists who had formed the bedrock of an emerging national school. British art and British identity were inextricably linked; the castles, cathedrals and ruined abbeys that were the subject of countless watercolours of the late eighteenth and early nineteenth centuries symbolised British pride, strength and independence from the Continent. The storms, showers and windy gusts, so appropriately rendered in the watercolour medium, spoke of the British love of the outdoors, their resilience and optimism. For too long, it seemed, the subject had been dominated by one artist, J. M. W. Turner, and one critical voice, that of John Ruskin, promoting an excessively laborious and literal response to nature's variety.

Bacon entered the field at a moment of diversity and widening horizons. The anti-establishment battles of the 1880s in favour of the new French art, led by the New English Art Club on the one hand and by J. M. Whistler on the other, were leading to the gradual acceptance of the Impressionist æsthetic.[1] English watercolours occupied a fascinatingly ambiguous position. They were found to possess many of the same qualities of freshness and spontaneity, lightness of touch and the embracing of the passing moment that were celebrated in Monet or Renoir, but, as part of a British visual heritage, they pushed back against any easy espousal of innovations emerging from France.[2]

Before committing himself to his watercolour collection, Bacon had acquired numerous prints by Dutch artists of the Hague School and the Barbizon artist Jean-François Millet, which were considered the height of modernity in the 1860s and 1870s.[3] At some stage, he amassed

an enormous number of Japanese woodcuts, which only began to be appreciated in advanced artistic circles in the 1860s; the 324 he donated to the British Museum in 1907 must have been acquired over several decades and included some exceptionally rare early examples. They are a testament to Bacon's acumen and tenacity, but also to the importance to him of deep and lasting friendship, since one of the leading watercolour scholars, Laurence Binyon at the British Museum, had also recently taken over responsibility for the Oriental collections, and was determined to build one of the world's greatest collections of these prints; with Bacon's significant contribution, he succeeded.[4]

Laurence Binyon was one of a small but significant group of professional scholars who transformed understanding of the field of English watercolour painting during the very years that Bacon was collecting, a period stretching roughly from 1895 to 1914. J. L. Roget's monumental *A History of the 'Old Water-colour' Society* appeared in 1891, scrupulously documenting dozens of artists who formed the backbone of what was proclaimed as a distinctly British art form. This followed hard on the heels of the first significant attempt to survey the emergence of the medium as an independent means of expression, *The earlier English water-colour painters* by the poet and critic Cosmo Monkhouse. In his final chapter, Monkhouse recognised the value of considering this historic practice in the light of the latest developments but declared that Turner's 'impressions' meant 'something very different from the impressions of the modern impressionists'.[5] For him the outstanding exponent of this approach was William Müller:

> [t]he impressions he painted were the impressions of the eye and of the moment, and he painted them at once in a sketch, and when he made a picture of the sketch, strove to preserve its freshness unimpaired, either by elaboration or added sentiment.[5]

The year 1891 was a watershed in another respect. The Winter Exhibition of the Royal Academy included a watercolour room for the first time, allowing the general public to see a strong survey of John Robert Cozens, Girtin, Turner, Cotman and others. The Royal Academy seemed to take this lead still further the following year, when the watercolour rooms were specifically devoted to a selection of 'studies, and sketches from nature'.

Despite a lack of direct evidence, there is every likelihood that Hickman Bacon saw this exhibition, although he did not begin collecting watercolours in earnest until a couple of years later. It is striking, nonetheless, that all the artists who came to form the core of his collection were the same ones represented at the Royal Academy in 1892: the four already mentioned from 1891, with the addition of Cox, De Wint and Bonington.

That is not to say that Bacon's taste was formed solely in response to these recent books and exhibitions; far from it. Having decided at a fairly early stage which artists were to him the central figures of the movement, he wanted to get to know them in the round. This led him to seek out works from all phases of their careers, but also to look in some detail at artists in their orbit. Thus, in addition to more than 15 works by Girtin, he assembled a really powerful group of watercolours by François Louis Thomas Francia. Francia spent many years in London as a refugee from the French Revolution, worked alongside Girtin, and, when he returned to France, was a vital

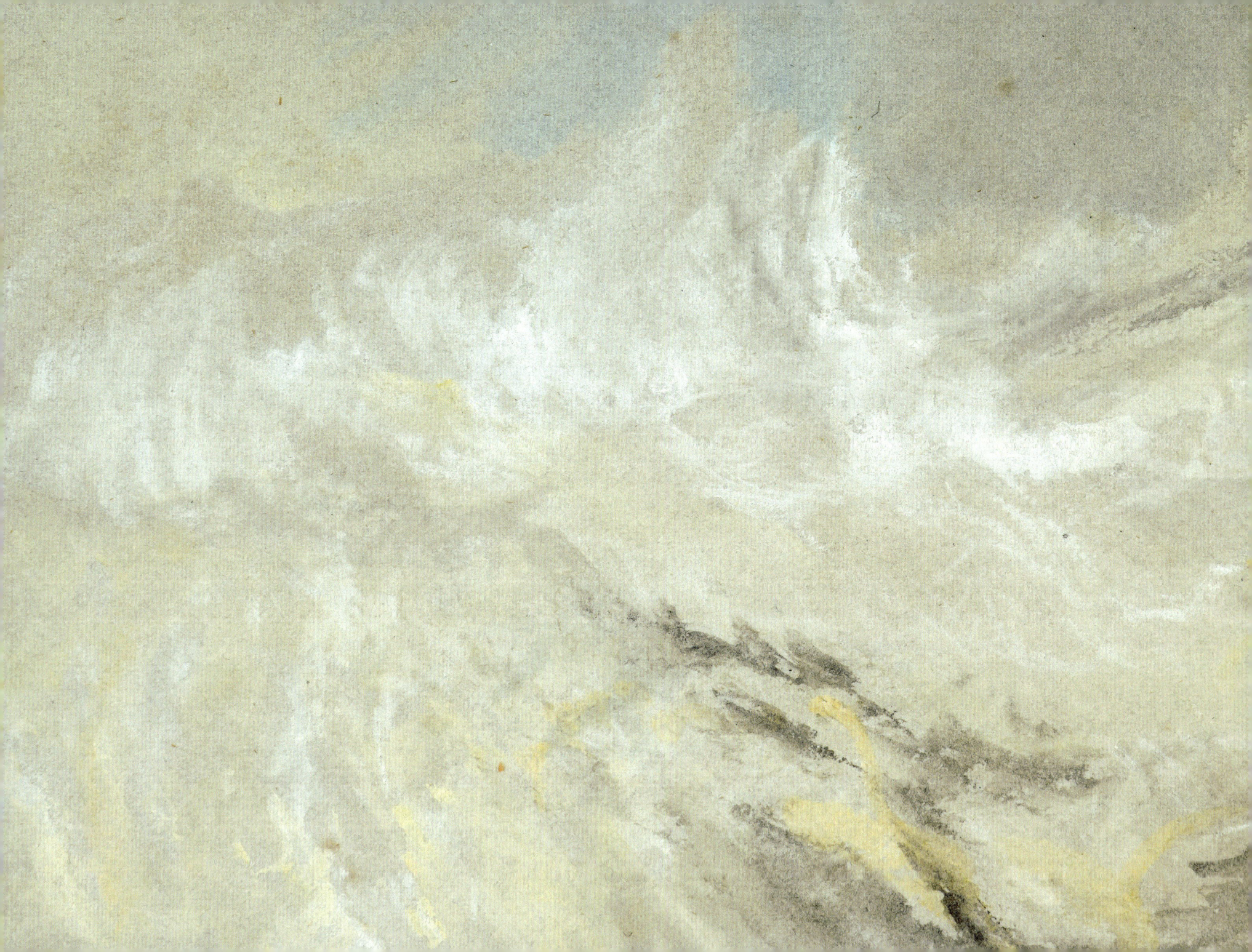

conduit in introducing Girtin's teachings to Bonington. The drawings and watercolours of Henry Edridge are today even less highly regarded than Francia's. However, a pencil drawing by Edridge in the British Museum of Girtin sketching out of doors stands as evidence that the two went out drawing together. Edridge is an acutely sensitive draughtsman, and his nature studies make a valuable foil to Girtin's more vigorous shorthand

Much as Hickman Bacon's collection is today celebrated for its many sketches and studies by Turner, ultimately, it was not these which gave their owner the greatest pleasure. In April 1913, Bacon visited Tom Girtin, the artist's great-grandson, to look at an early Cotman Girtin was thinking of buying and, on Bacon's advice, had taken home on approval for the weekend. On hearing the news that Girtin decided to keep it, Bacon wrote, 'I confess that I feel more permanently satisfied with [Cotman's] work of about 1805 than with that of any other artist – except perhaps Girtin's latest work. I prefer them to Turner's work at that time. I think they are simpler and more masculine.'[6] Quite what Bacon understood by the term 'masculine' is not straightforward to unravel, but it seems to have something to do with the clarity and definition of Cotman's mature idiom, the pronounced linear element in the design of his 1805 watercolours, together with his economy and sureness of touch in the use of colour. These were the very characteristics of Cotman's style which became all the rage in the 1920s and 1930s, permeating British visual culture from the avant-garde watercolours of Paul Nash to the vivid posters promoting railway travel across the length and breadth of the country.

It appears that Bacon had already relaxed his own unwritten rule regarding loans from his collection in favour of the Tate Gallery in 1922. Alongside their exhibition of John Sell Cotman, Bacon lent a selection of his 50 or so works by the artist, which were displayed in a separate room.[7] Several of the larger Cotmans along with works by John Robert Cozens, Girtin and Francia were in storage in the basement of the Tate Gallery when the Thames breached the Embankment in January 1928 and flooded the storeroom. Bacon was not in London at the time, and his good friend, the collector and scholar Paul Oppé, went to assess the situation. On being told that his watercolours had survived with little damage, Bacon's reaction was generous and philosophical, to say the least; 'I think Providence must disapprove of my lending things to exhibition – as you will doubtless remember my poor "Sharo" paintings being burnt at the Burlington Club only 3 or 4 years ago'.[8] Six weeks later, he again invoked Providence, now meaning some more personal force operating in the universe. Bacon reveals himself to have been the very opposite of the possessive hoarder the private collector can sometimes appear. 'The drawings should not have been flooded, had Providence willed otherwise – and as it is, He was fully entitled to cause anything He pleased to happen to them.'[9]

Nowadays, individual items and groups of works from the Hickman Bacon collection appear in major exhibitions all over the world. The present exhibition, consisting solely of a selection of the watercolours that he acquired, has an added dimension, beyond the appeal of the individual works: the personality of the collector himself. As the curator Francis Hawcroft expressed it in 1962, in the first detailed survey of the collection, his choices remain as 'a great tribute to his perception, individual tastes and intelligent judgement'.[10]

1. Kenneth McKonkey, *Impressionism in Britain*, Barbican Art Gallery 1995

2. Bruce Laughton, writing of Wilson Steer's first exhibition with the London branch of the Paris dealer Goupil in 1894, goes so far as to refer to 'francophobia'; *Philip Wilson Steer 1860-1942*, Oxford 1971, p. 50

3. Bacon's private papers indicate that in April 1897 he received a parcel of 23 etchings by Israels, Mauve and Maris from the Goupil Gallery, on approval. They are all marked with a tick, despite some having the added annotation, 'have this already'. A few months later he was billed for 27 etchings by Israels alone. In July 1895, Robert Dunthorne supplied him with eight etchings by Millet

4. Laurence Binyon, *A catalogue of Japanese and Chinese woodcuts preserved in the Sub-Department of Oriental Prints and Drawings in the British Museum*, London 1916

5. Cosmo Monkhouse, *The earlier English watercolour painters*, London 1890, p. 139

6. Letter of 9 April 1913, Girtin Archive in the Department of Prints and Drawings, British Museum; see Timothy Wilcox, 'The Hickman Bacon Collection of English watercolours' in *Turner and his contemporaries: The Hickman Bacon Watercolour Collection*, Kendal, 2012, p. 12. For Girtin's letter of the previous day, see Jessica Feather, 'A new 'golden age'? The 'modern' landscape watercolour' in Kim Sloan, (ed) *Places of the mind. British watercolour landscapes, 1850-1950*, London 2017, p. 223. The watercolour in question, a view of Bolton Abbey c. 1804, now in a private collection, is reproduced in David Hill, *Cotman in the North*, London 2005, p. 42

7. The full extent of Bacon's Cotman collection was revealed in the *Exhibition of the works of John Sell Cotman* at the Ferens Art Gallery, Hull in 1938, which numbered 54 items, though several of the attributions would not be sustained today

8. Bacon was perhaps referring to the Burlington Fine Arts Club exhibition *Counterfeits, imitations and copies of works of art*, London 1924, but he is not named among the lenders in the catalogue

9. Paul Mellon Centre for Studies in British Art, Oppé Papers, letters of 10 January and 2 March 1928

10. Francis W. Hawcroft, 'English water-colours and drawings in the collection of Sir Edmund Bacon, Bart.', *The Old Watercolour Society's Club, 37th Annual Volume*, London 1962, p. 33

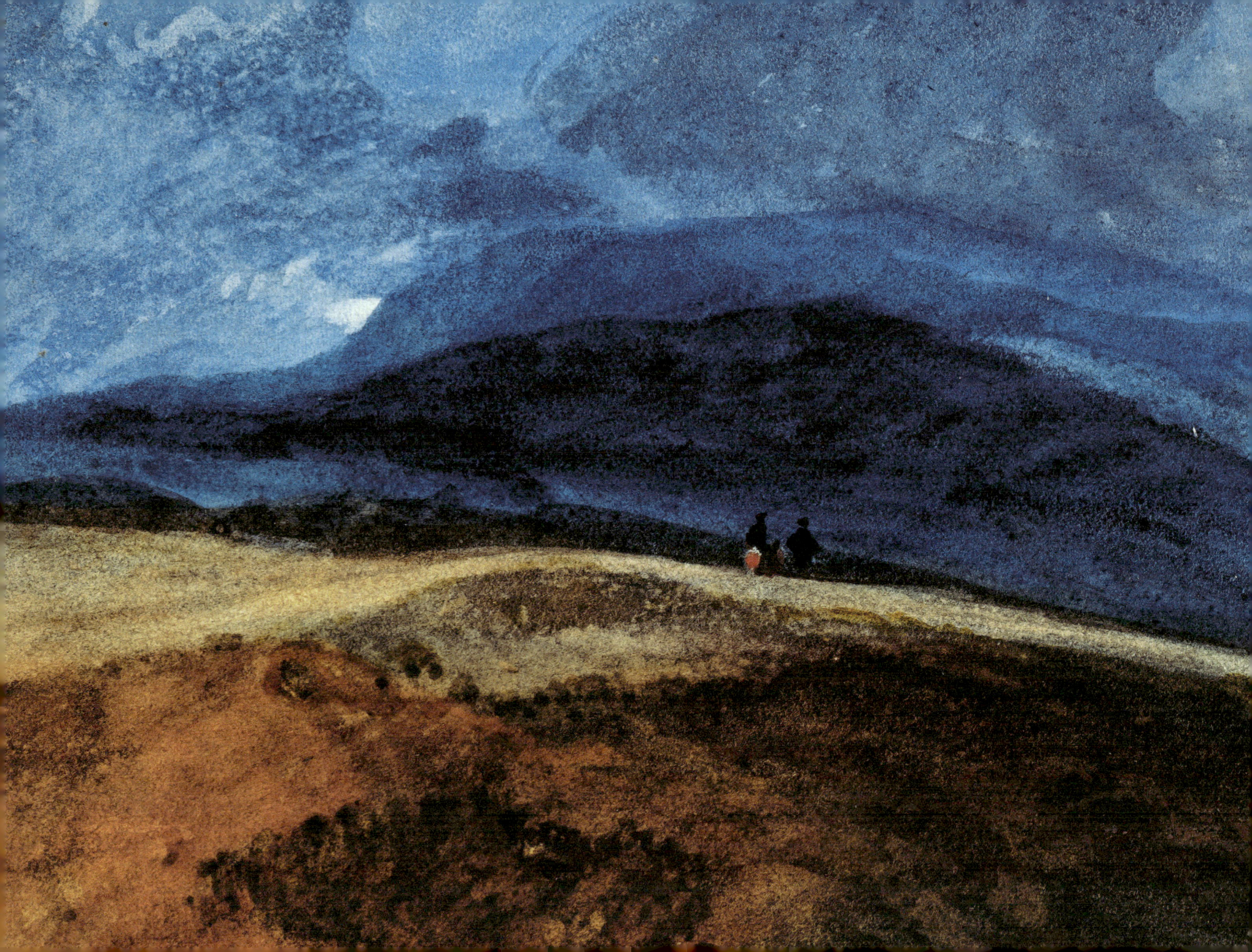

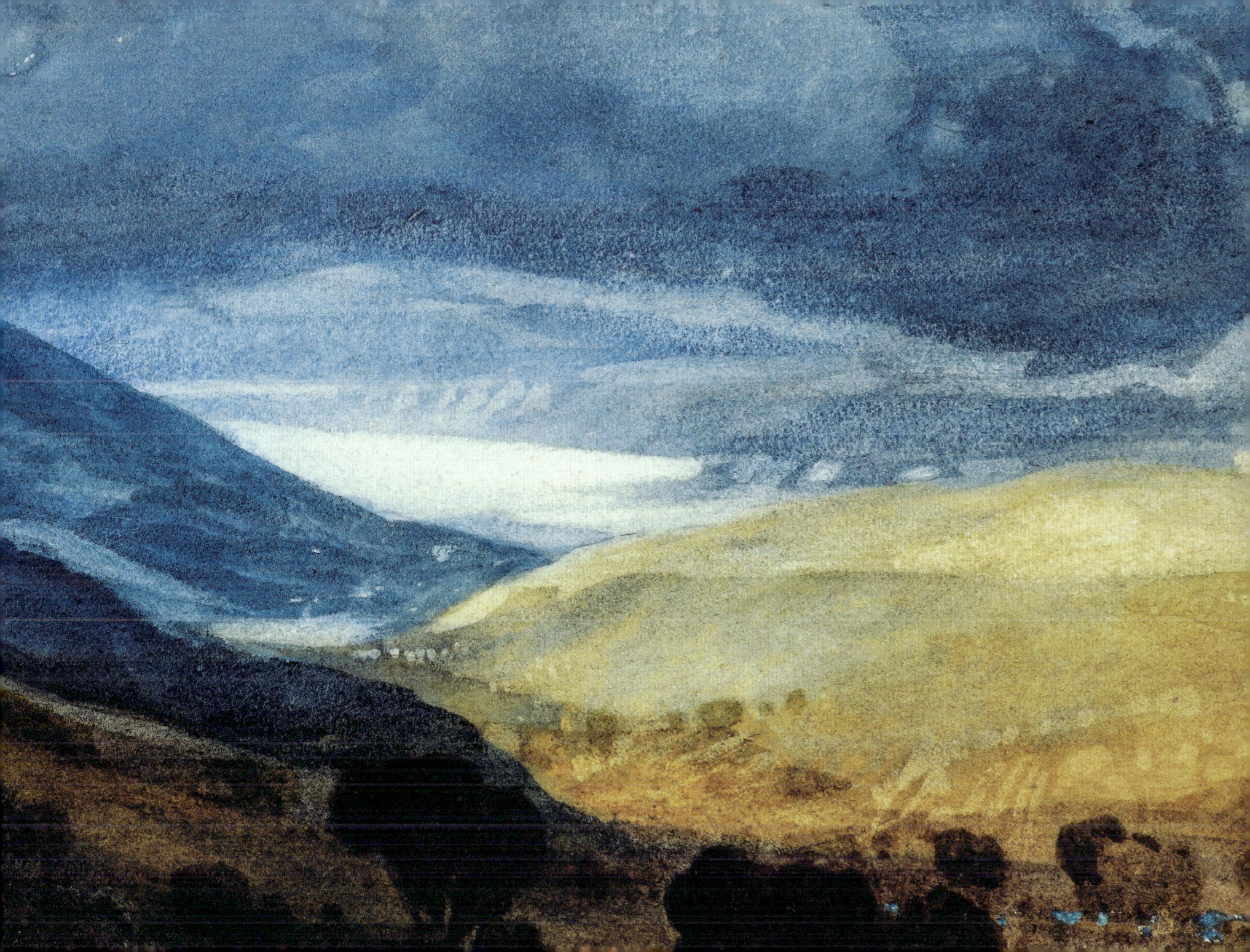

1. John Robert Cozens
In the Tyrol near Brixen, 1790
watercolour on paper
37.2 x 53.6 cm

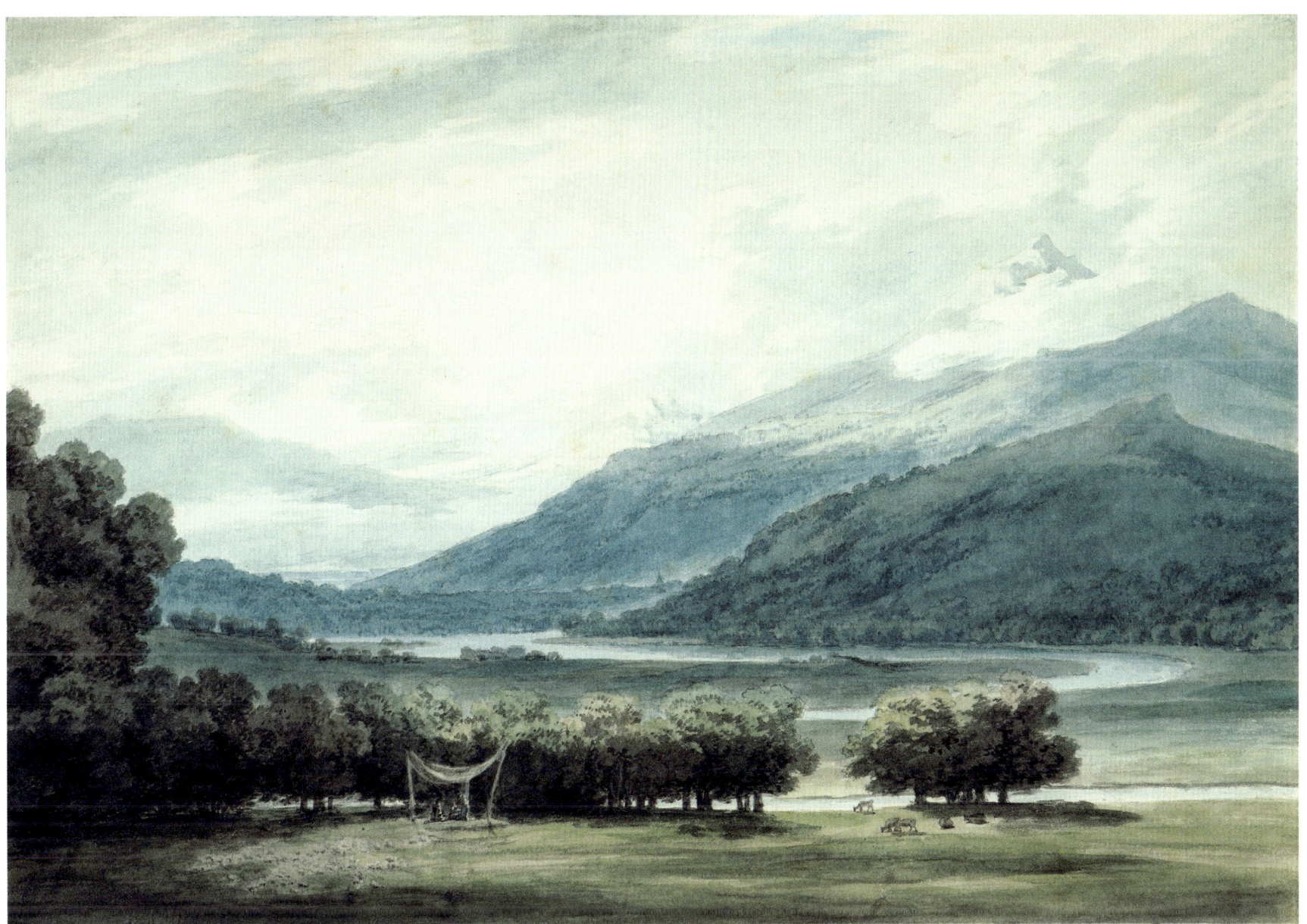

2. Joseph Mallord William Turner
Bath from Kingsdown Hill, 1791-2
watercolour, pencil and ink on paper
17.4 x 26.5 cm

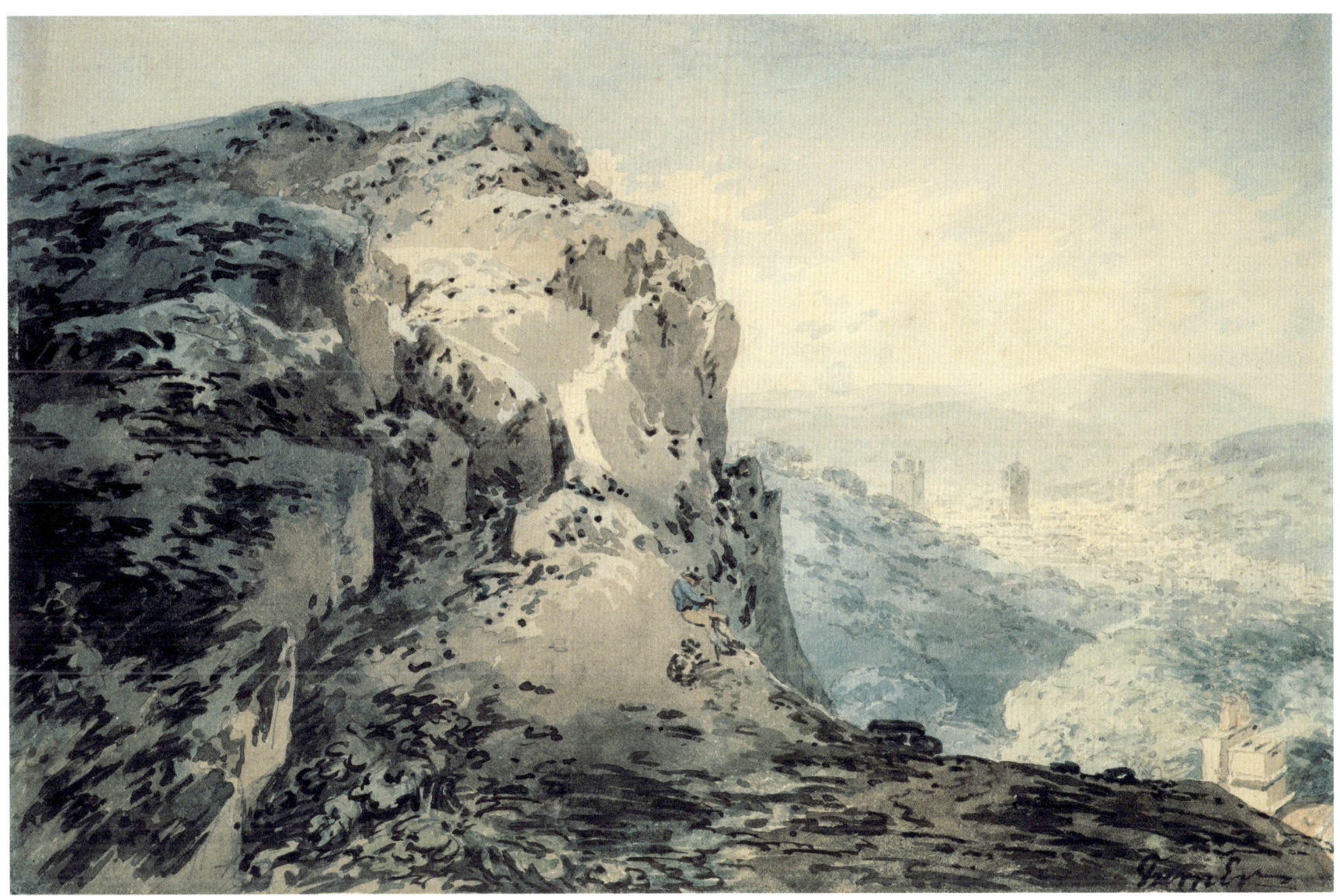

3. Joseph Mallord William Turner
Malmesbury Abbey, 1791
pen and brown ink and watercolour on paper
19.1 x 26.2 cm

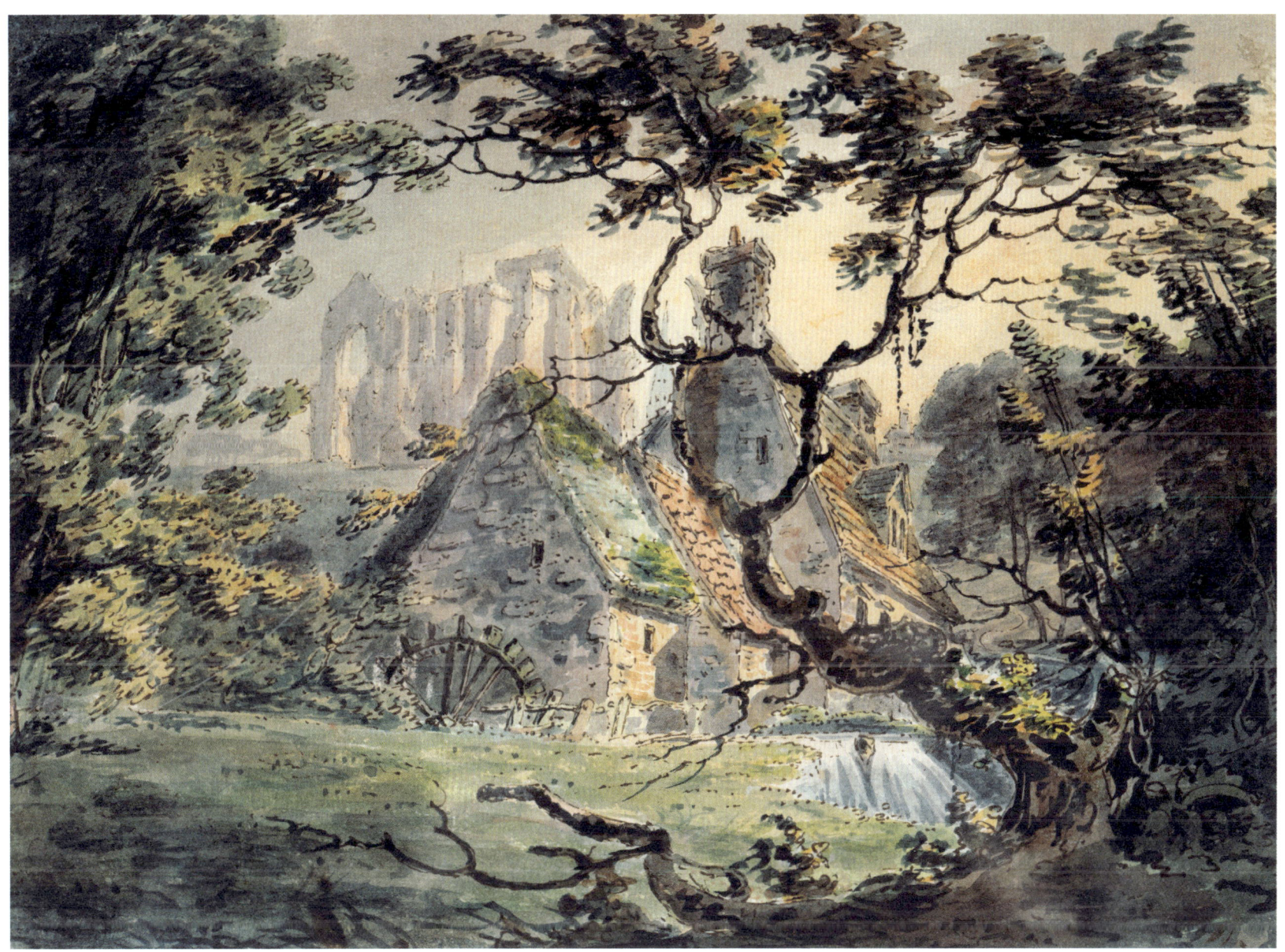

4. Thomas Girtin
Windsor Park and Castle, c. 1796-8
pencil and watercolour on paper
20.5 x 27 cm

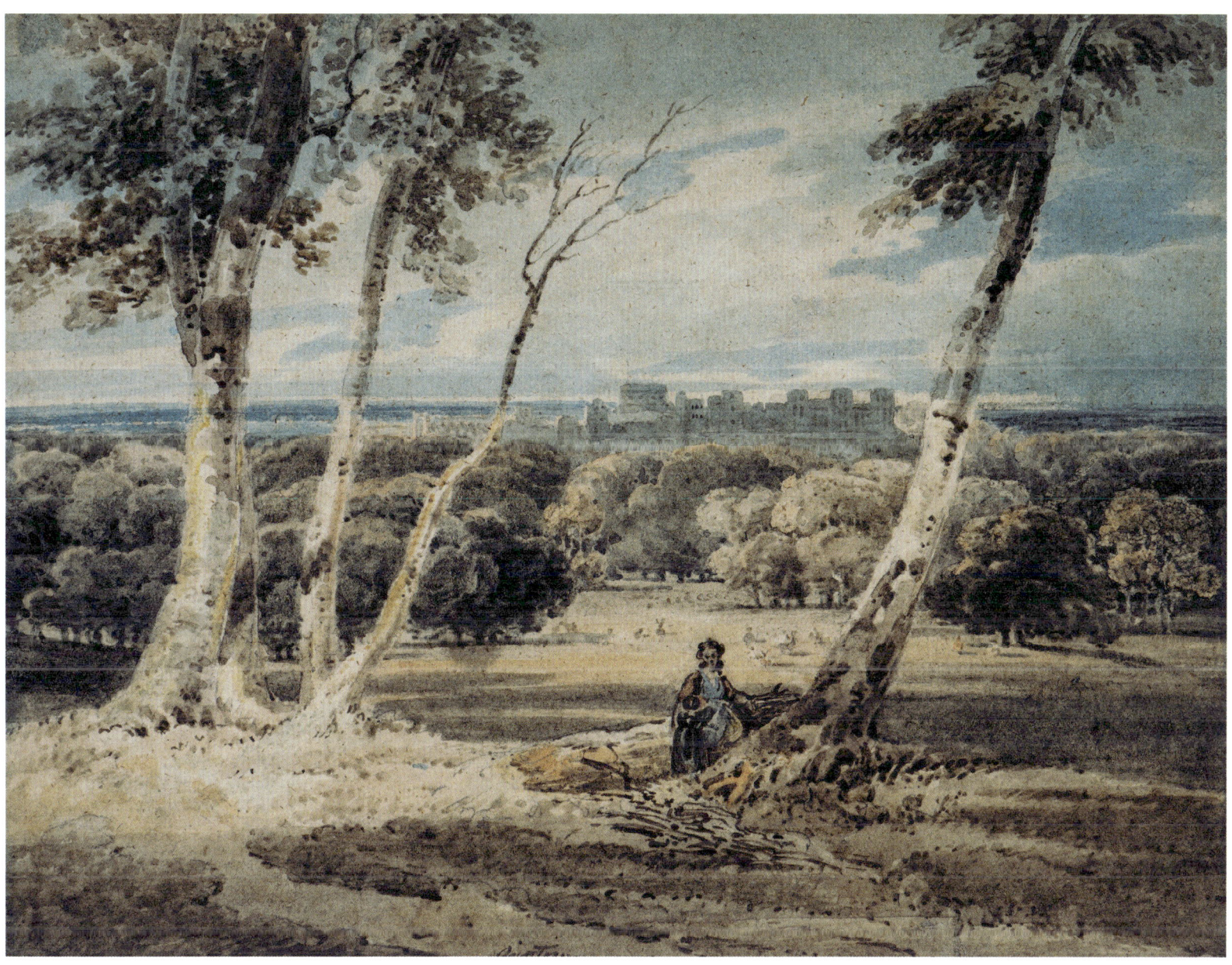

5. Thomas Girtin
Warkworth Castle, c. 1800
watercolour on paper
33.3 x 53.8 cm

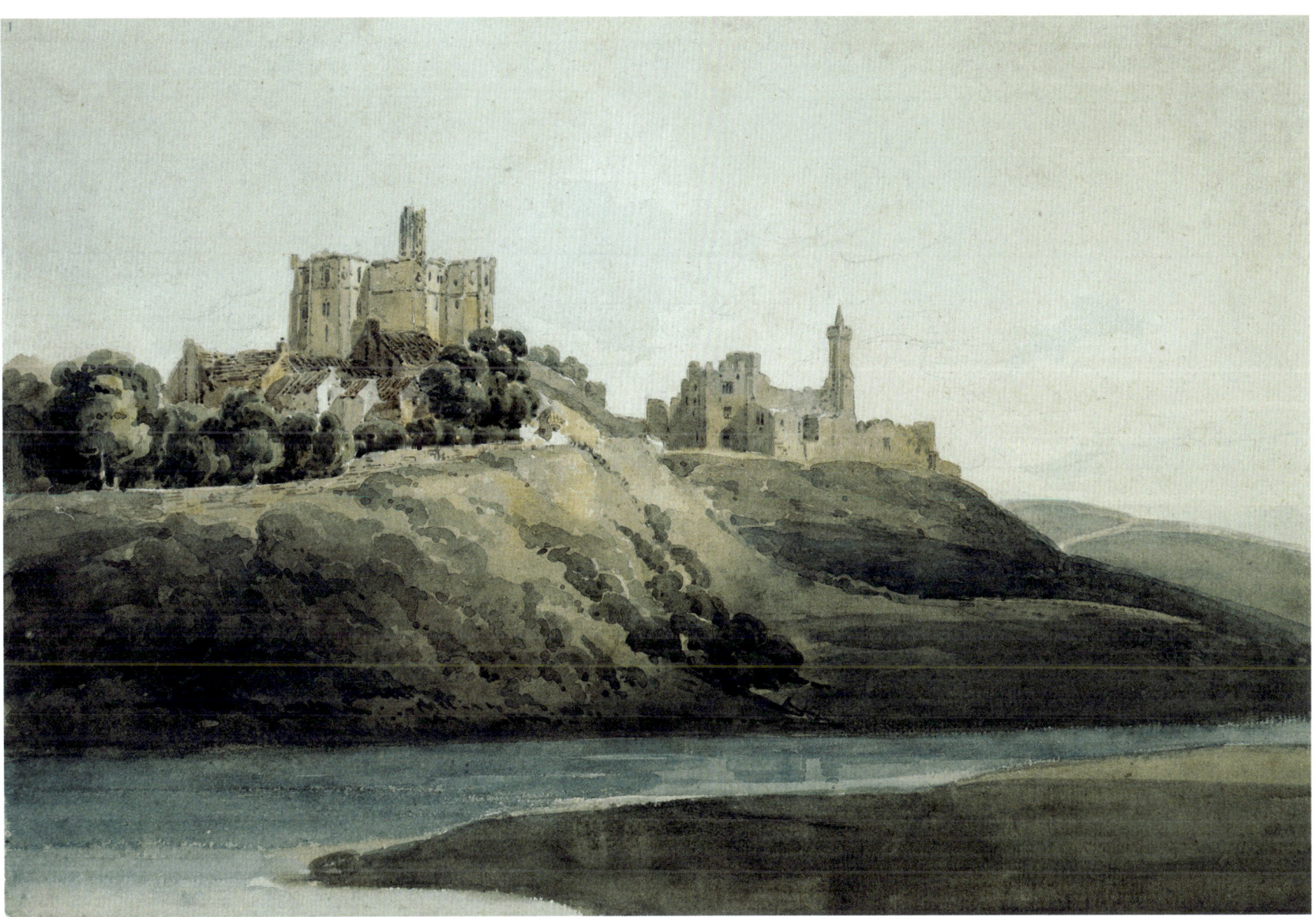

6. Joseph Mallord William Turner
Durham Castle and Cathedral, c. 1801
pencil and watercolour on paper
39.2 x 26.9 cm

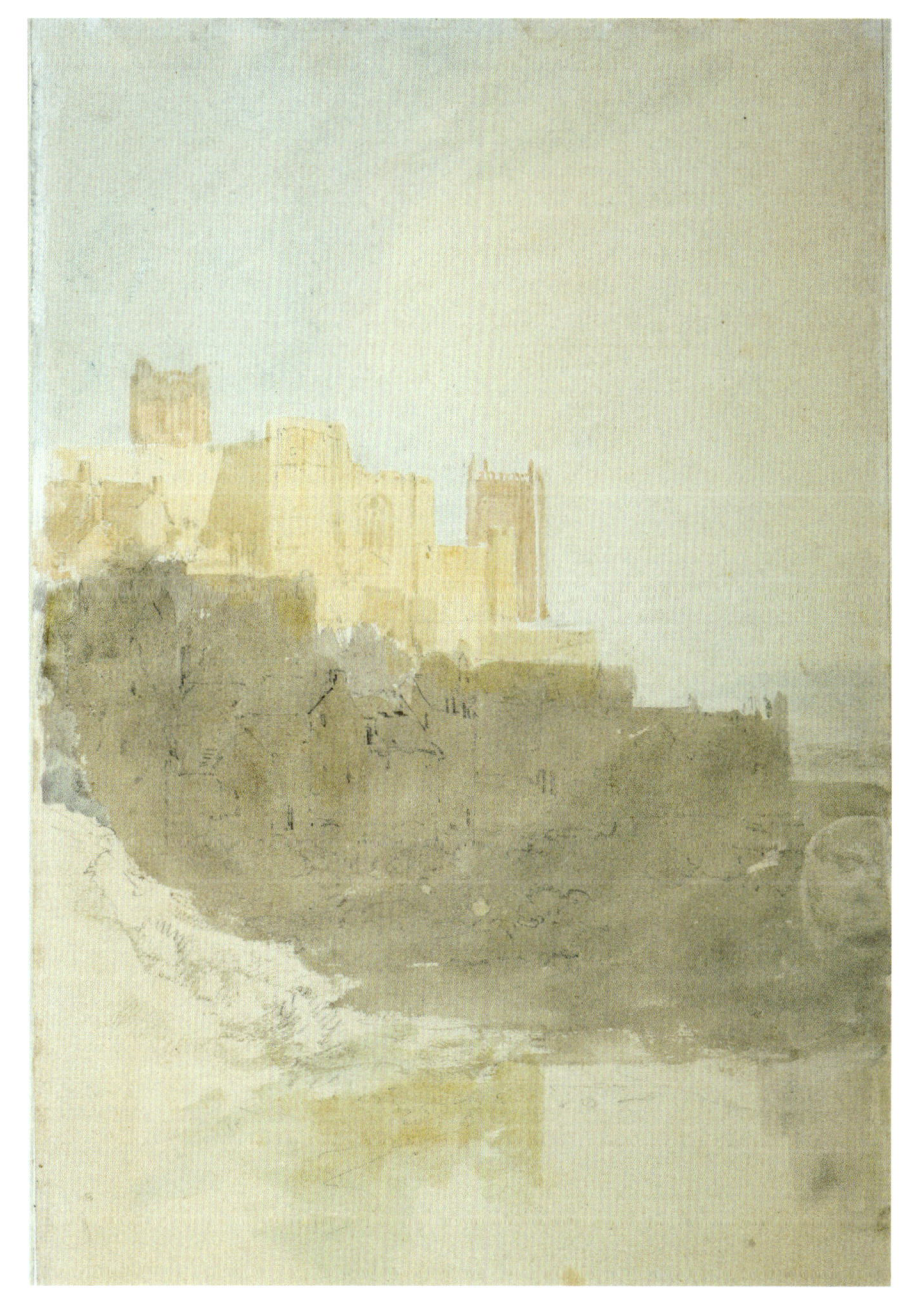

7. Thomas Girtin
View on the Wharfe, c. 1801
watercolour on paper
31.5 x 52.7 cm

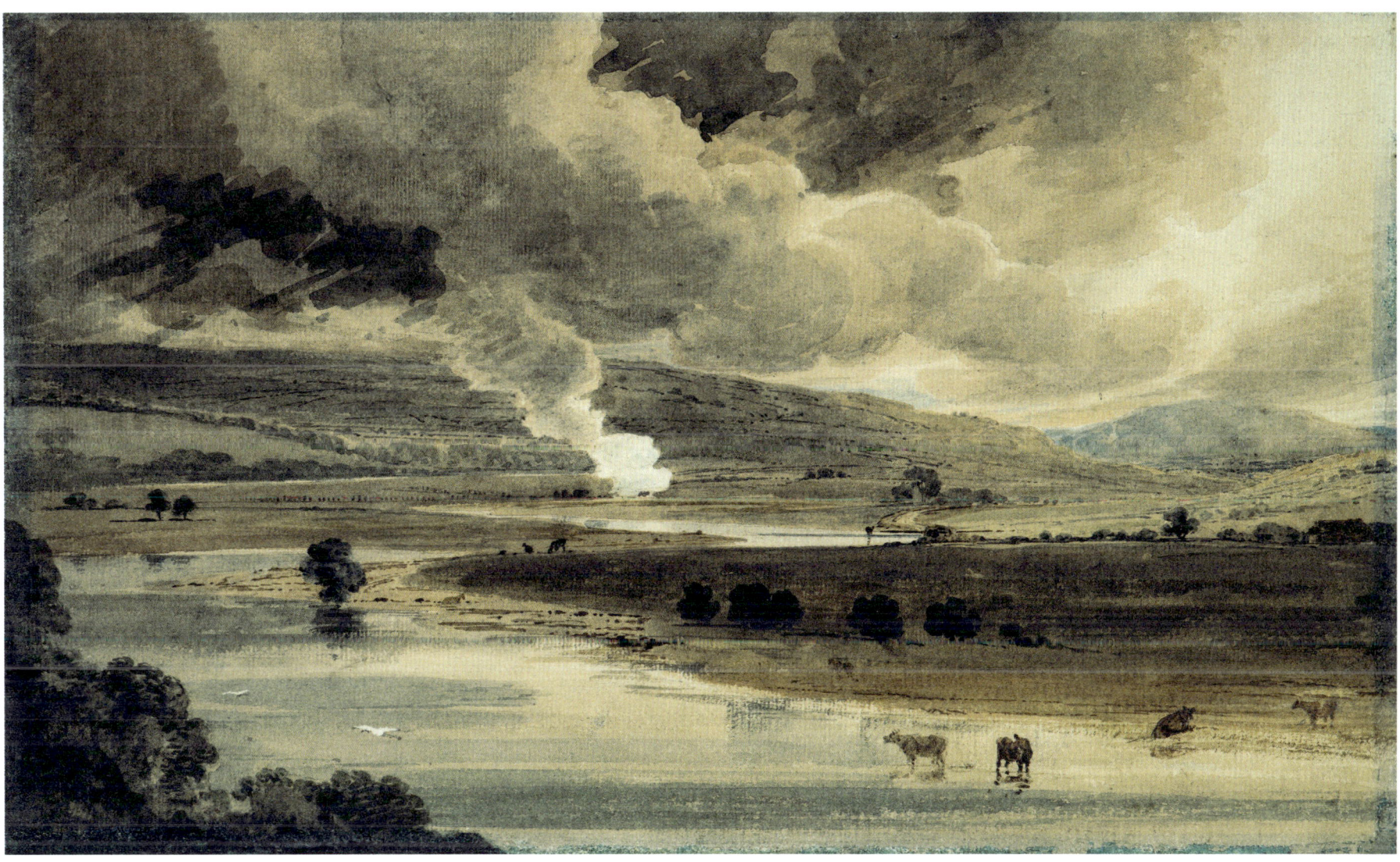

8. Joseph Mallord William Turner
Glacier des Bossons, Chamonix, 1802
pencil and watercolour with gouache on white paper prepared with a grey wash
32 x 47.6 cm

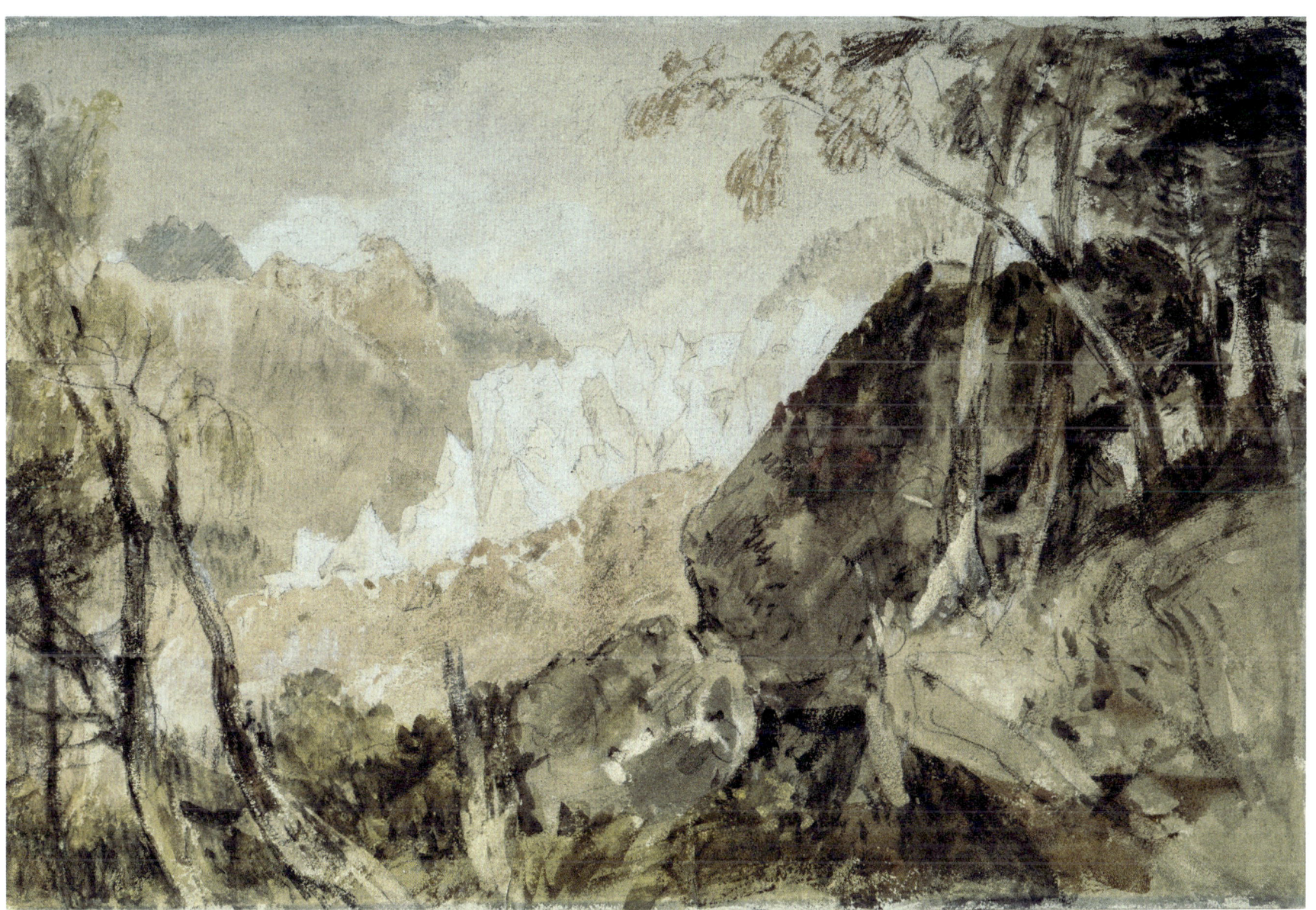

9. John Sell Cotman
Brecknock (now Brecon), c. 1801
watercolour with scratching out on paper
37.6 x 54.6 cm

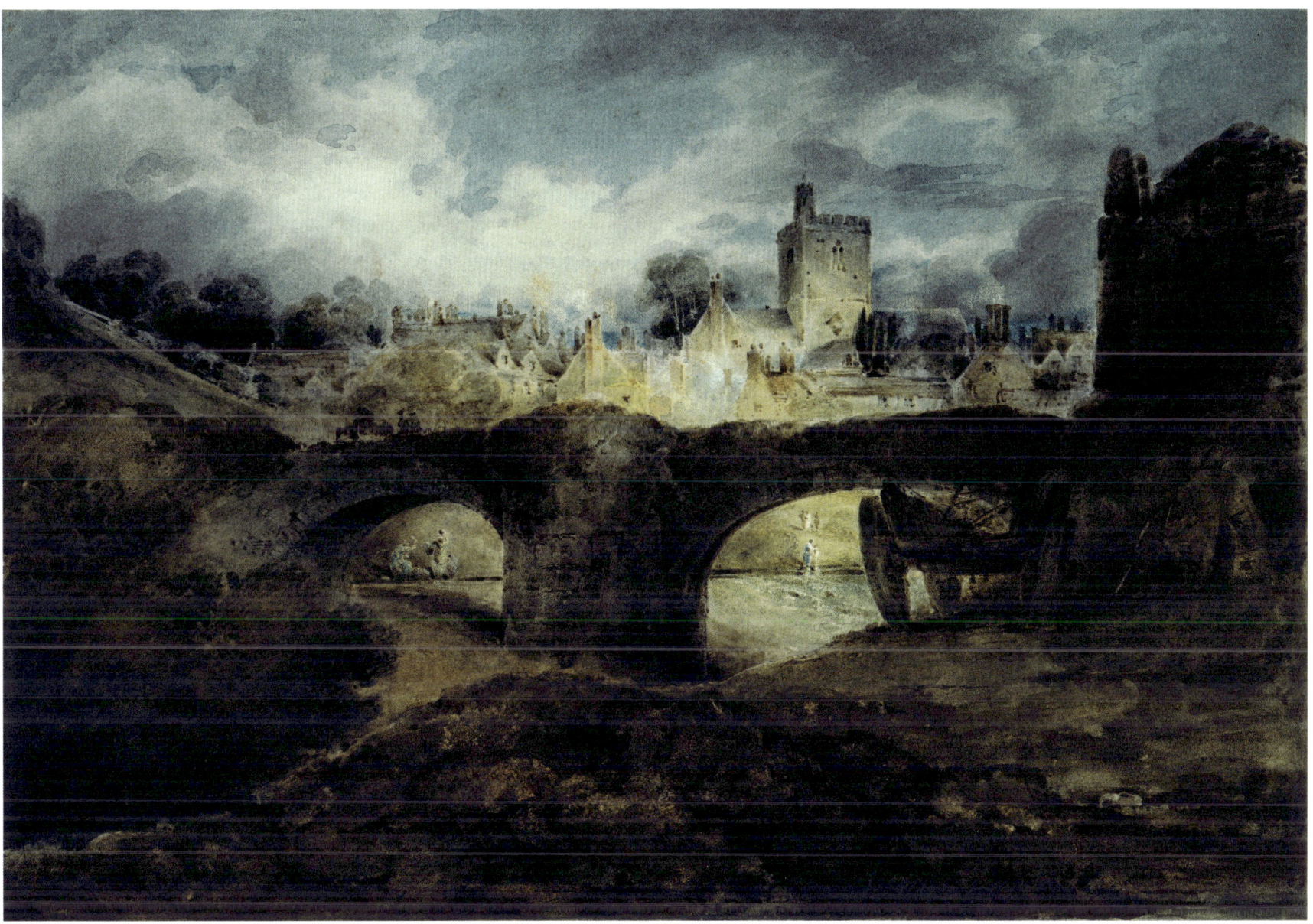

10. John Sell Cotman
Bedlam Furnace at Coalbrookdale, c. 1802
watercolour on paper
26 x 48.6 cm

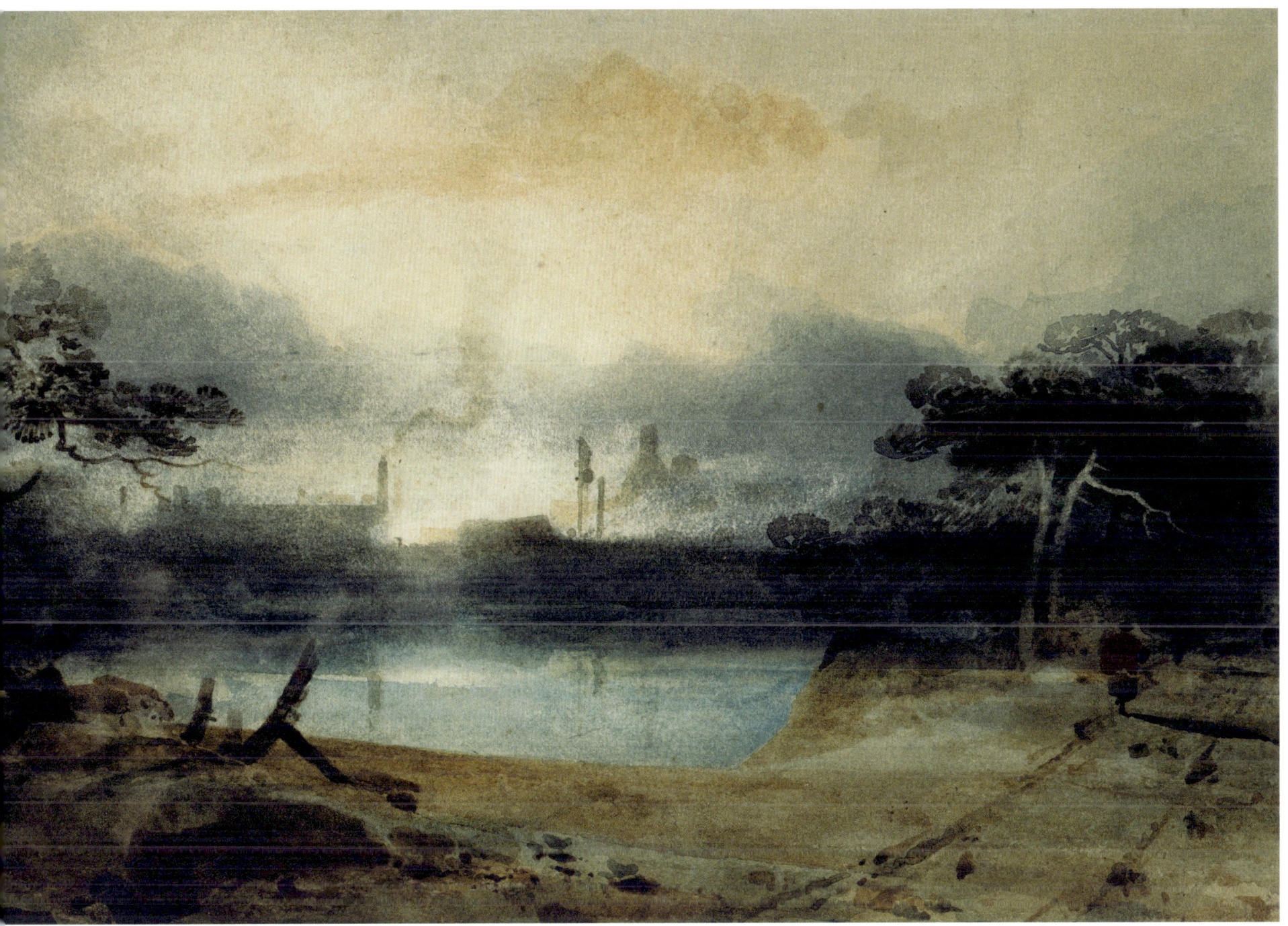

11. John Sell Cotman
A Waterfall in Wales (perhaps on the River Llugwy), 1803
watercolour on paper
21.1 x 32.5 cm

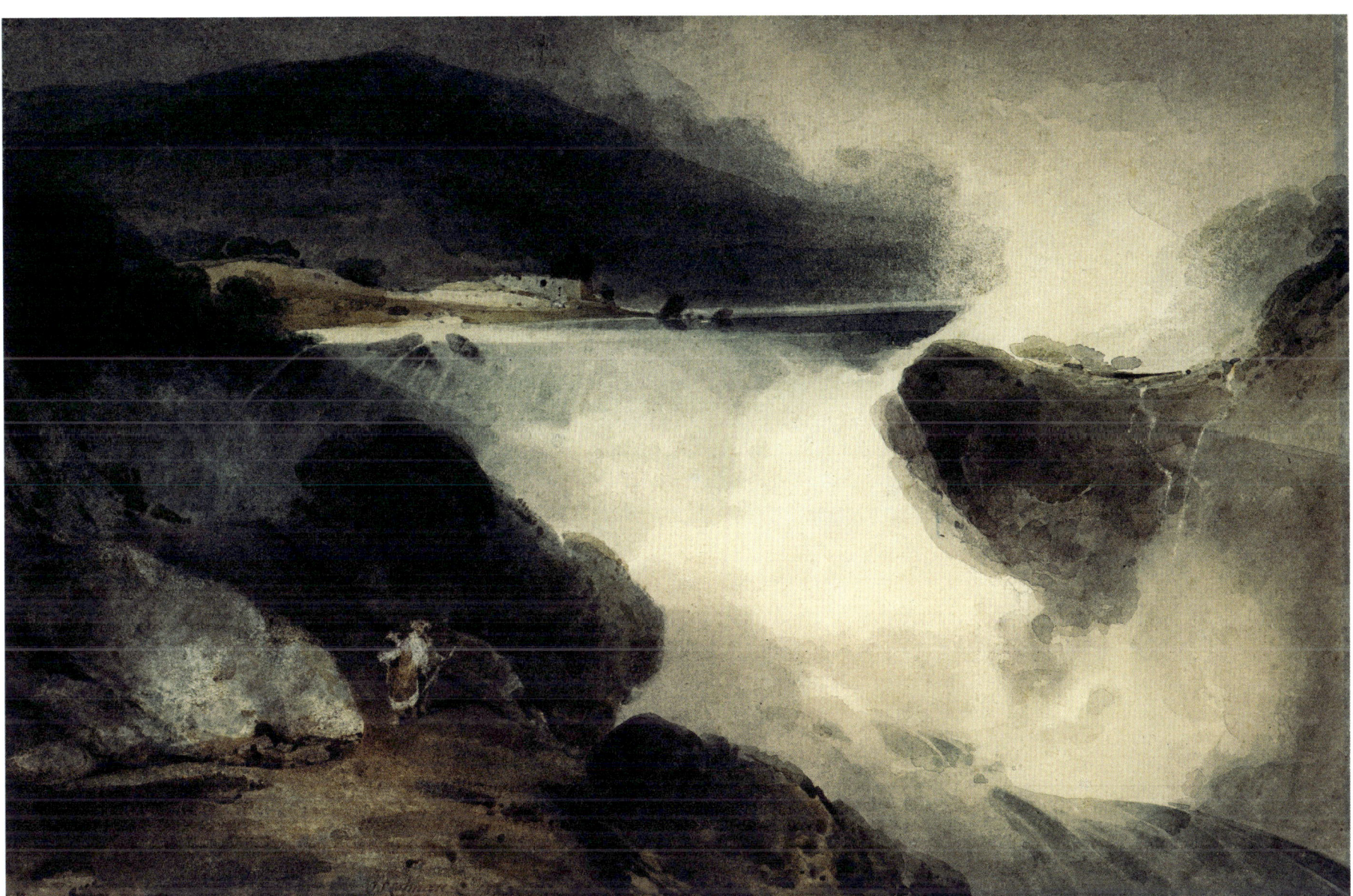

12. John Sell Cotman
Tintern Abbey by Moonlight, c. 1802
watercolour with pen and brown ink on paper
39.1 x 26.4 cm

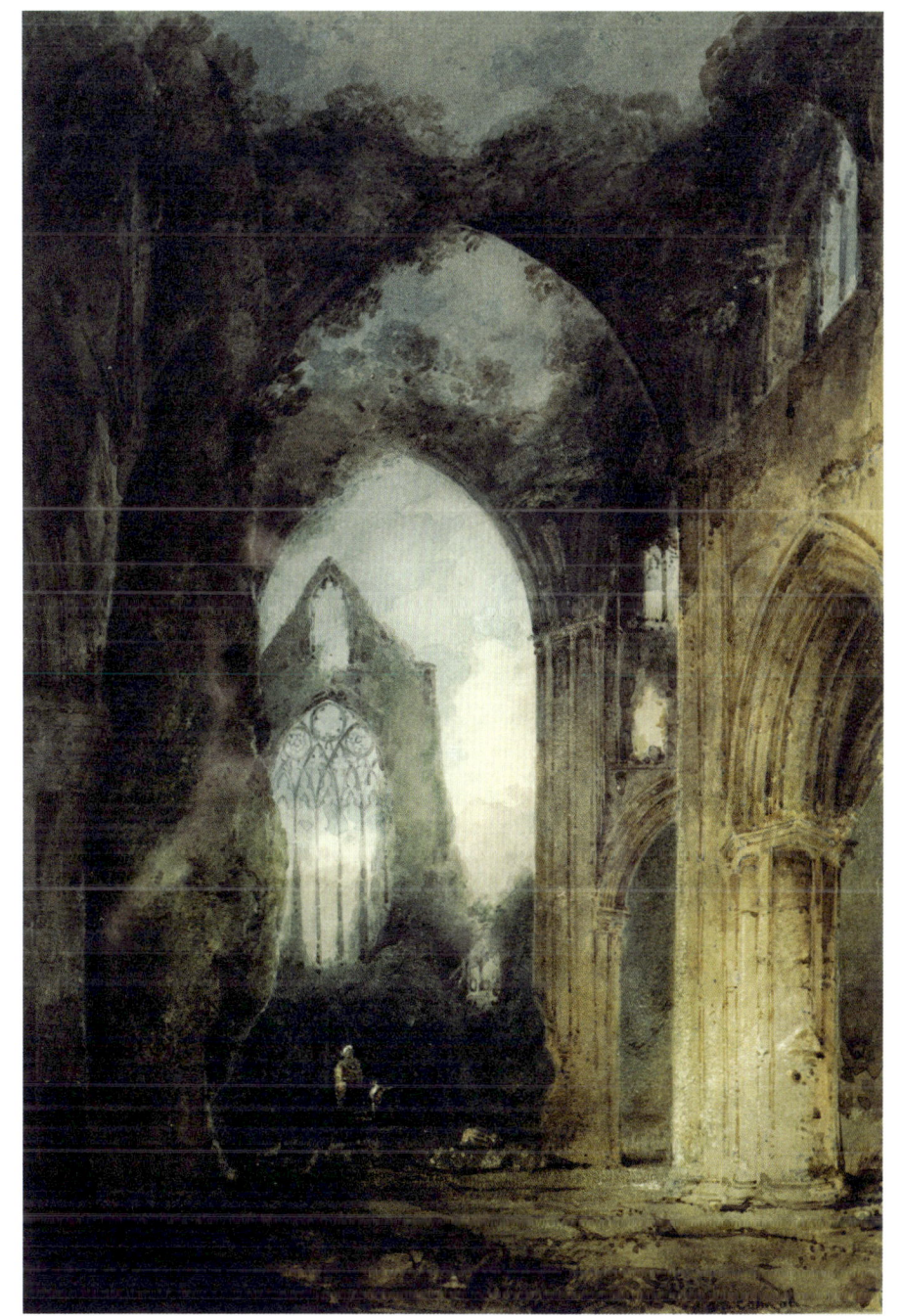

13. John Sell Cotman
A Screen, Norwich Cathedral, c. 1807-8
pencil and watercolour on paper
33 x 22.9 cm

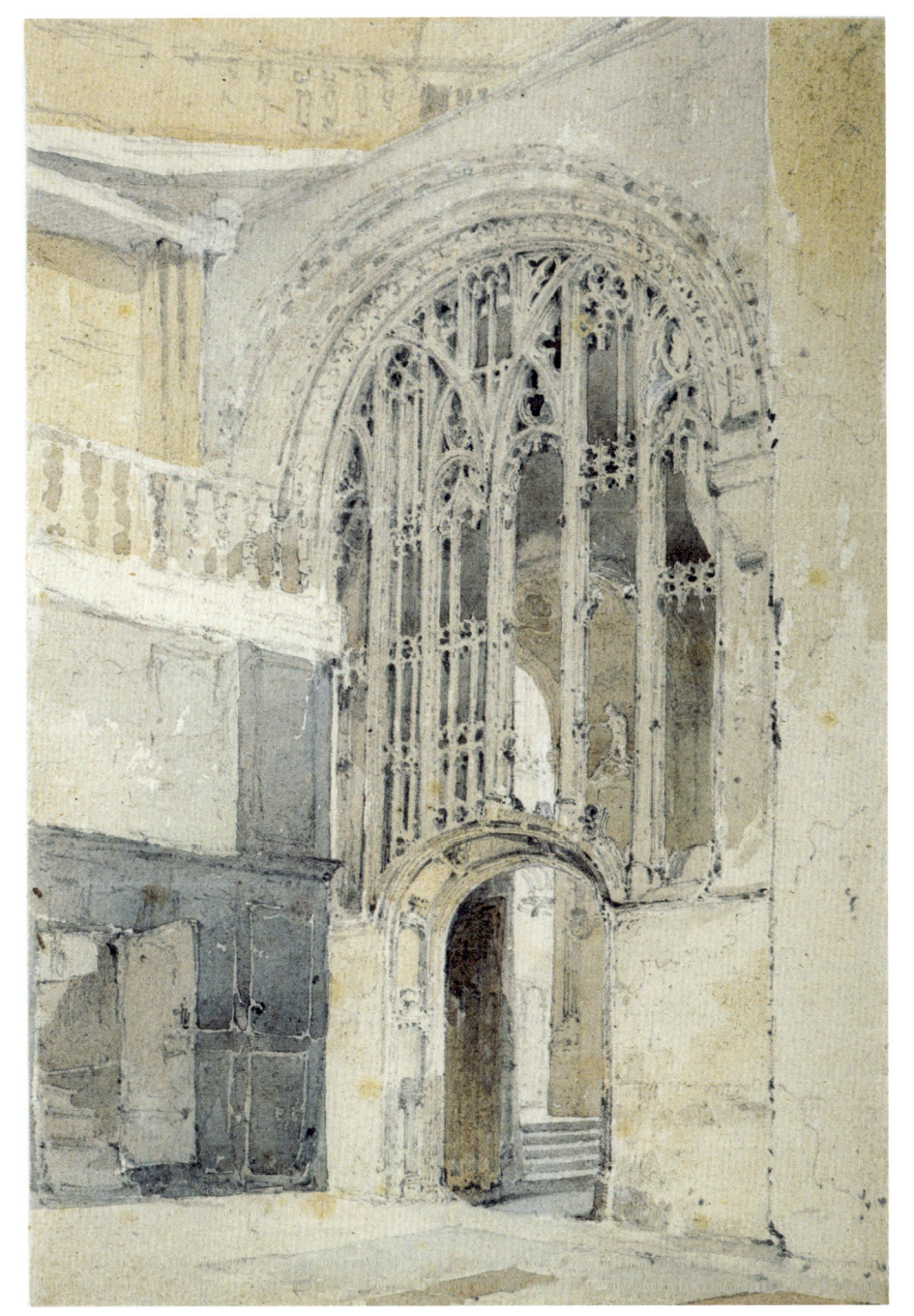

14. John ('Old') Crome
A Blasted Oak, c. 1808-10
watercolour on paper
58.4 x 44.5 cm

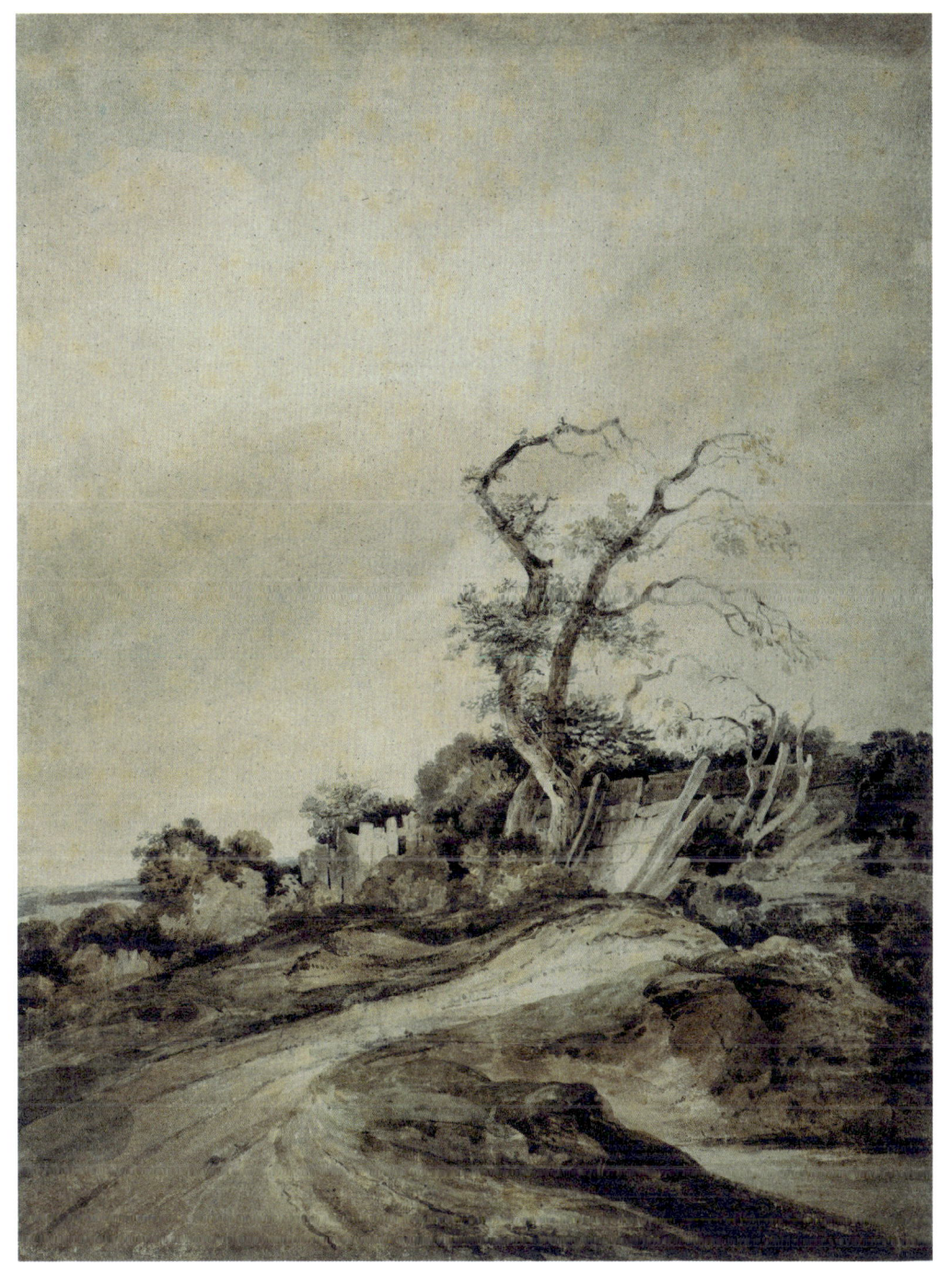

15. John Sell Cotman
Trees near the River Greta, 1805
pencil, watercolour and touches of blue gouache on paper
33 x 22.9 cm

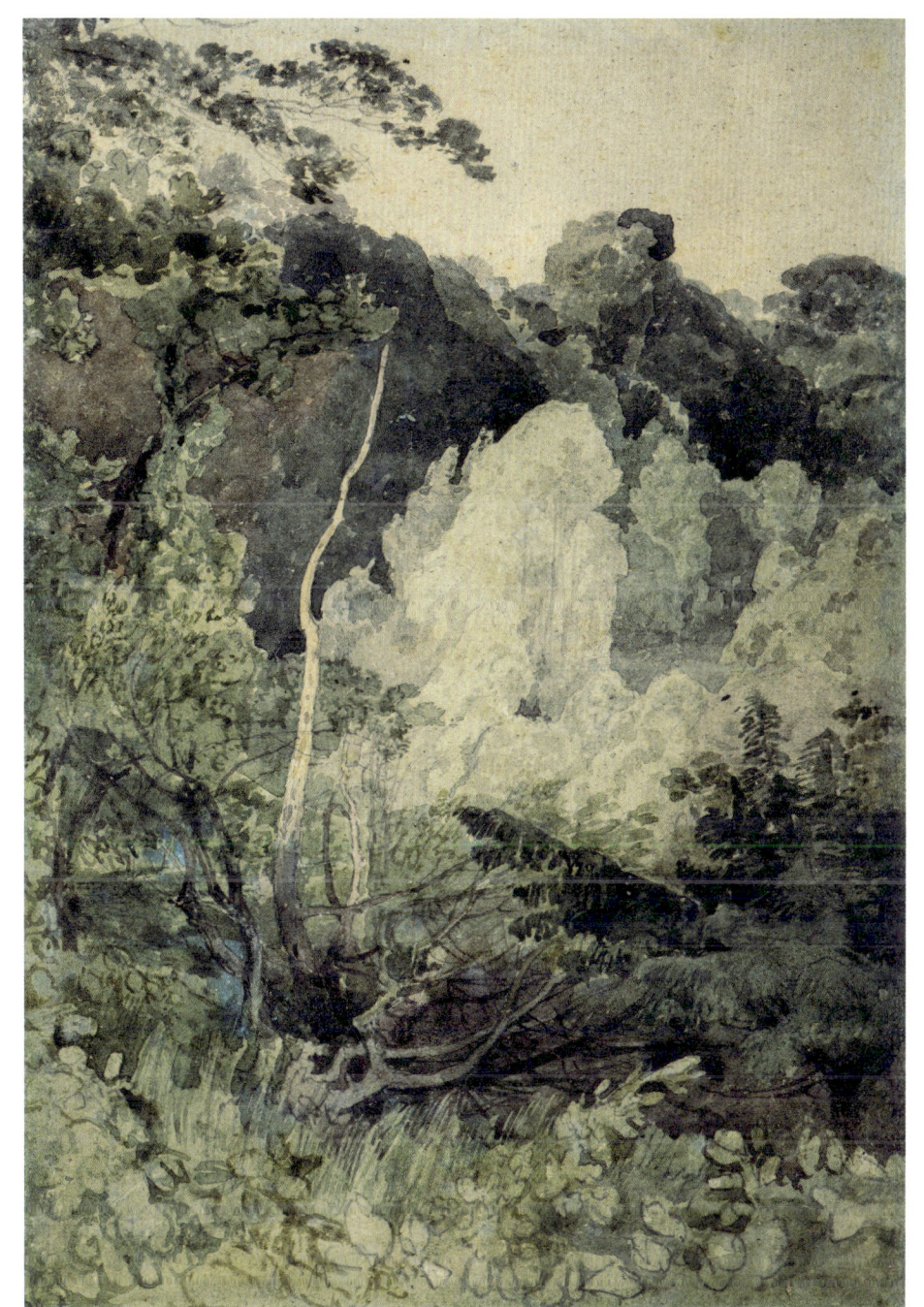

16. John Sell Cotman
New Bridge, Durham, 1805
pencil and watercolour on paper
43.9 x 32.5 cm

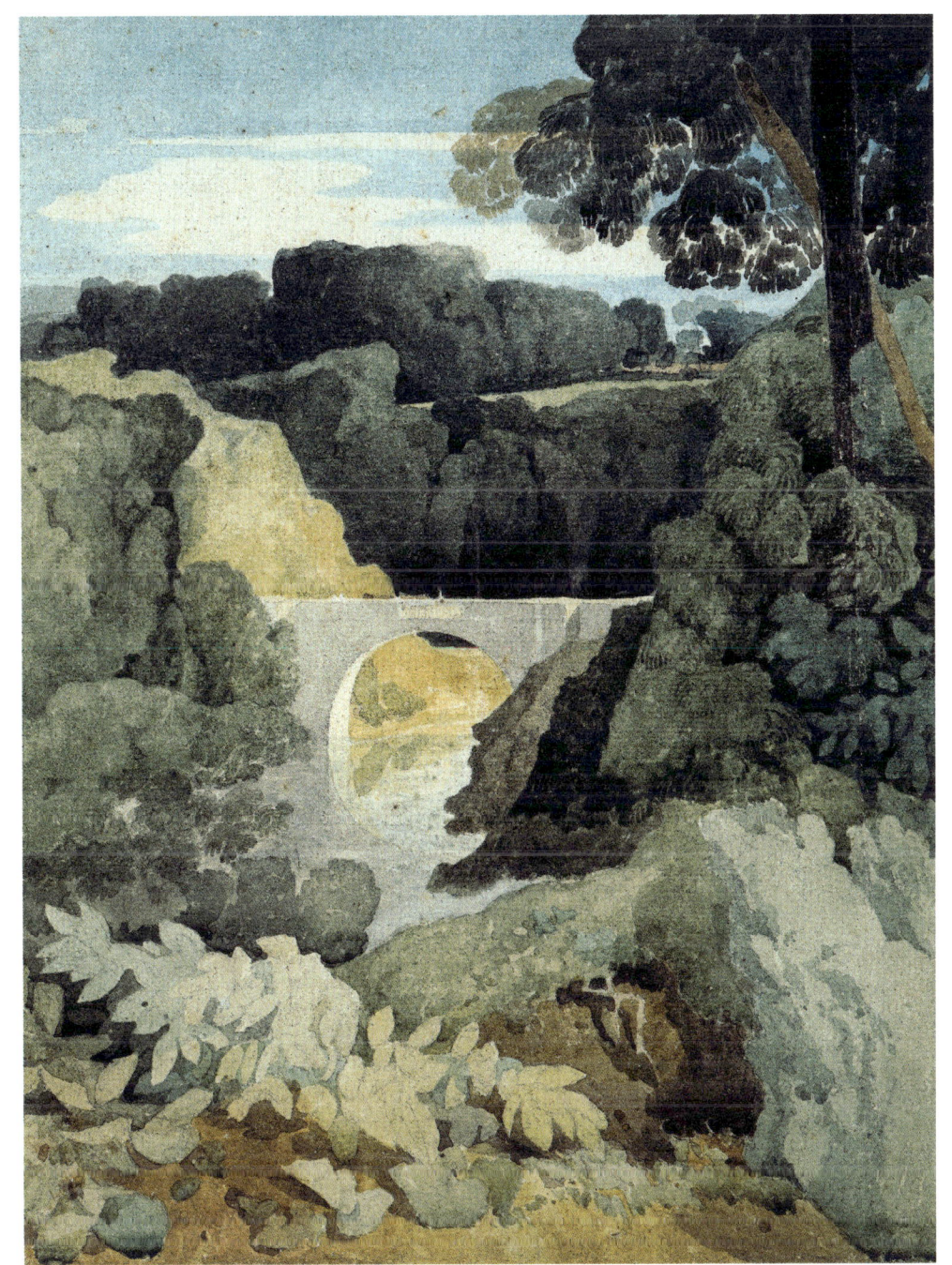

17. Henry Edridge
Study of Old Houses, c. 1810
watercolour on paper
26 x 21.3 cm

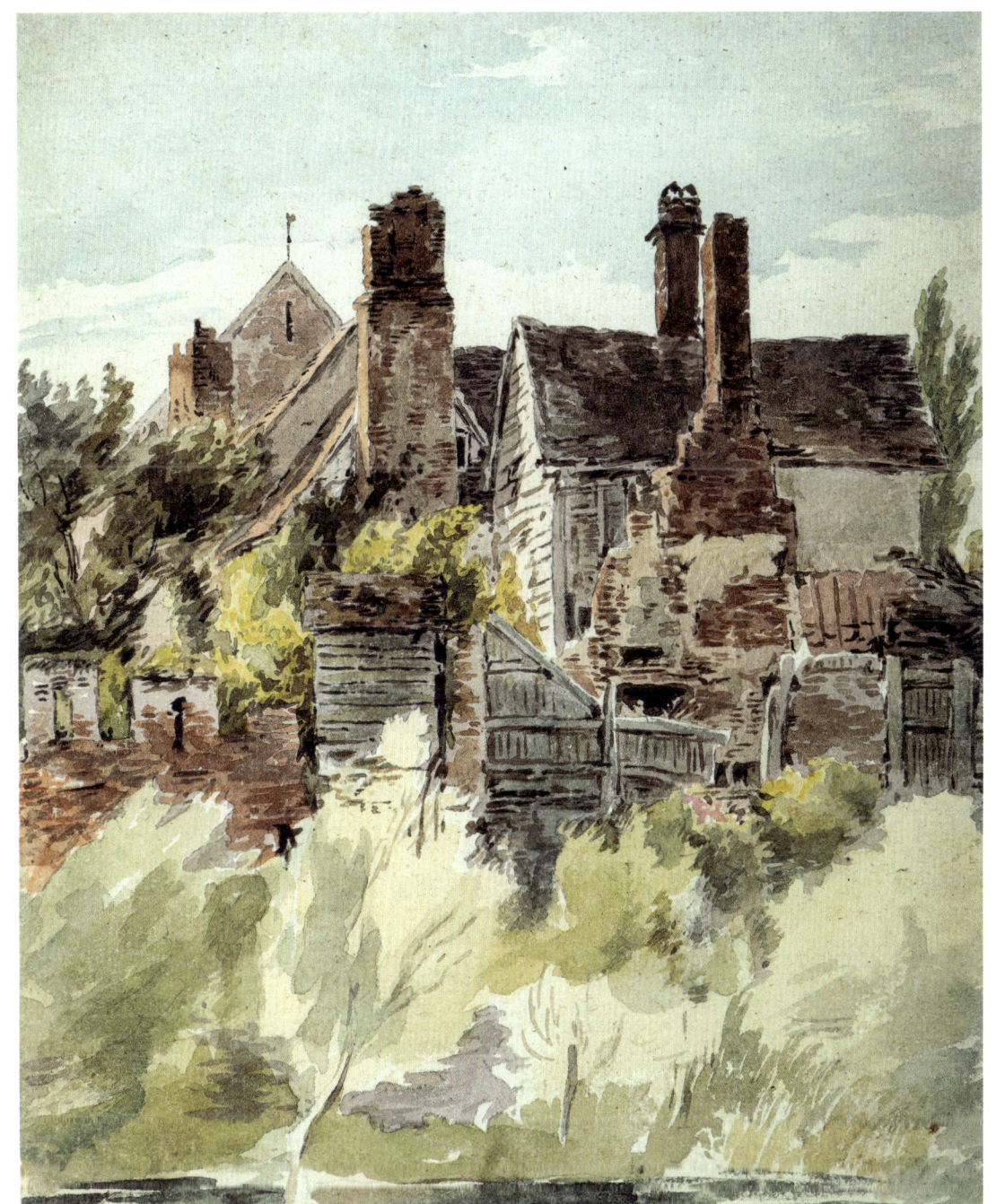

18. François Louis Thomas Francia
Figure on a Wooden Bridge, c. 1810
watercolour on paper
33.5 x 26.5 cm

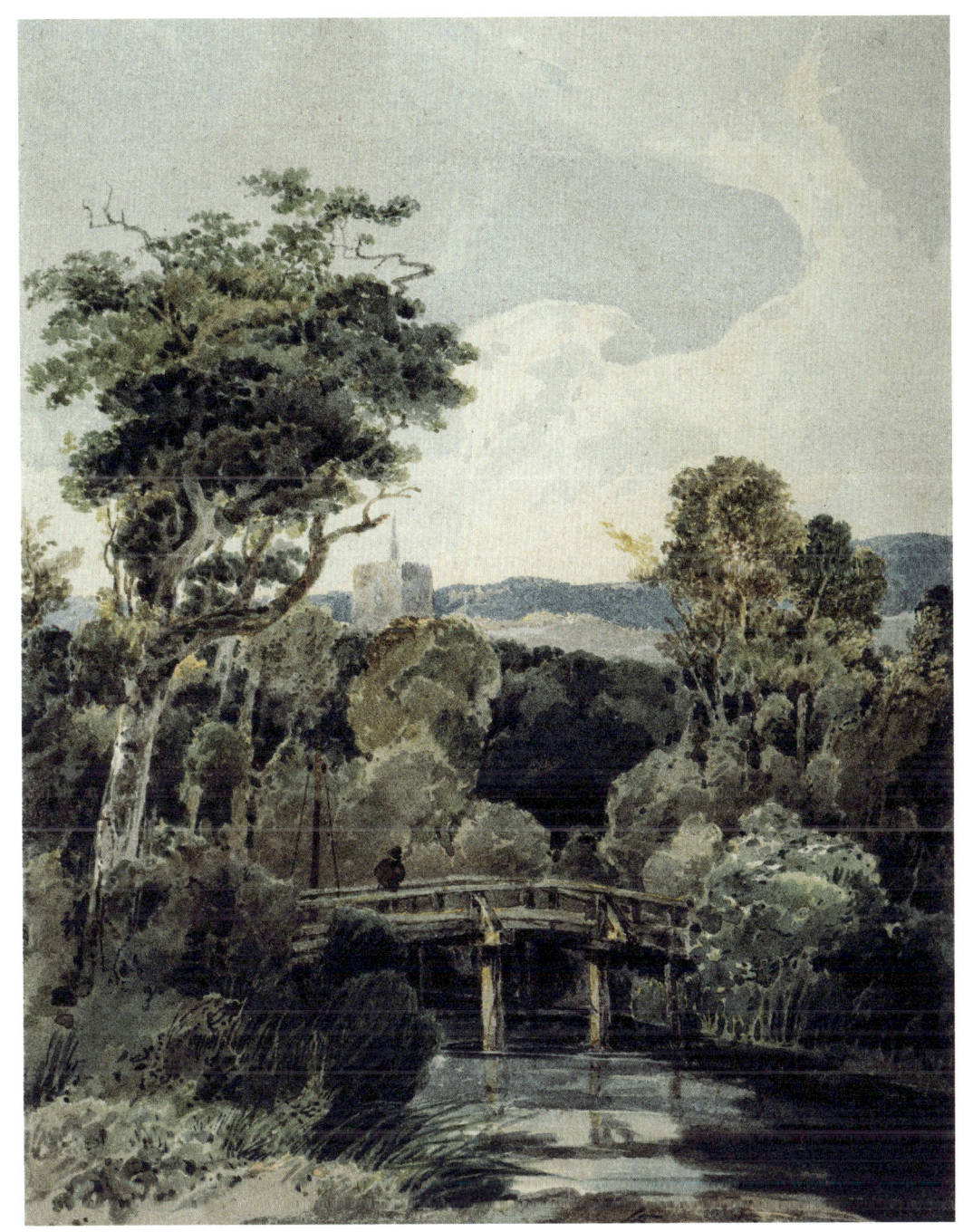

19. John Sell Cotman
Richmond, Yorkshire, c. 1805
pencil and watercolour on paper
33.9 x 44.1 cm

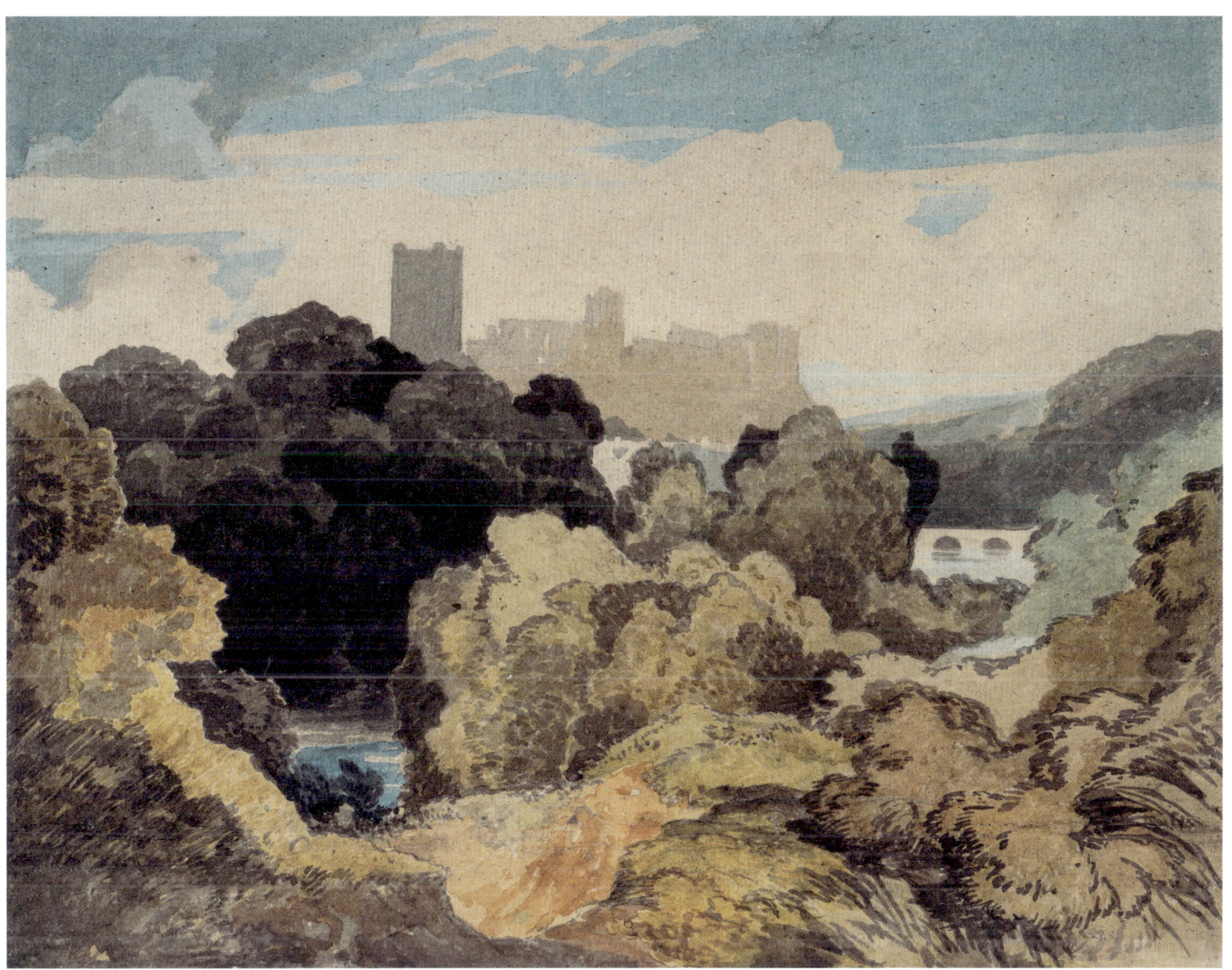

20. John Sell Cotman
Cattle Watering, c. 1808-10
pencil and watercolour on paper
22.8 x 32.3 cm

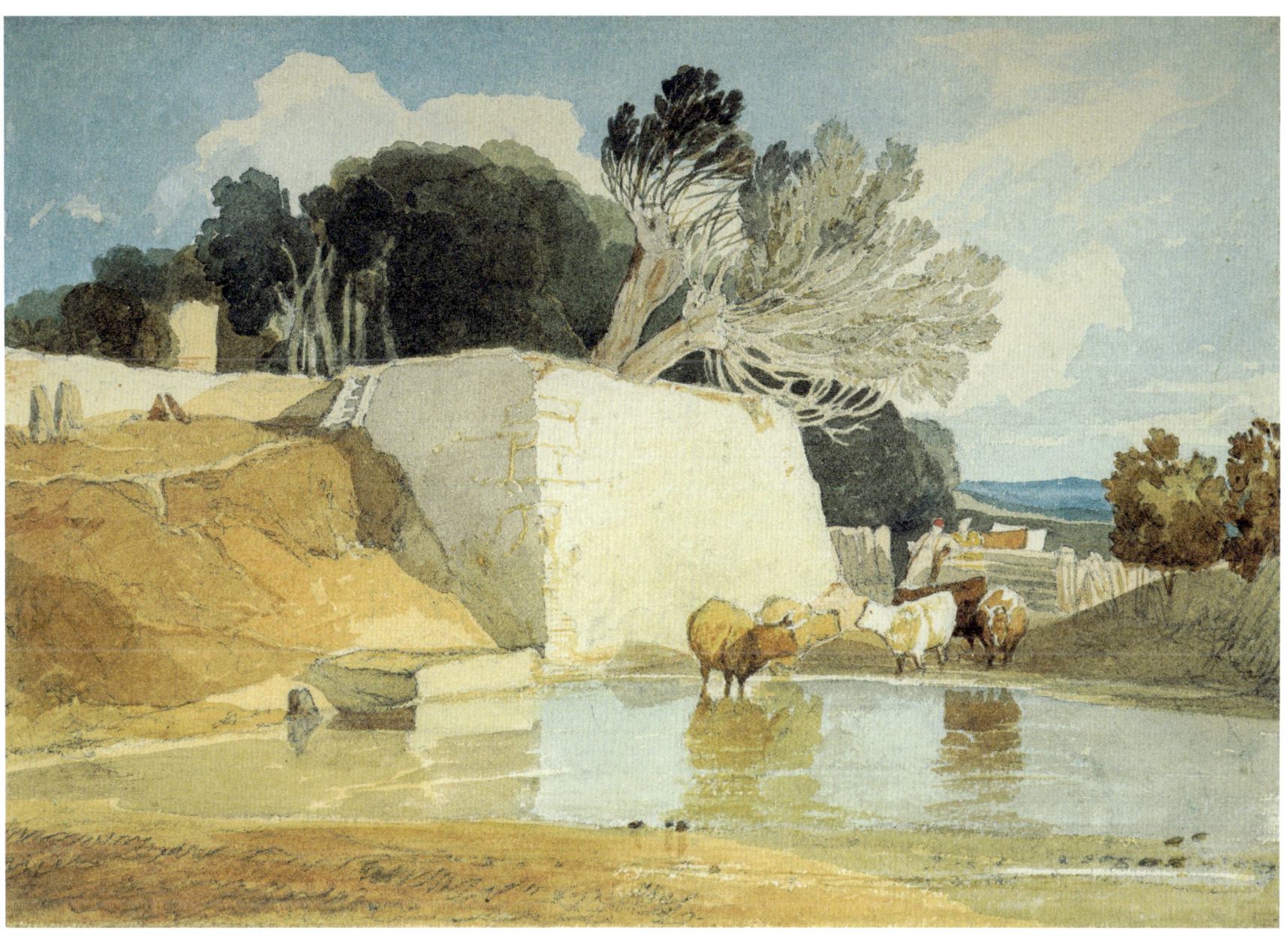

21. John Sell Cotman
Beached Barge near Battersea Bridge, c. 1809
watercolour on paper
33 x 28.8 cm

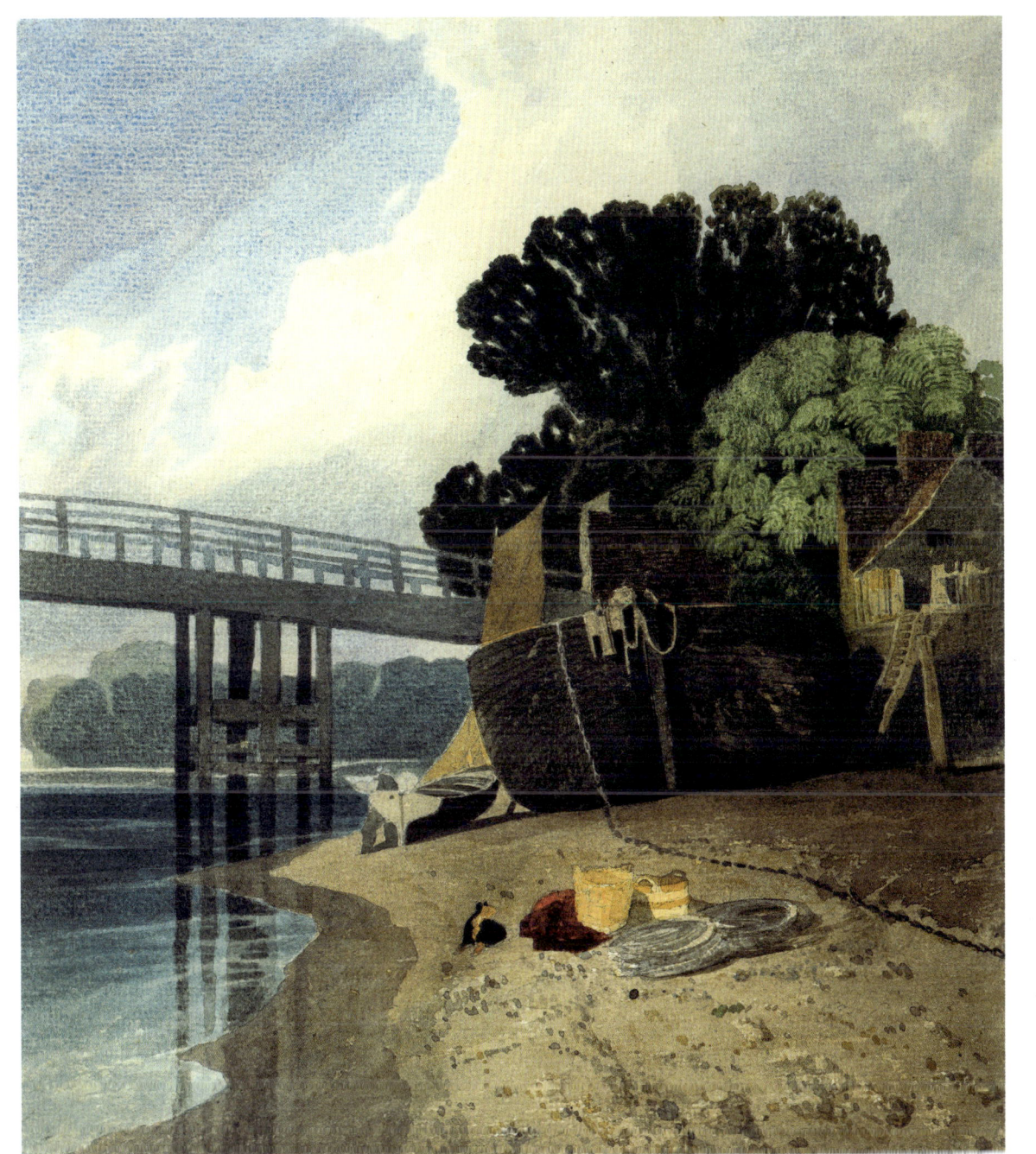

22. Joseph Mallord William Turner
A Squall off a Jetty, c. 1813 or early 1820s
watercolour and pencil on paper
16.3 x 23.1 cm
reproduced approximately life-size

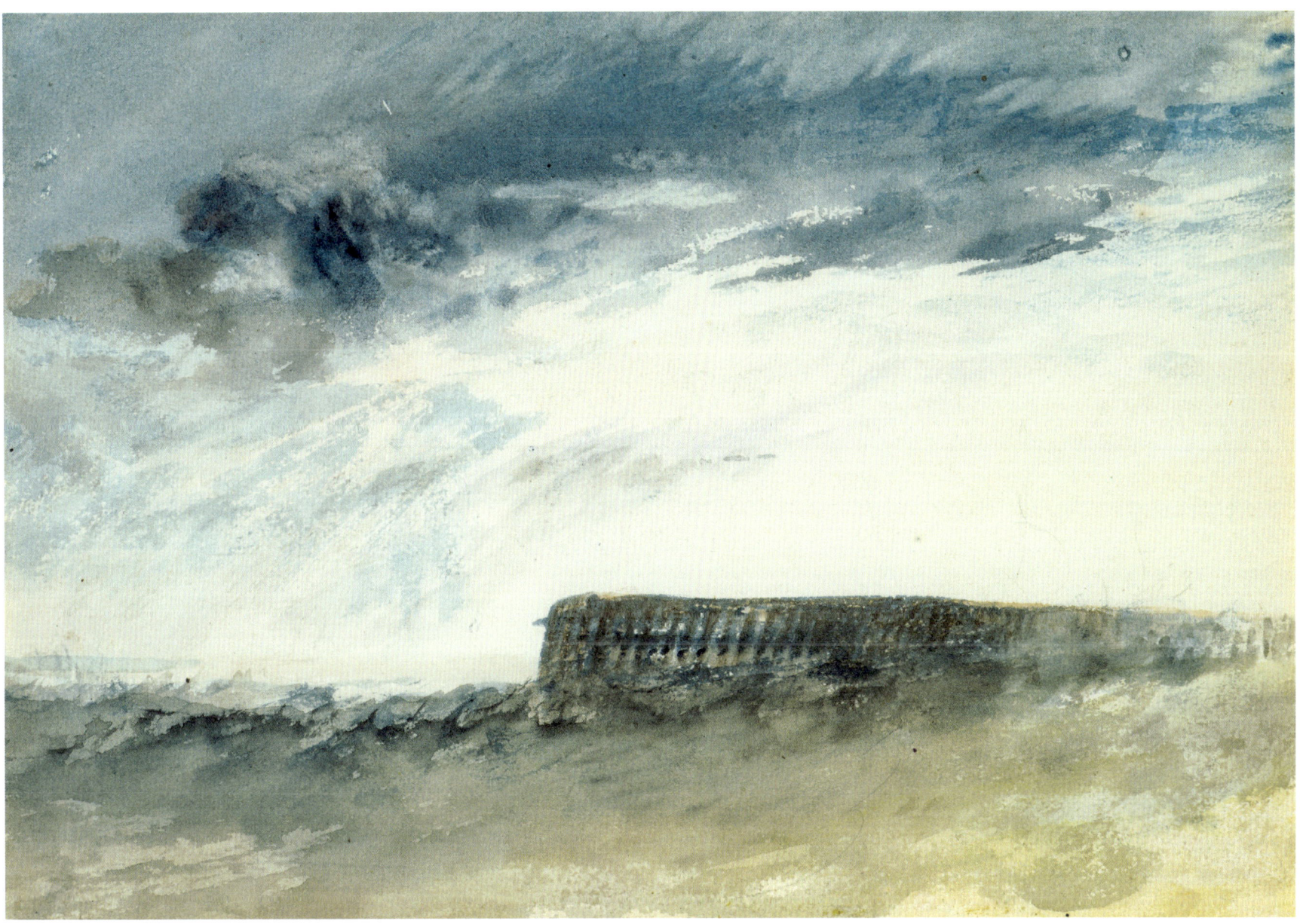

23. Joseph Mallord William Turner
A Boat and Red Buoy in a Rough Sea, c. 1835-40
watercolour and gouache on blue paper
13.9 x 19 cm
reproduced approximately life-size

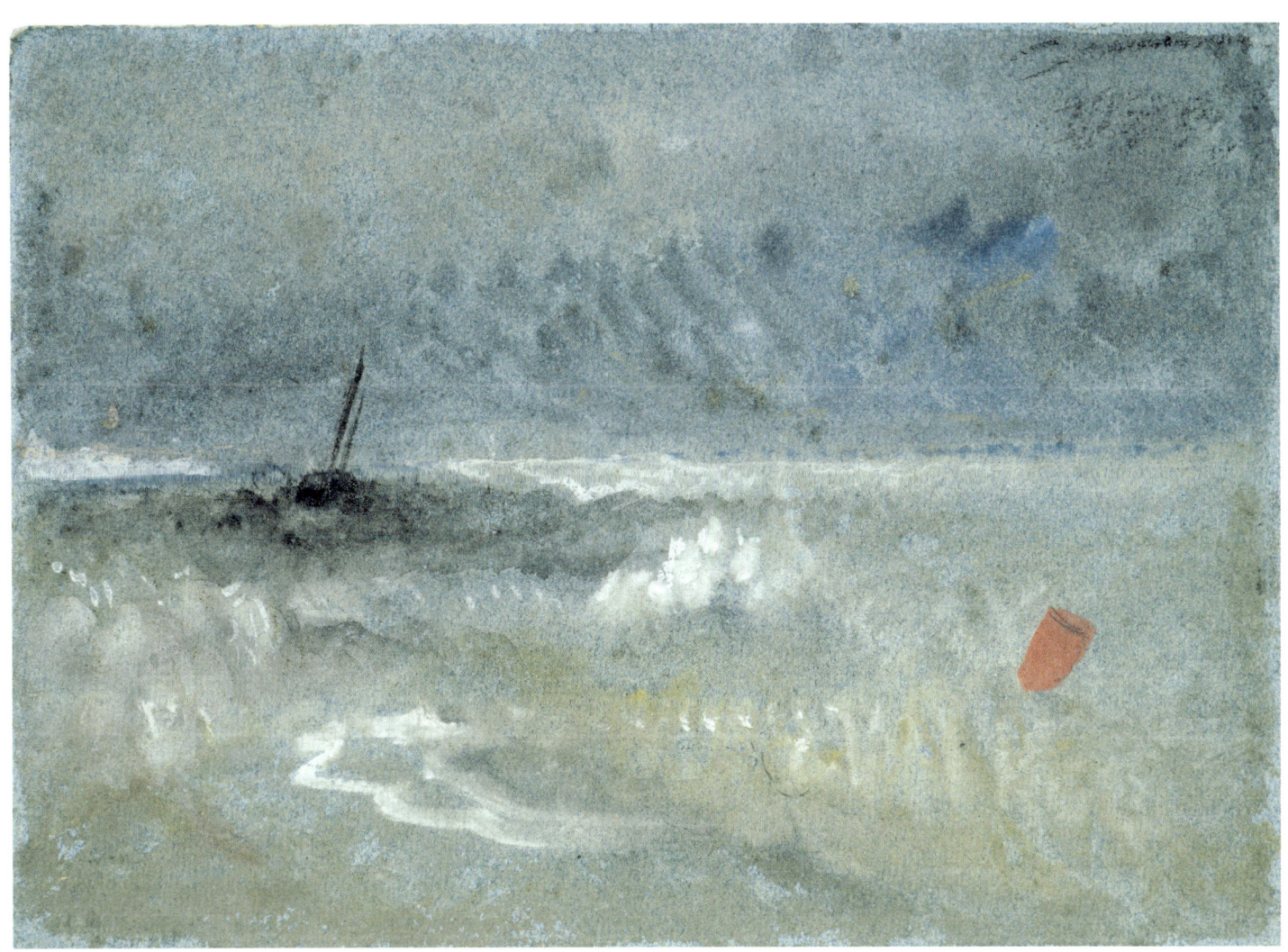

24. Joseph Mallord William Turner
Sunset over the Sea, 1830s or 40s
watercolour on paper
18.2 x 26.5 cm

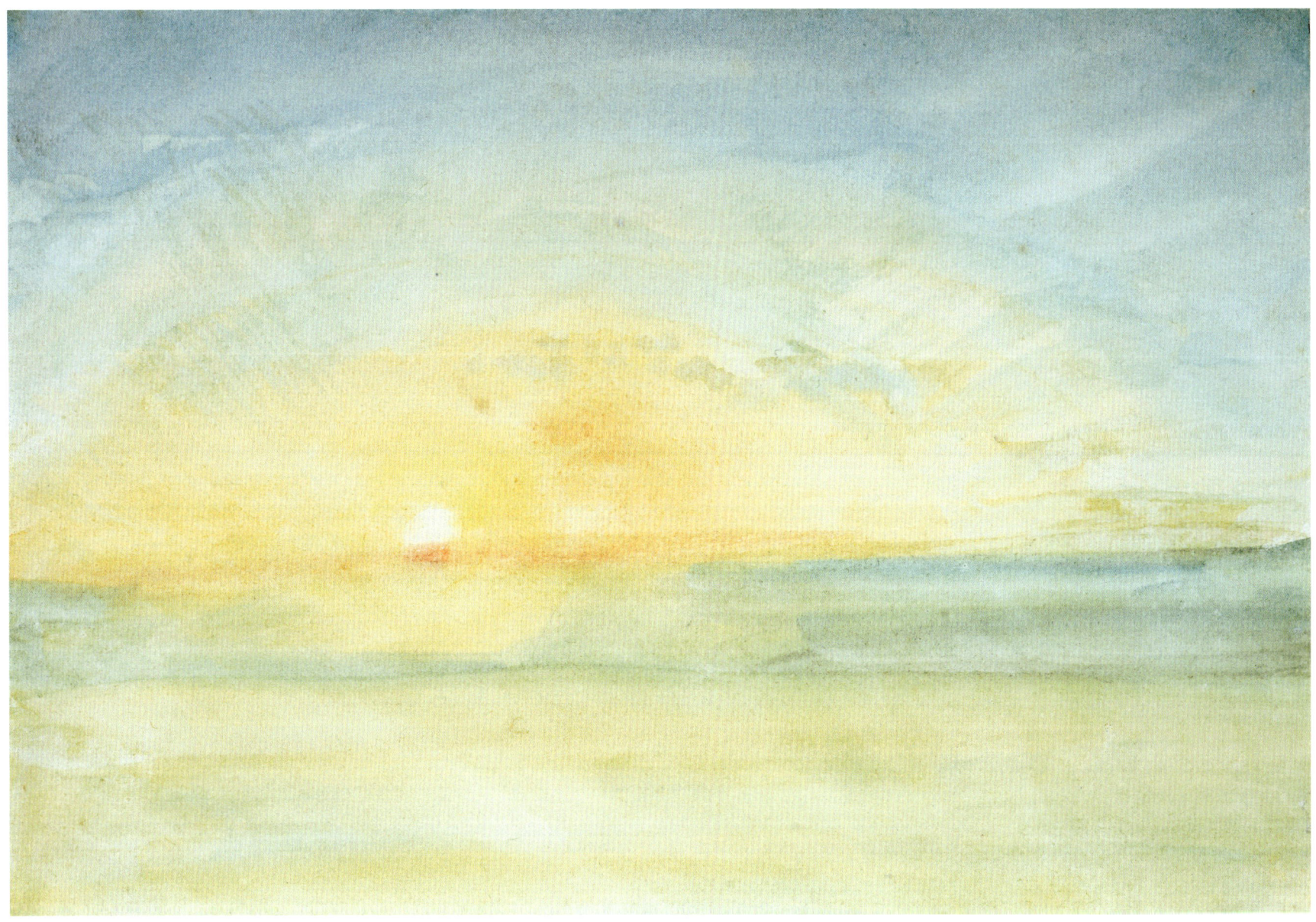

25. Joseph Mallord William Turner
Fishmarket on the Sands, c. 1840-5
pencil and watercolour with gouache on grey paper
13.9 x 19 cm
reproduced approximately life-size

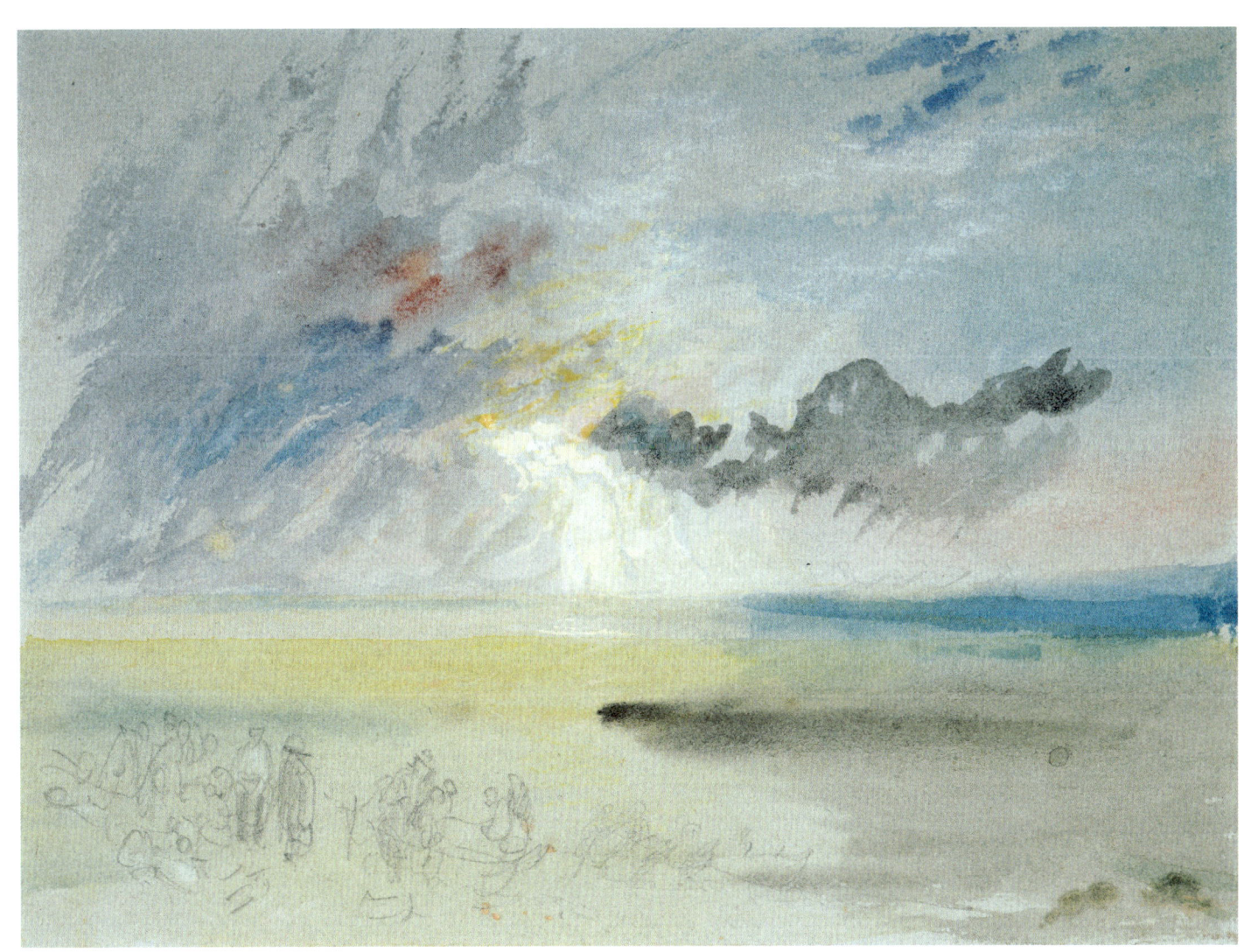

26. Joseph Mallord William Turner
A Rough Sea beating against Margate Jetty, c. 1840
pencil, stopping-out and watercolour with gouache on grey paper
19.3 x 28.8 cm

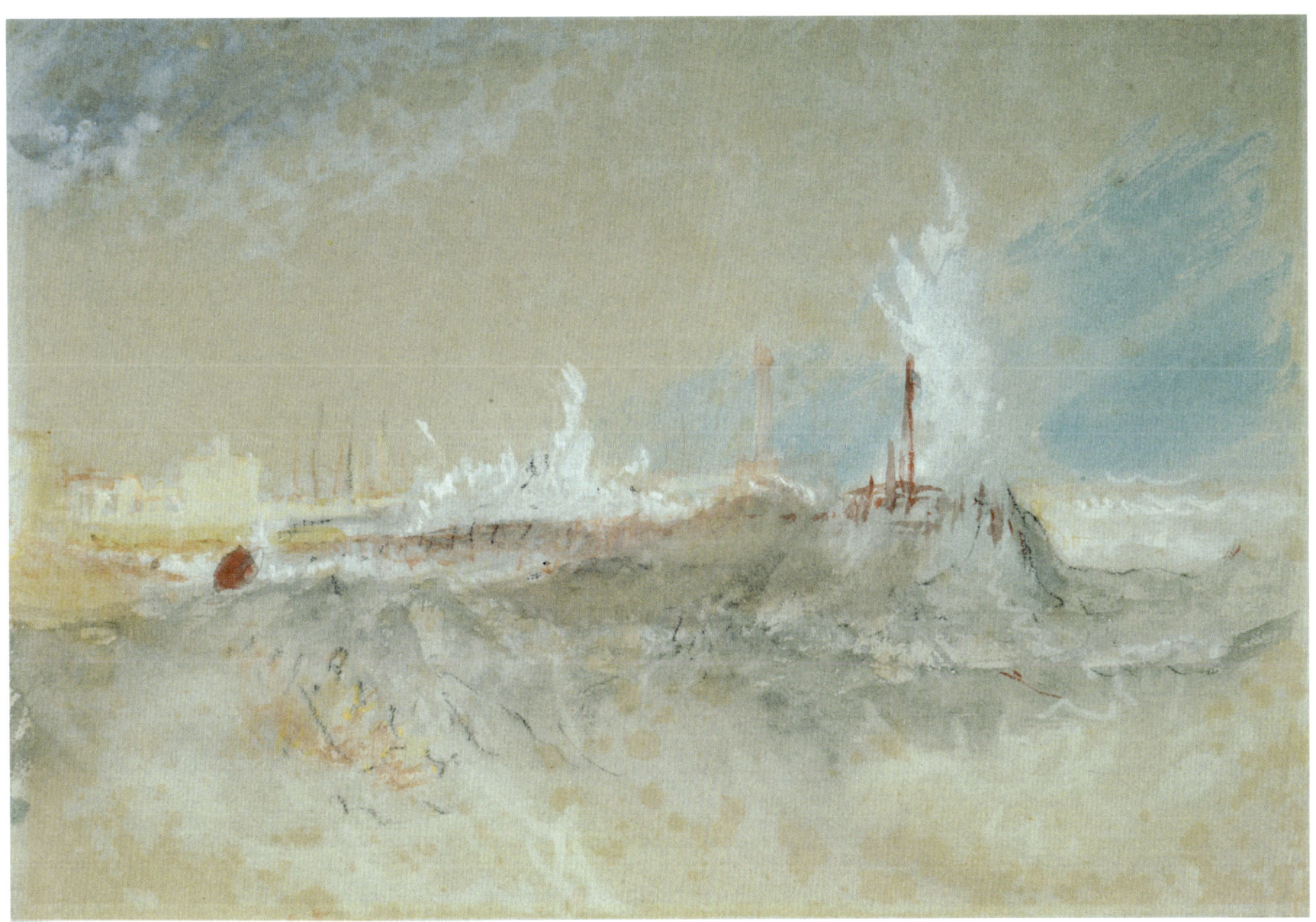

27. Joseph Mallord William Turner
Study of Waves, c. 1840
watercolour and gouache on grey paper
18.8 x 27.4 cm

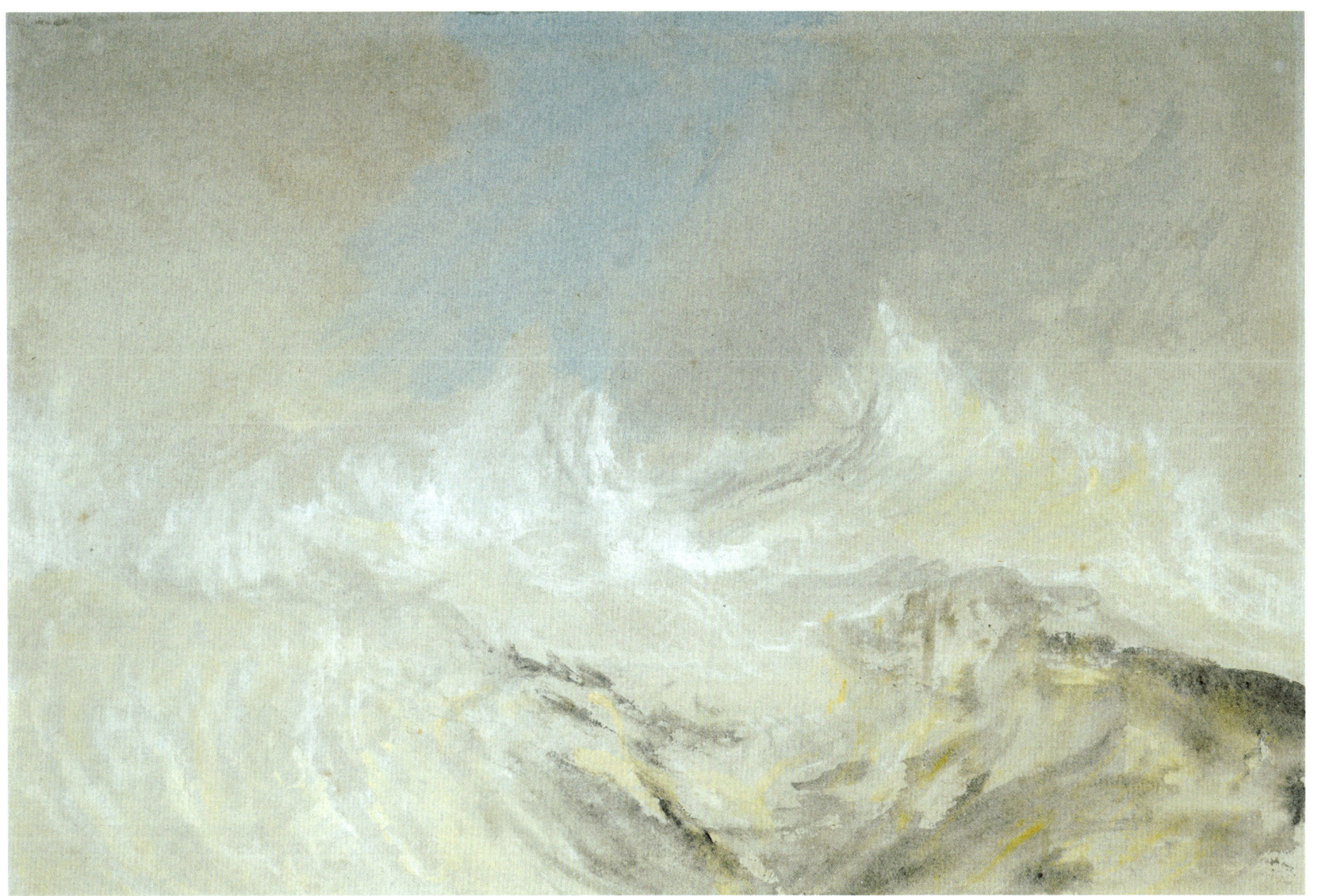

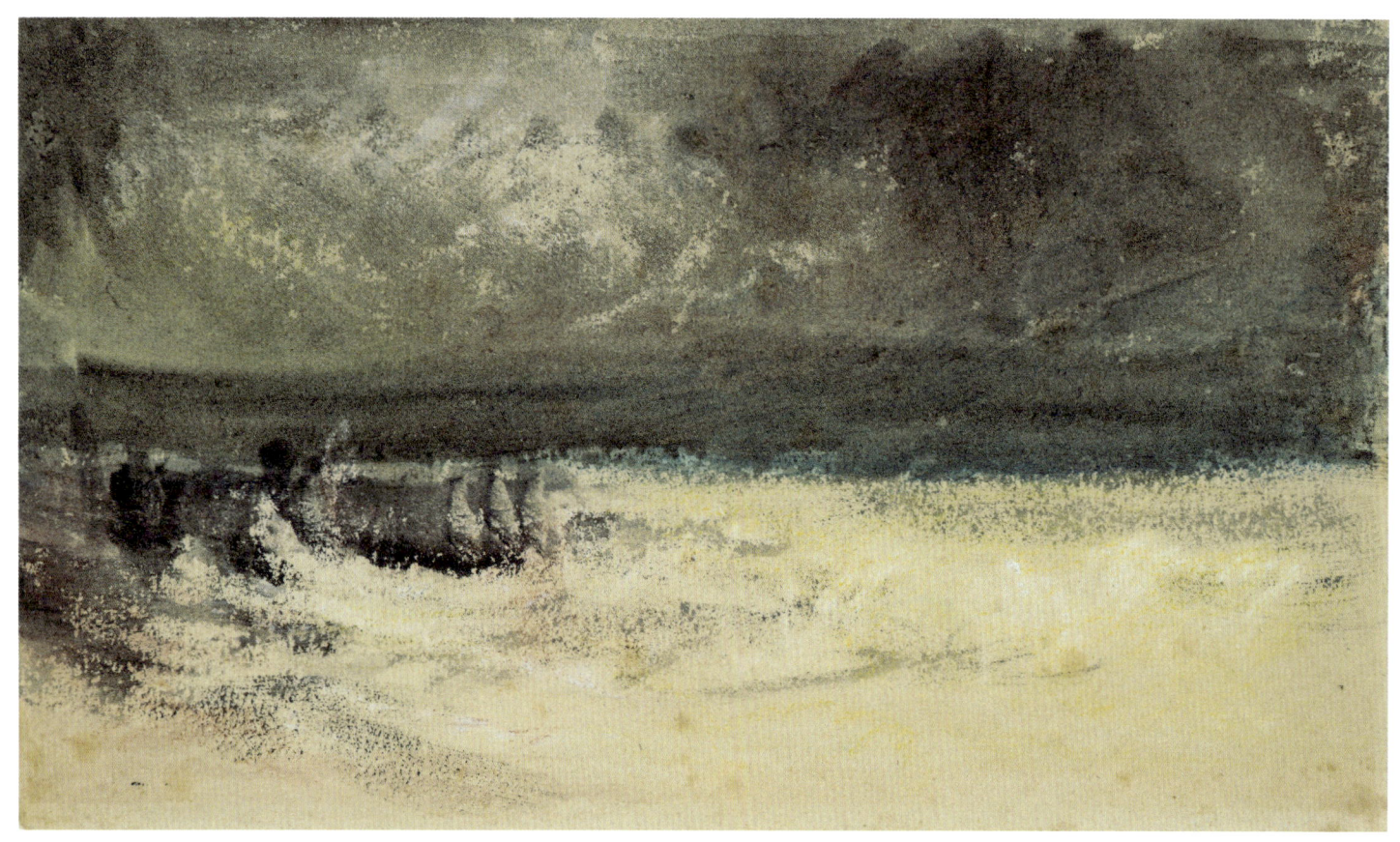

28, 29,30. Joseph Mallord William Turner
Three sketches originally from the same sheet, arranged vertically, c. 1835-40
watercolour on buff paper
Above: Waves breaking against a wooden groyne, 11.4 x 19.1 cm
Opposite top: A shore with a breakwater, 8.9 x 19.1 cm
Opposite below: Sunset at sea, 7.6 x 18.4 cm
reproduced approximately life-size

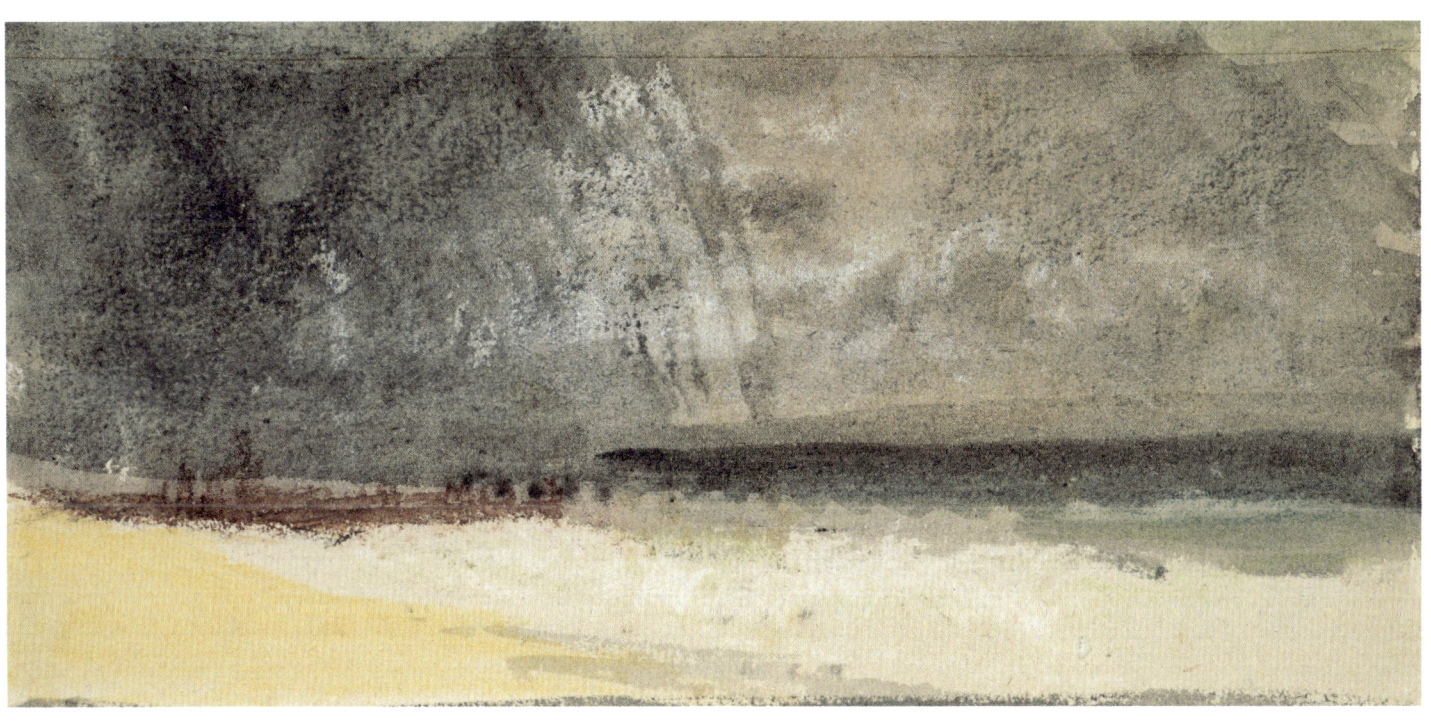

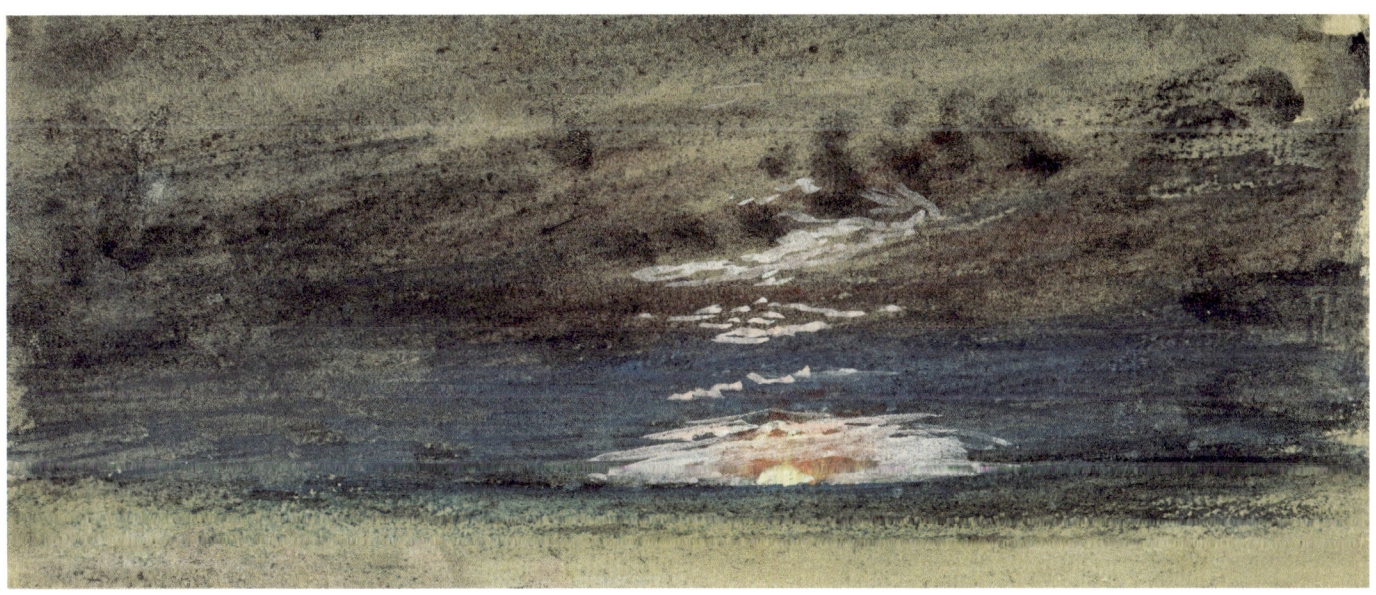

31. Joseph Mallord William Turner
Evening: Figures on a Beach, c. 1840
watercolour and gouache on buff paper
22.6 x 29.2 cm

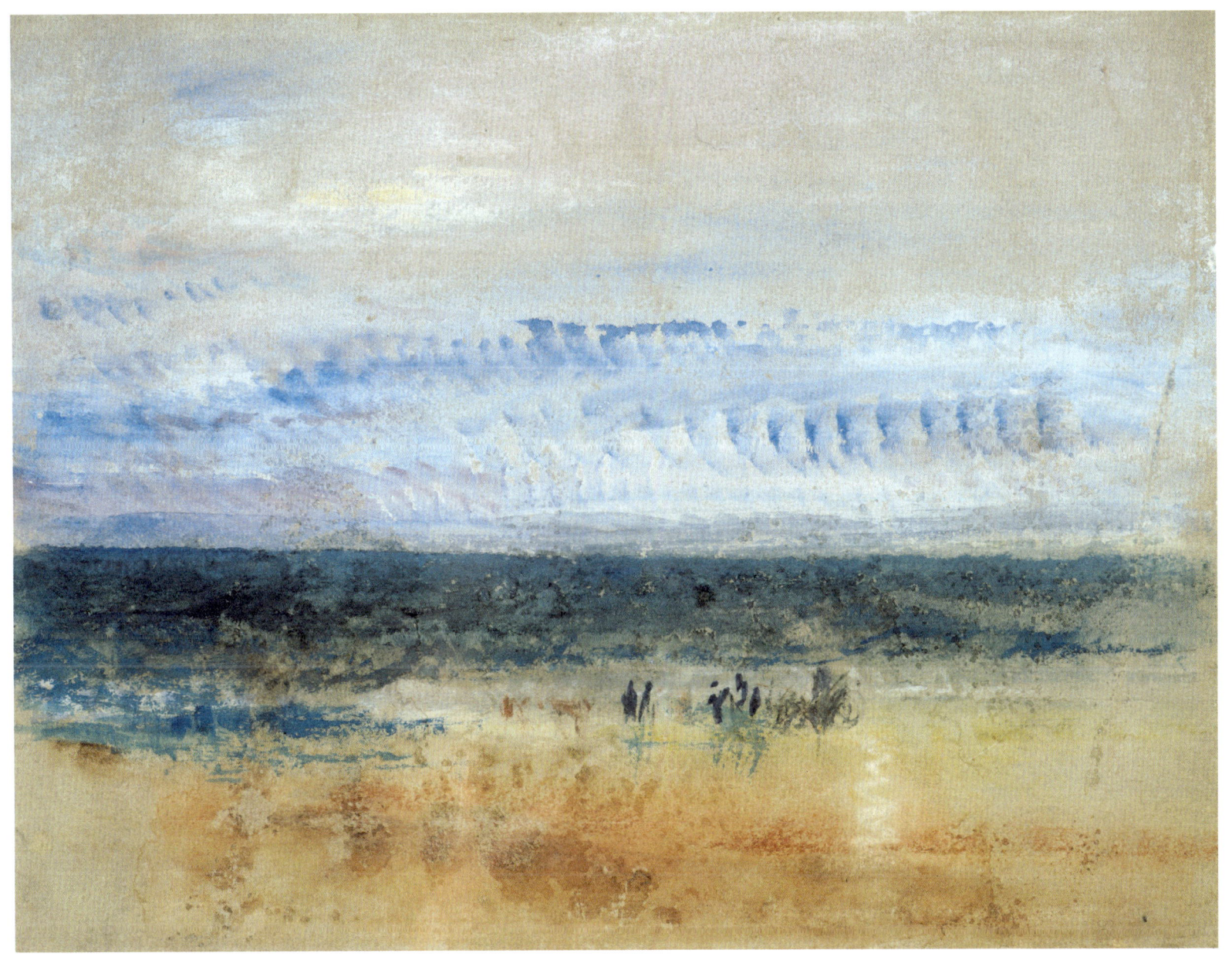

32. Joseph Mallord William Turner
A Low Sun, c. 1840
watercolour and gouache on buff paper
22.6 x 29.5 cm

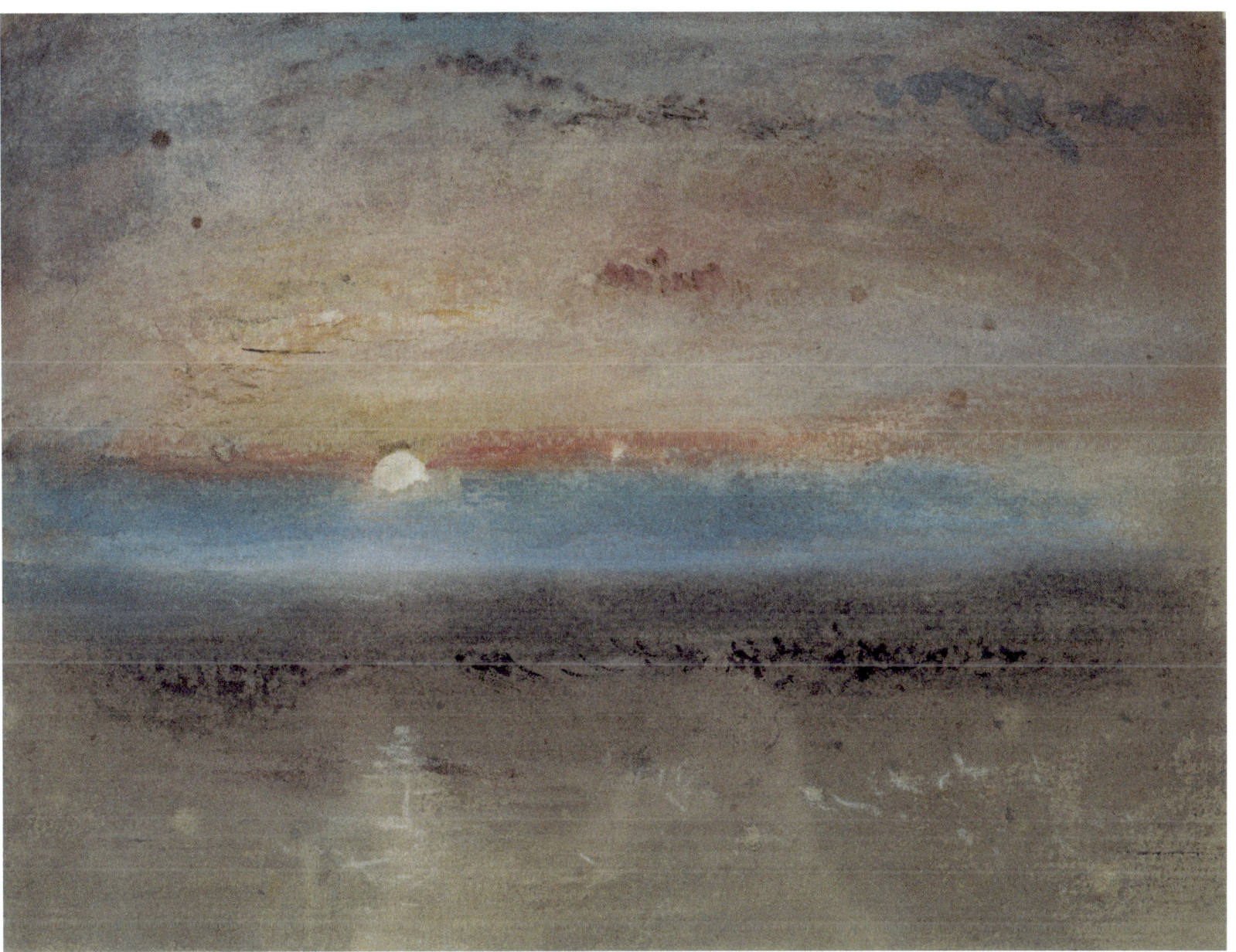

33. Joseph Mallord William Turner
Wreckers on the Shore, c. 1845
pencil and watercolour on paper
22.4 x 28.9 cm

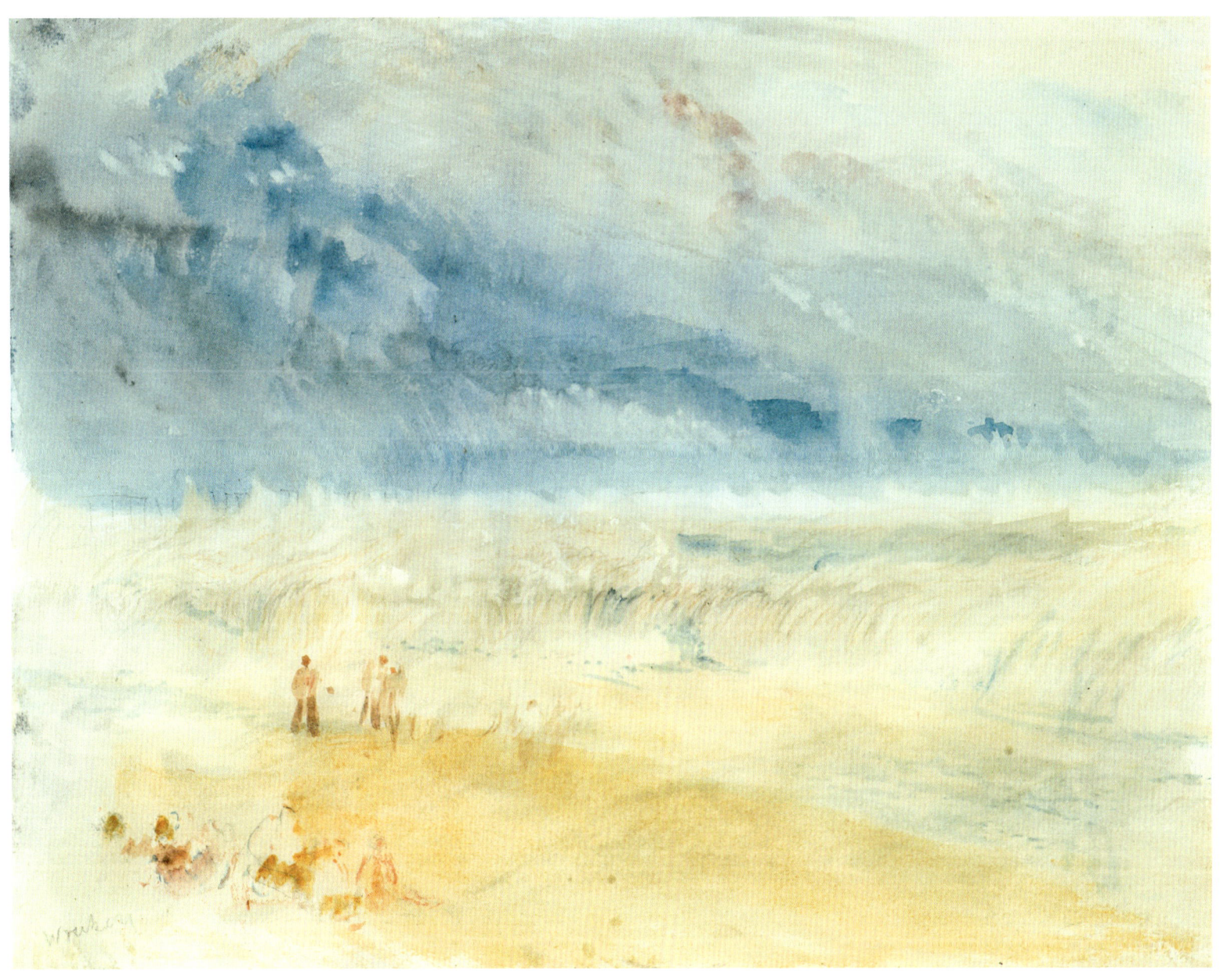

34. Joseph Mallord William Turner
Sky Study, c. 1845
watercolour on paper
22.8 x 29.5 cm

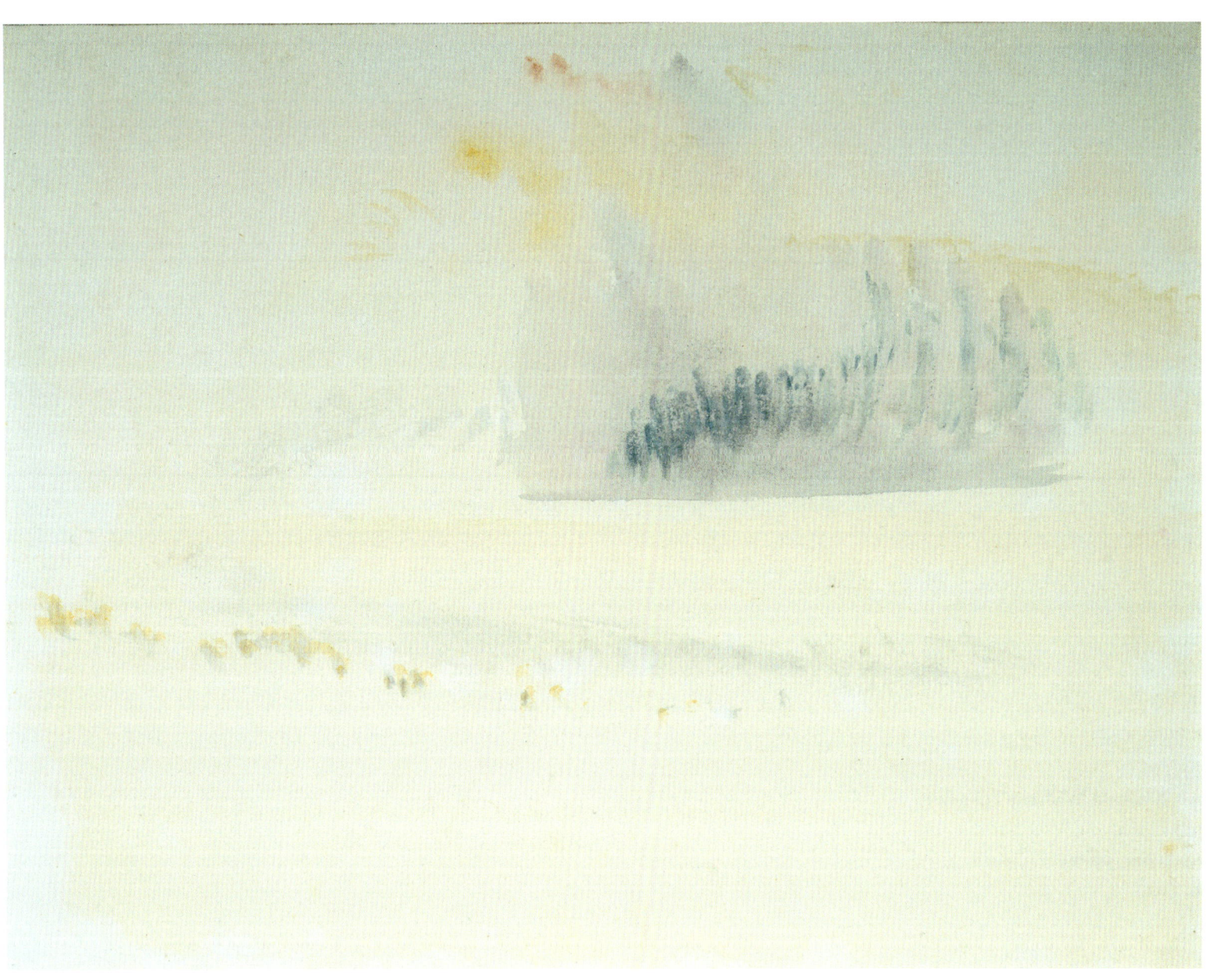

35. Joseph Mallord William Turner
Study of Clouds and Wet Sand, c. 1845
pencil and watercolour on paper
22.9 x 29.5 cm

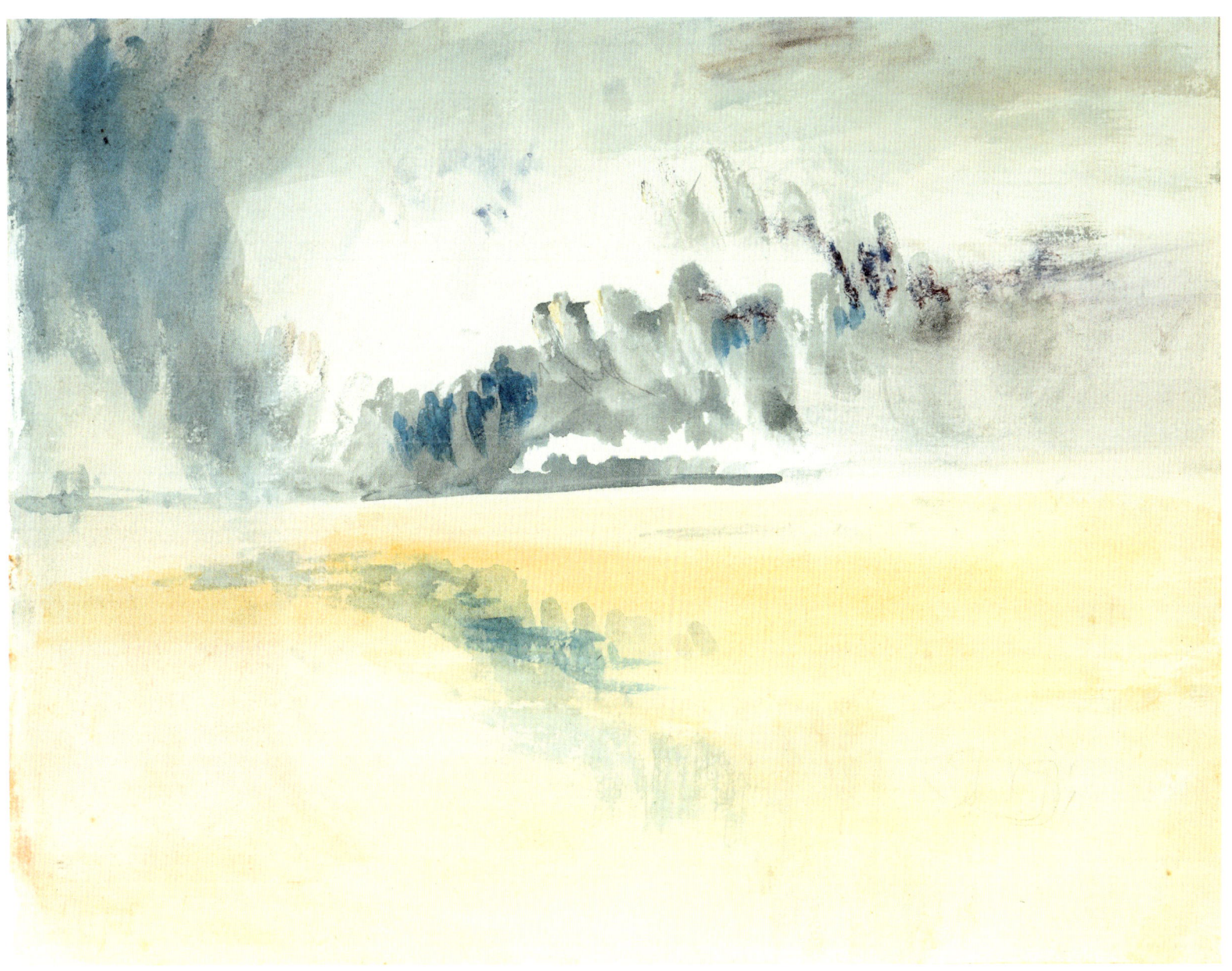

36. Joseph Mallord William Turner
Red and Blue Sunset Sky over the Sea, c. 1845
watercolour on paper
24.1 x 35.8 cm

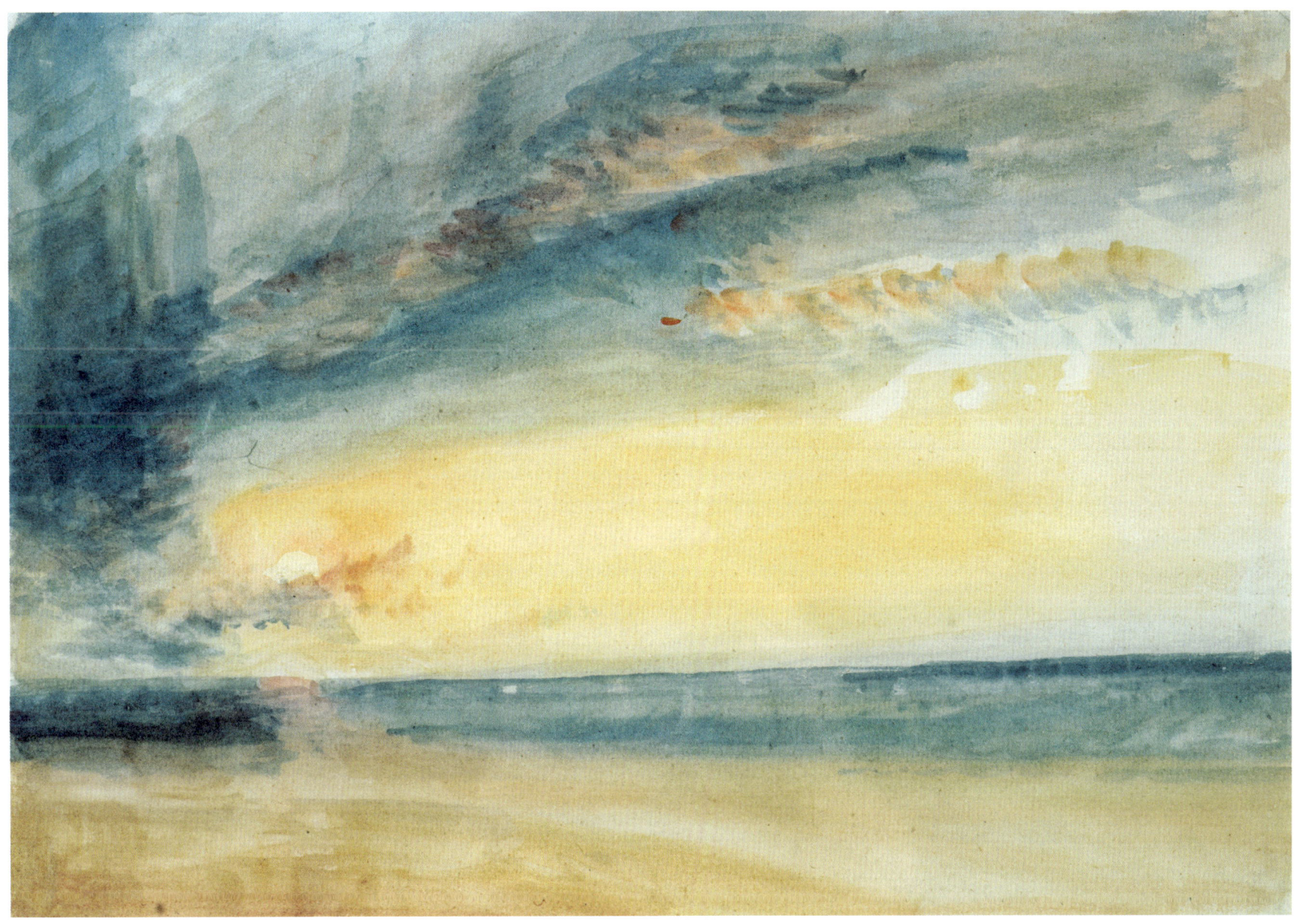

37. Joseph Mallord William Turner
A Steamboat and Crescent Moon, c. 1845
watercolour on paper
22.9 x 32.7 cm

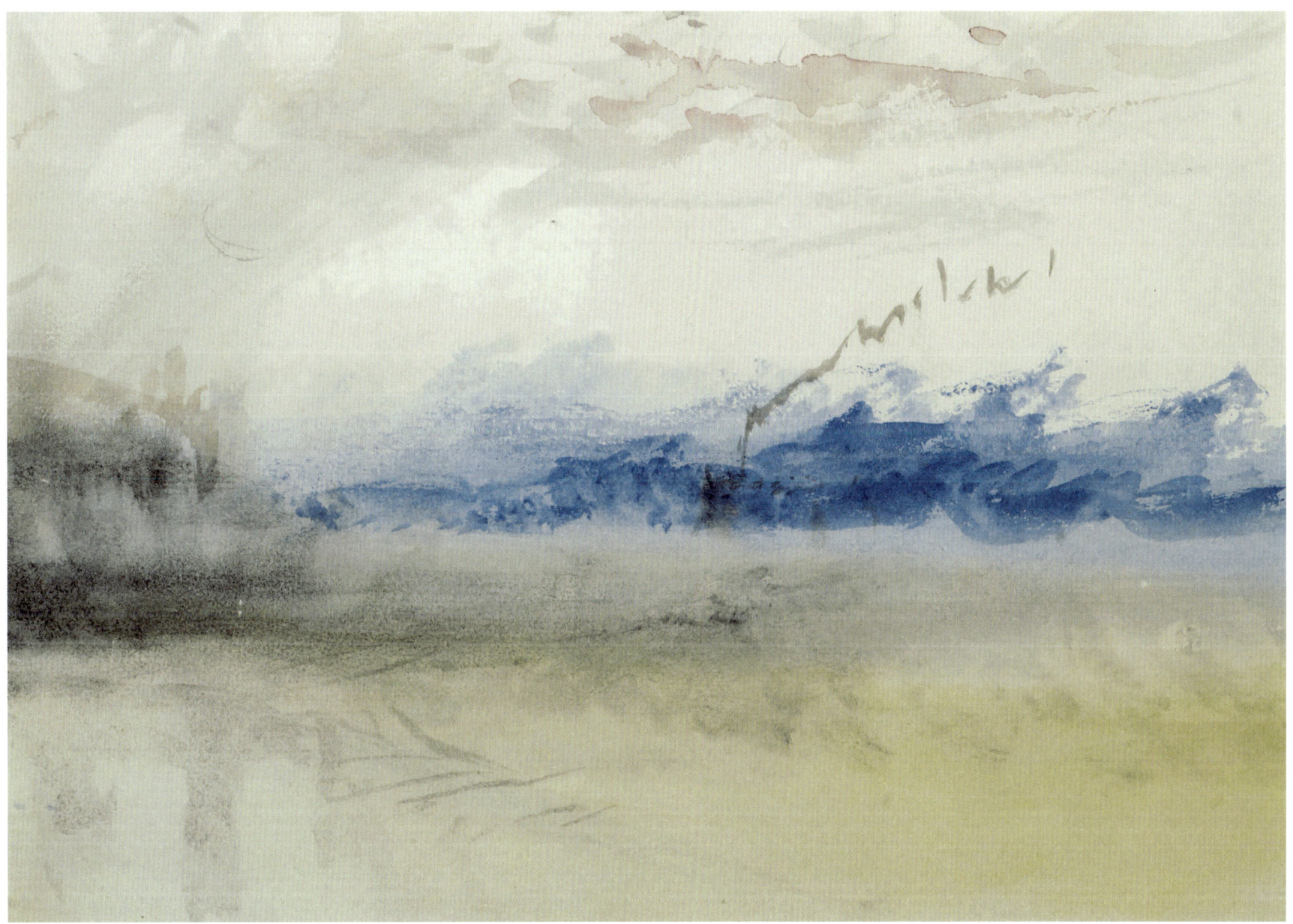

38. Joseph Mallord William Turner
A Cloudy Sky (or, Fire at Sea), c. 1845
watercolour and red chalk on paper
23 x 31.2 cm

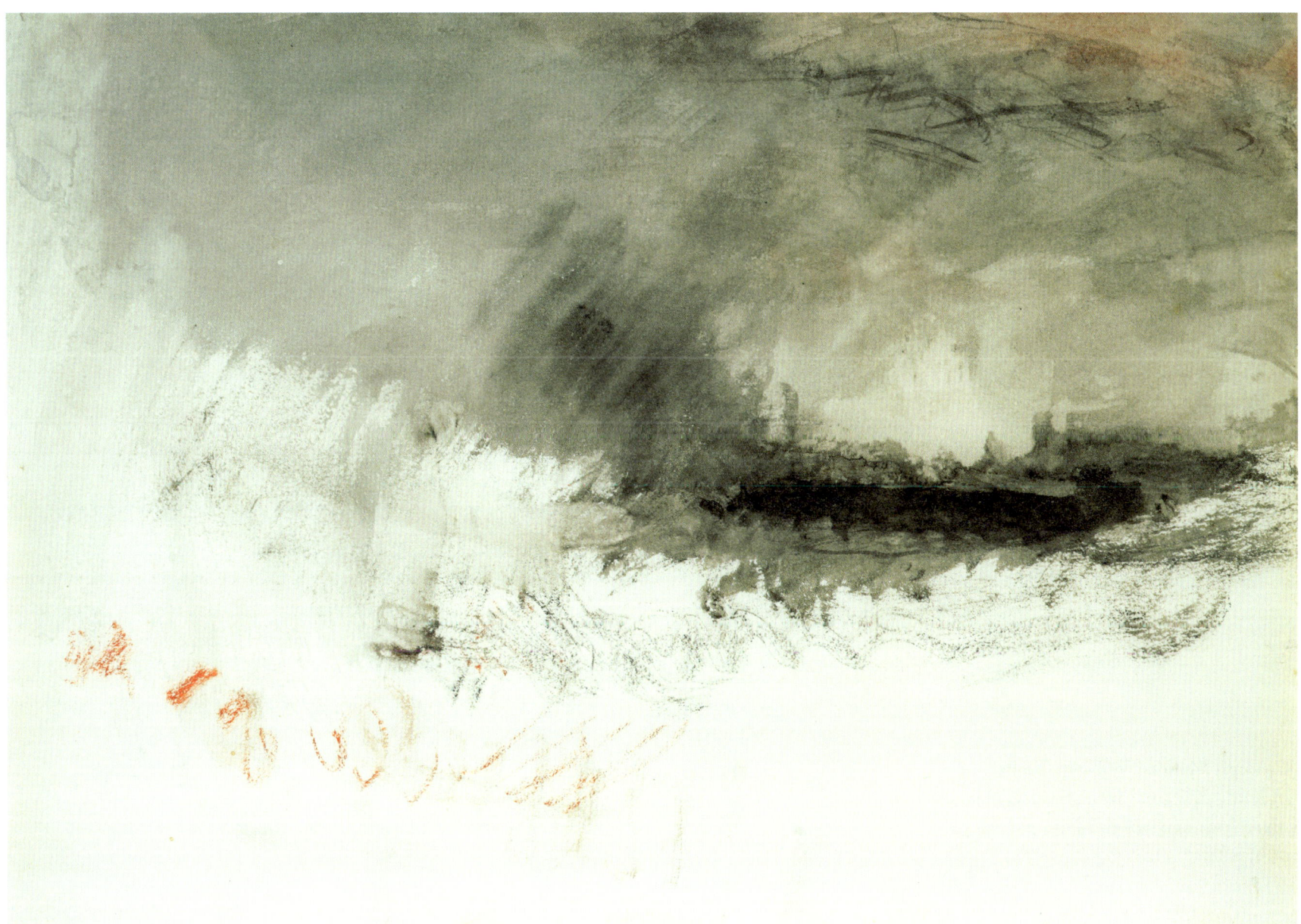

39. Joseph Mallord William Turner
Study of a Summer Sky at Margate, c. 1844-45
watercolour on paper
22.8 x 33 cm

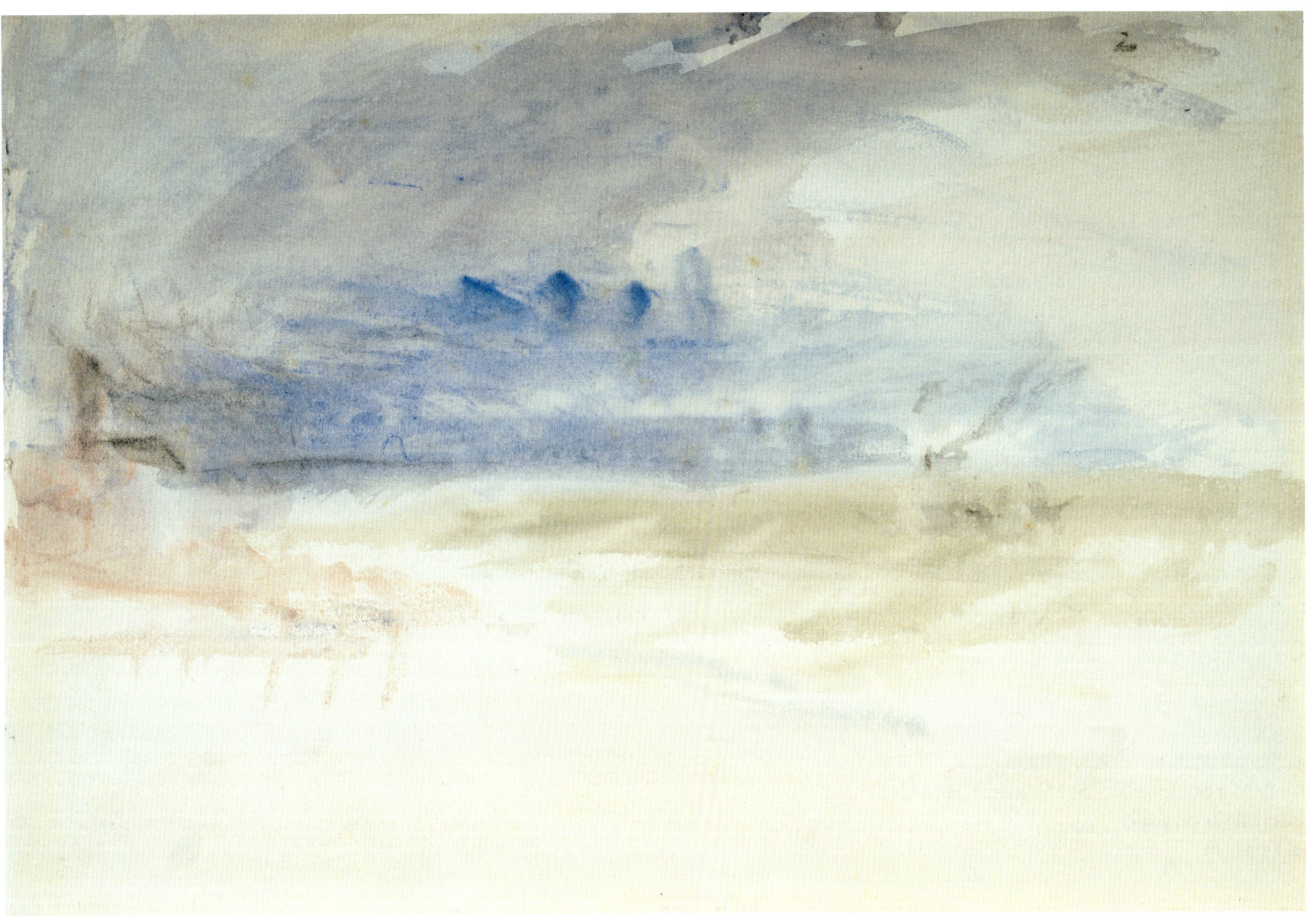

40. Joseph Mallord William Turner
Study of Sky, Sea and Shore, Margate, c. 1844-5
watercolour on paper
22.8 x 33 cm

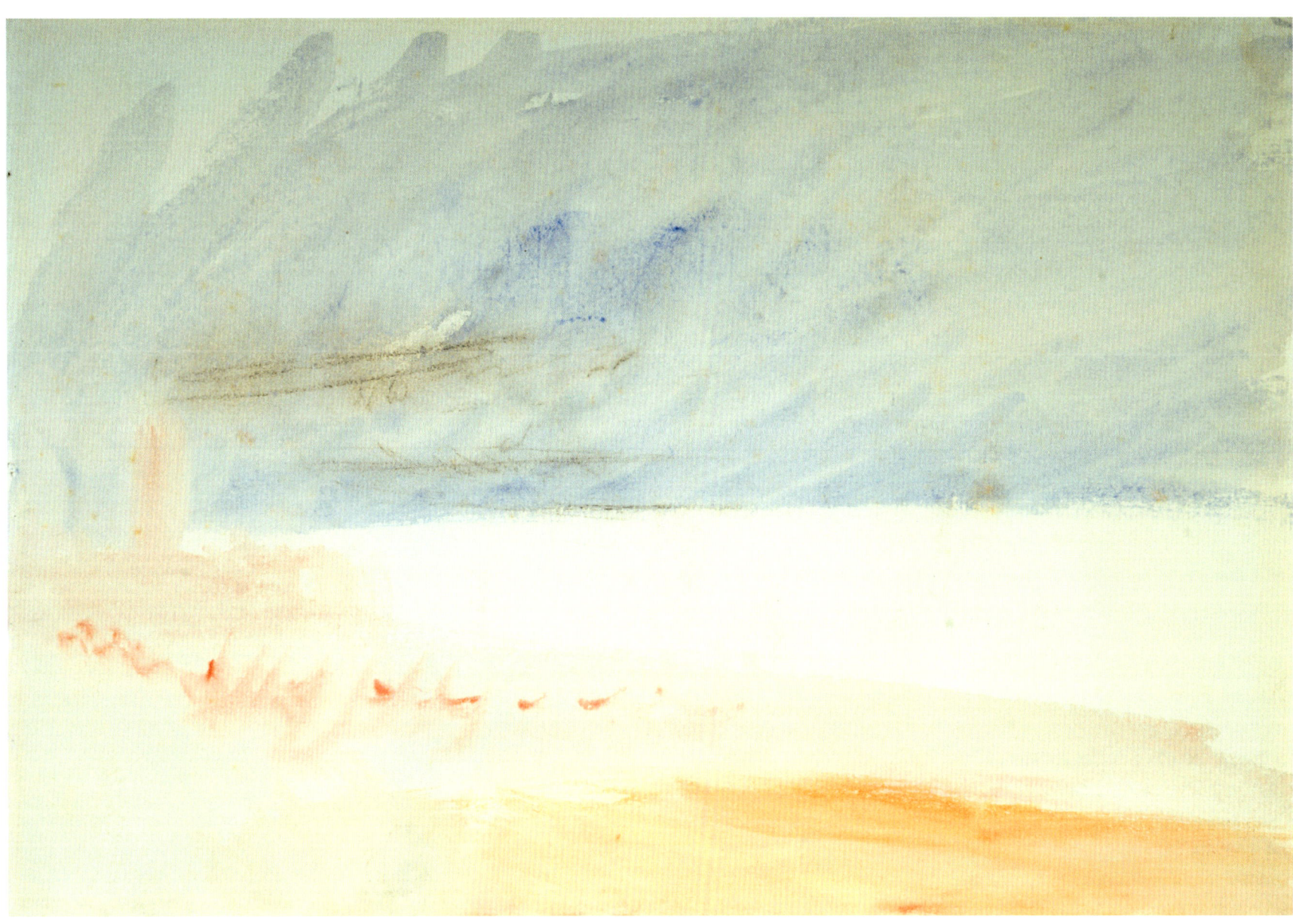

41. Joseph Mallord William Turner
'Fox Lugger' in a Storm off Margate, c. 1845
pencil and watercolour on paper
22.8 x 33 cm

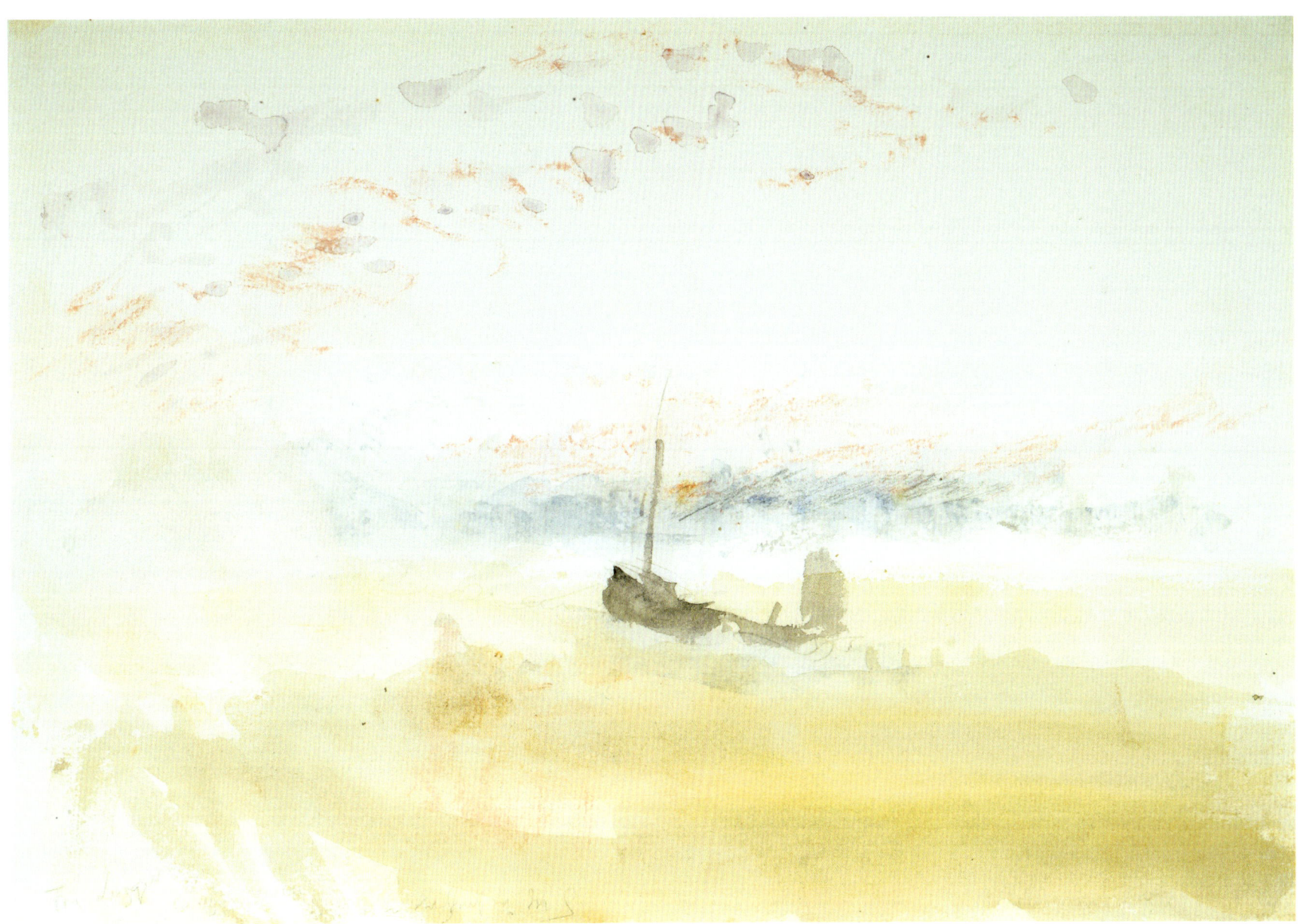

42. David Cox
Low Tide, ?1830s
watercolour and gouache on laid paper
17.5 x 28.2 cm

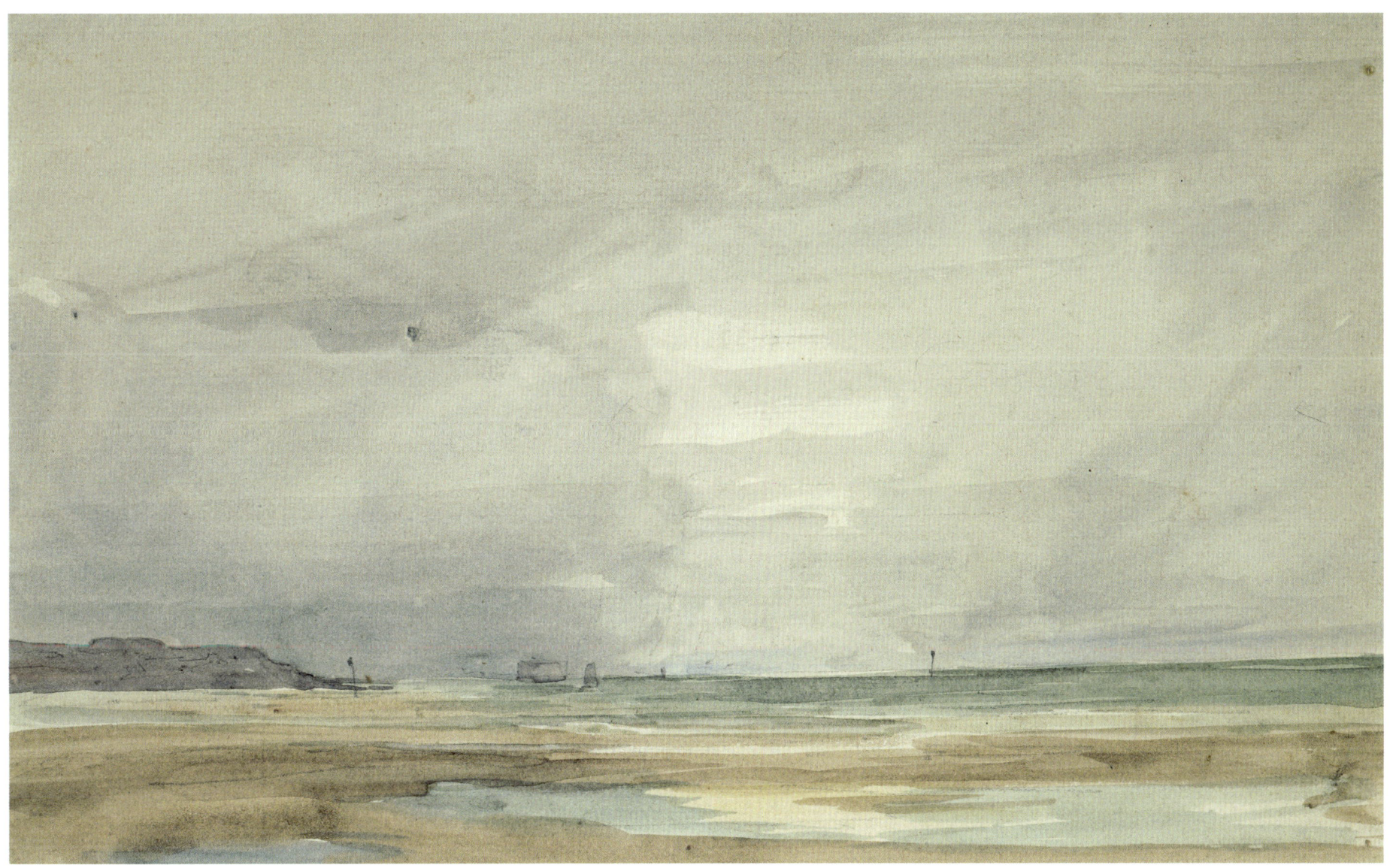

43. David Cox
Study of a Headland, Penmaenmawr, 1830s
watercolour on paper
26.7 x 36.7 cm

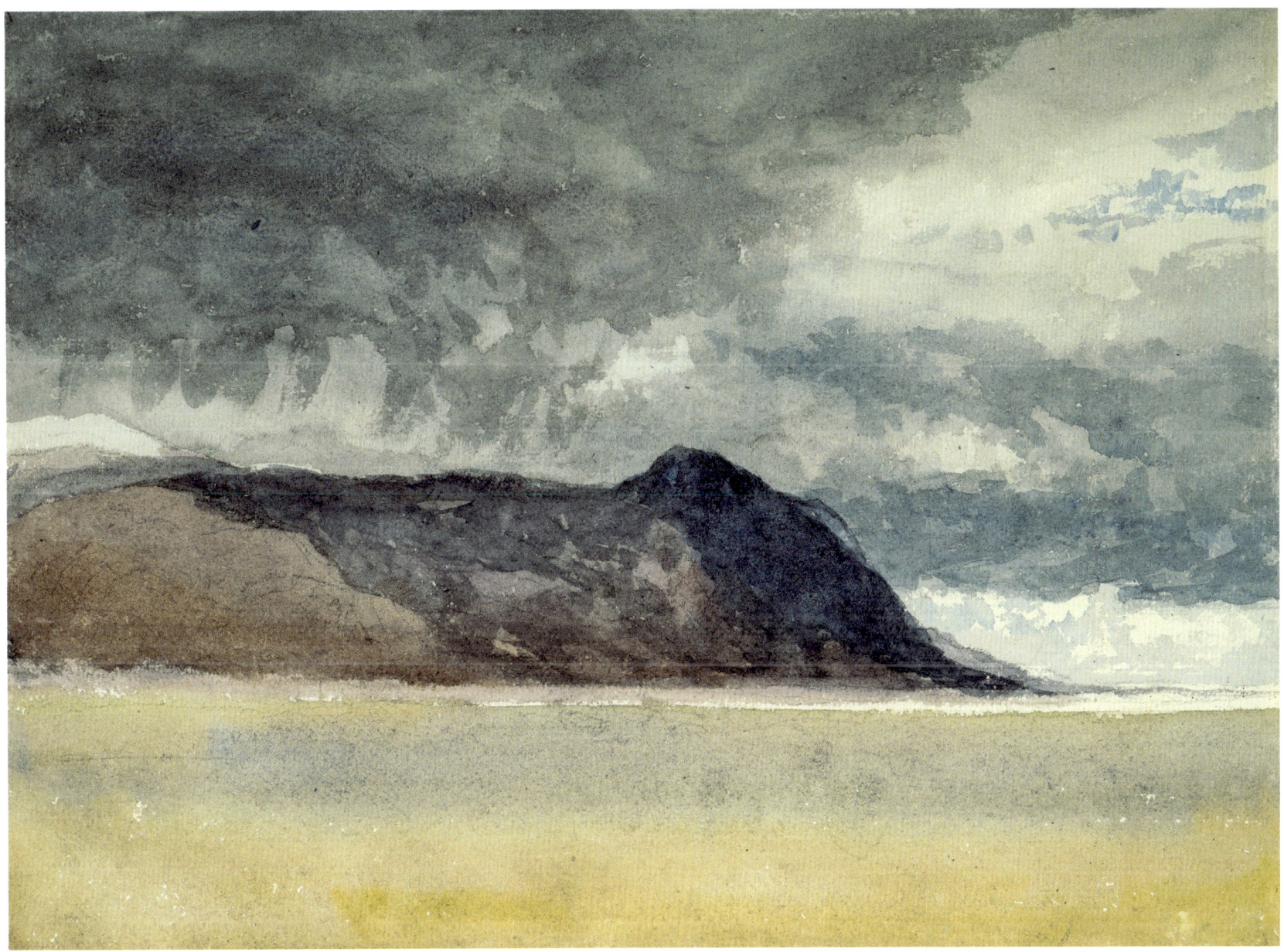

44. David Cox
A Wooded Landscape at Sunset, c. 1835
watercolour on paper
25 x 37.9 cm

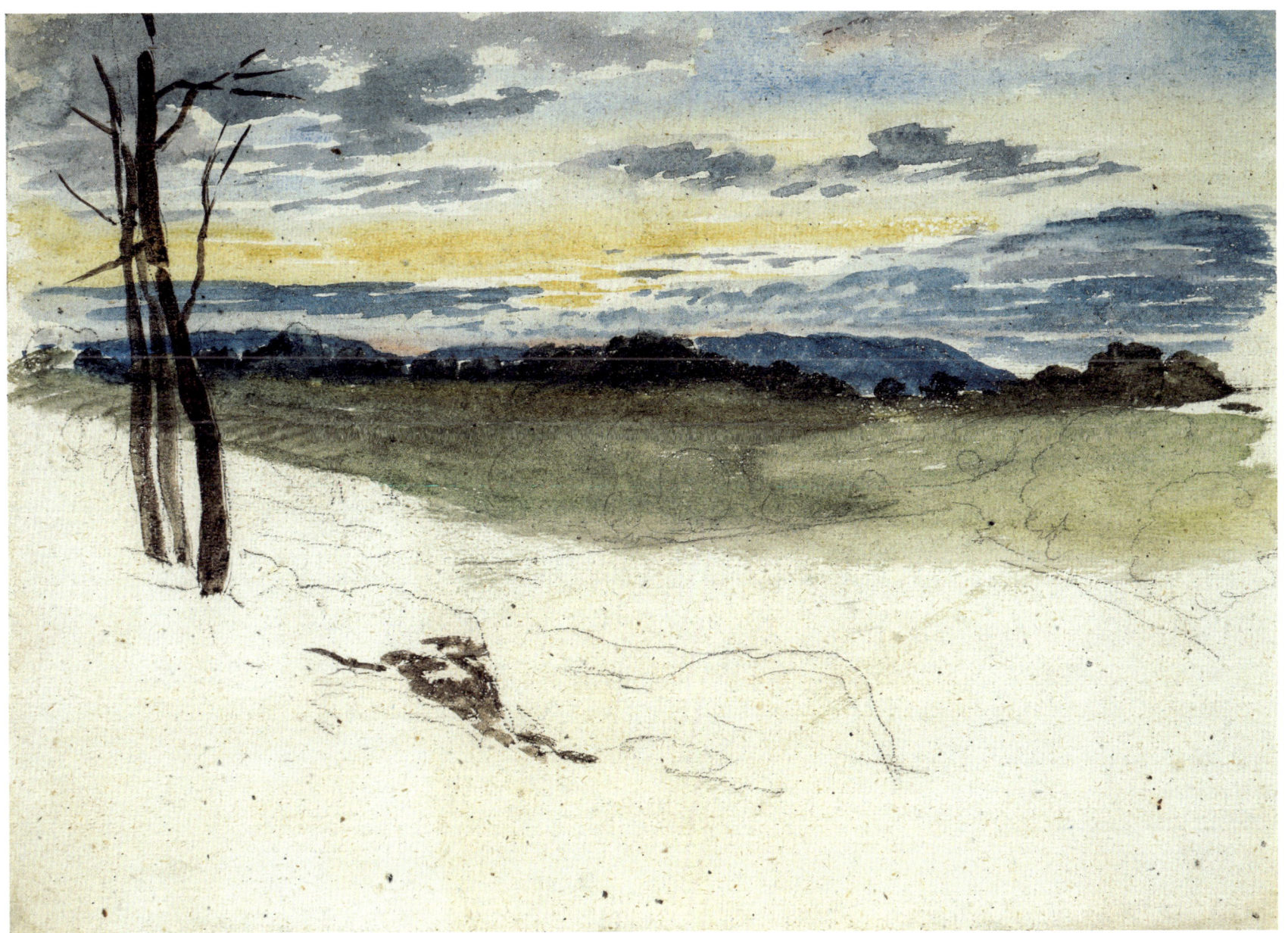

45. David Cox
Furness Abbey, 1830s
pencil, watercolour and gouache on paper
28.7 x 38.6 cm

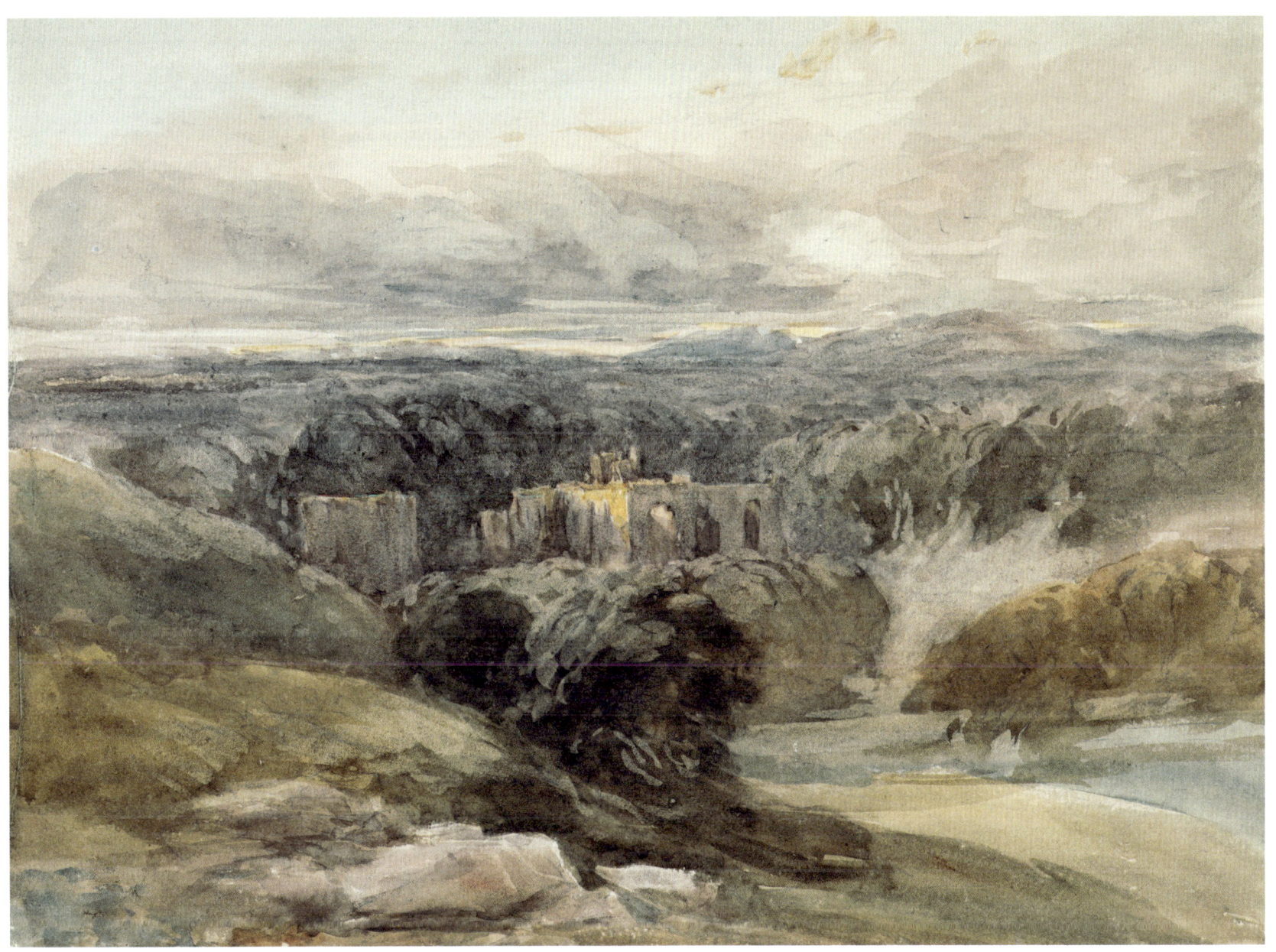

46. David Cox
Cattle Watering in a Wooded River (possibly the Wharfe
or the Dee), 1830s
black chalk and watercolour on two sheets of laid paper
19.6 x 43.1 cm

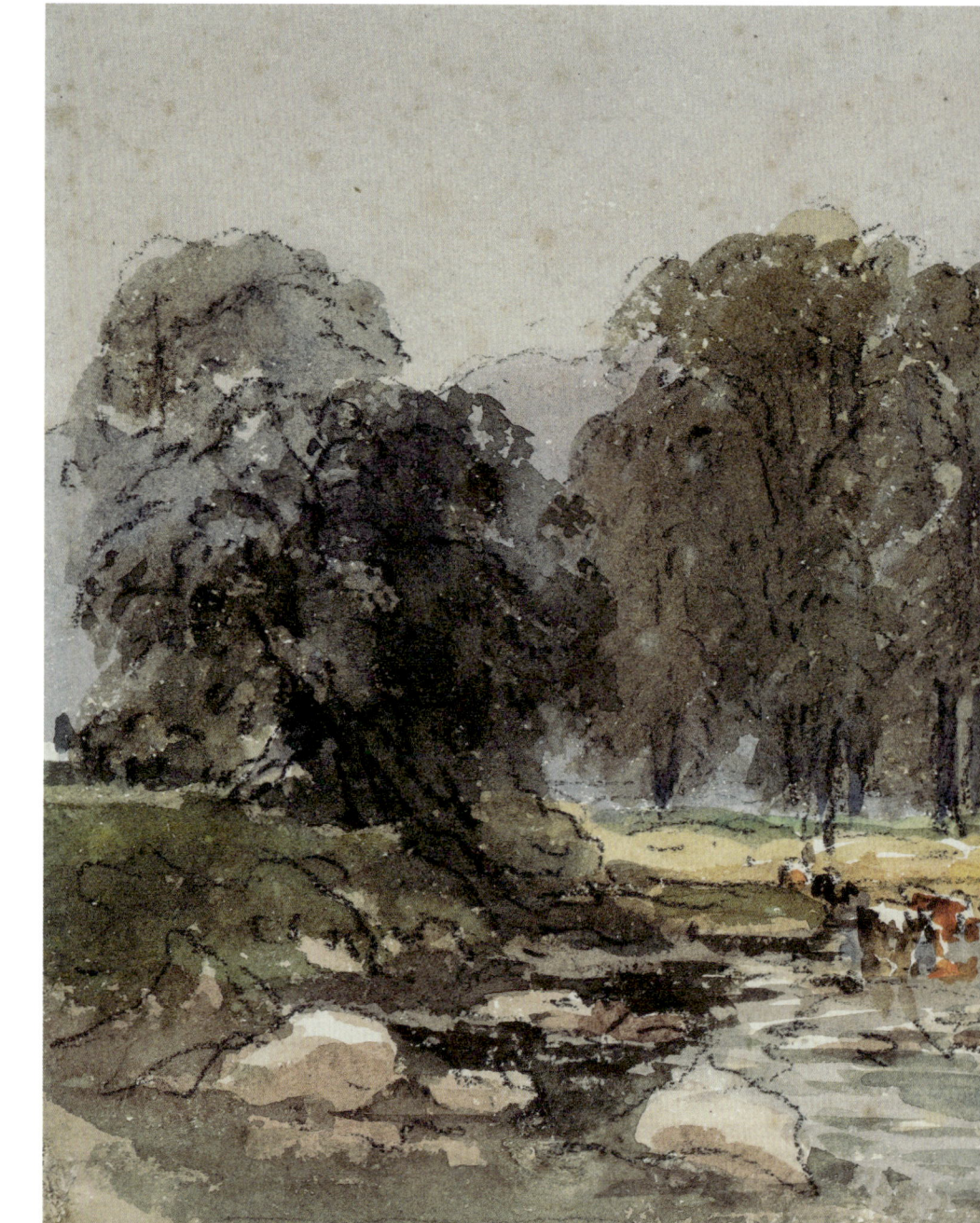

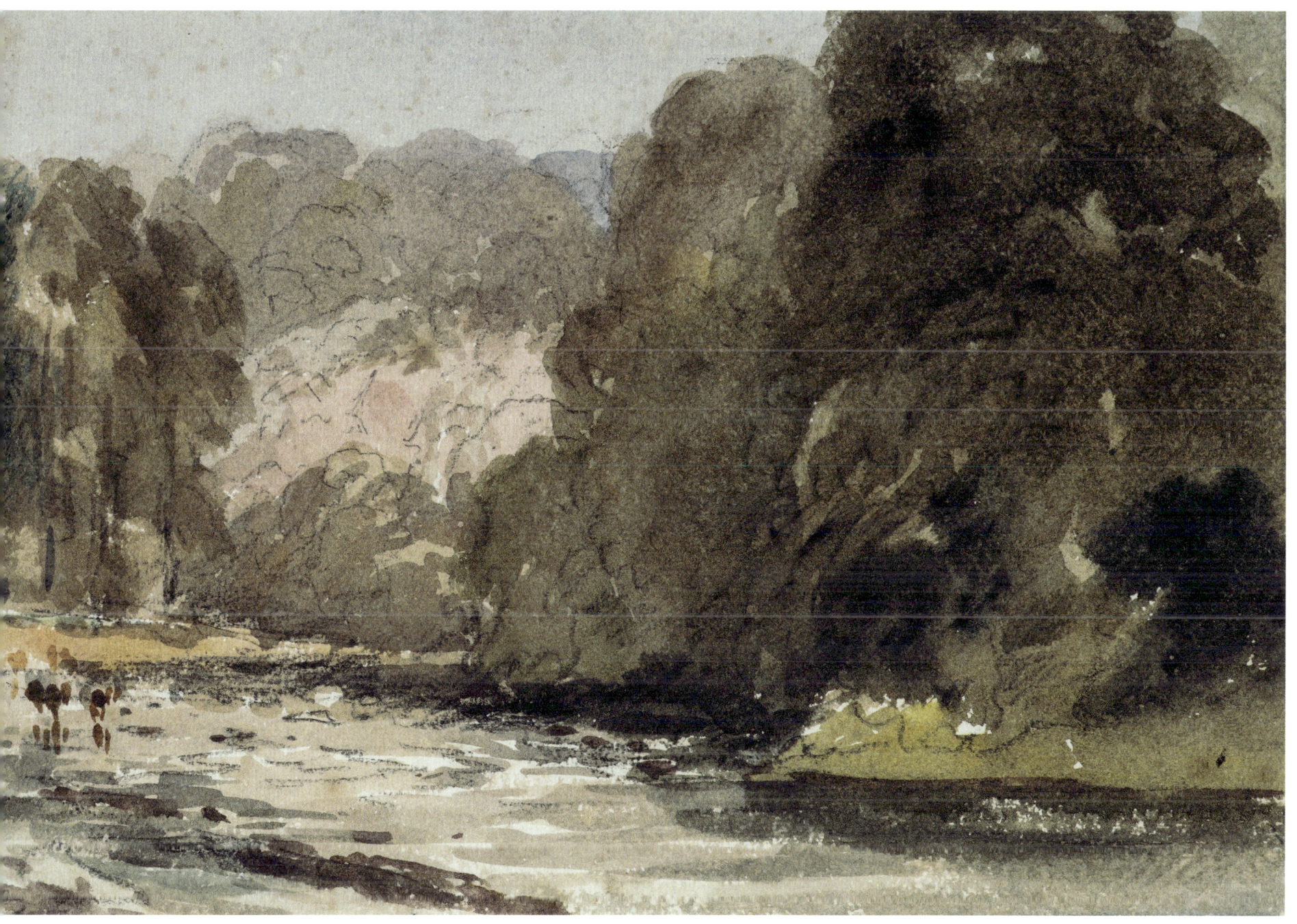

47. Peter De Wint
Trees by the River near Lowther, c. 1839-40
watercolour on paper
45 x 60.9 cm

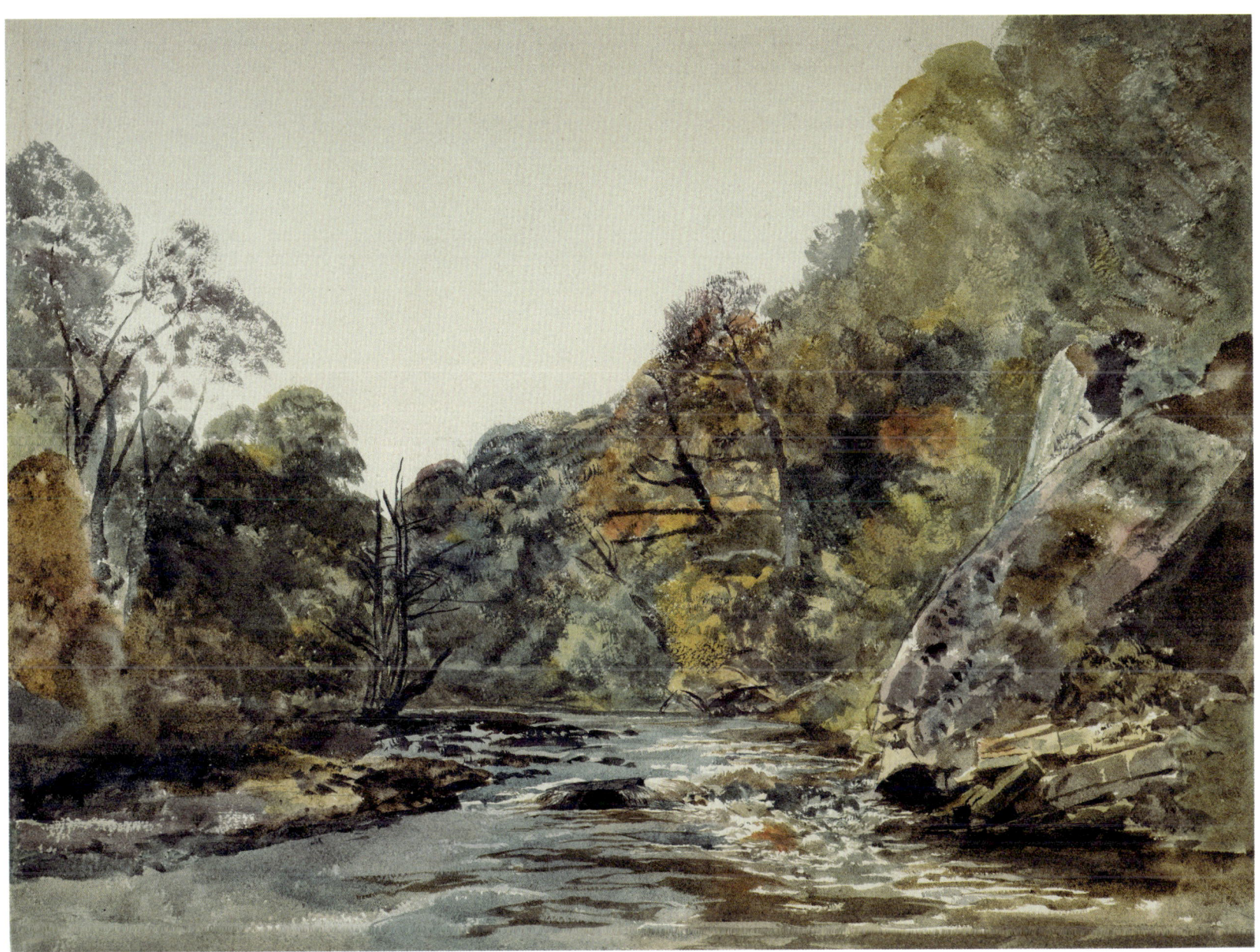

48. Peter De Wint
Landscape with Church Tower (formerly titled 'Matlock Tor'), c. 1840
watercolour on paper
35.6 x 54.6 cm

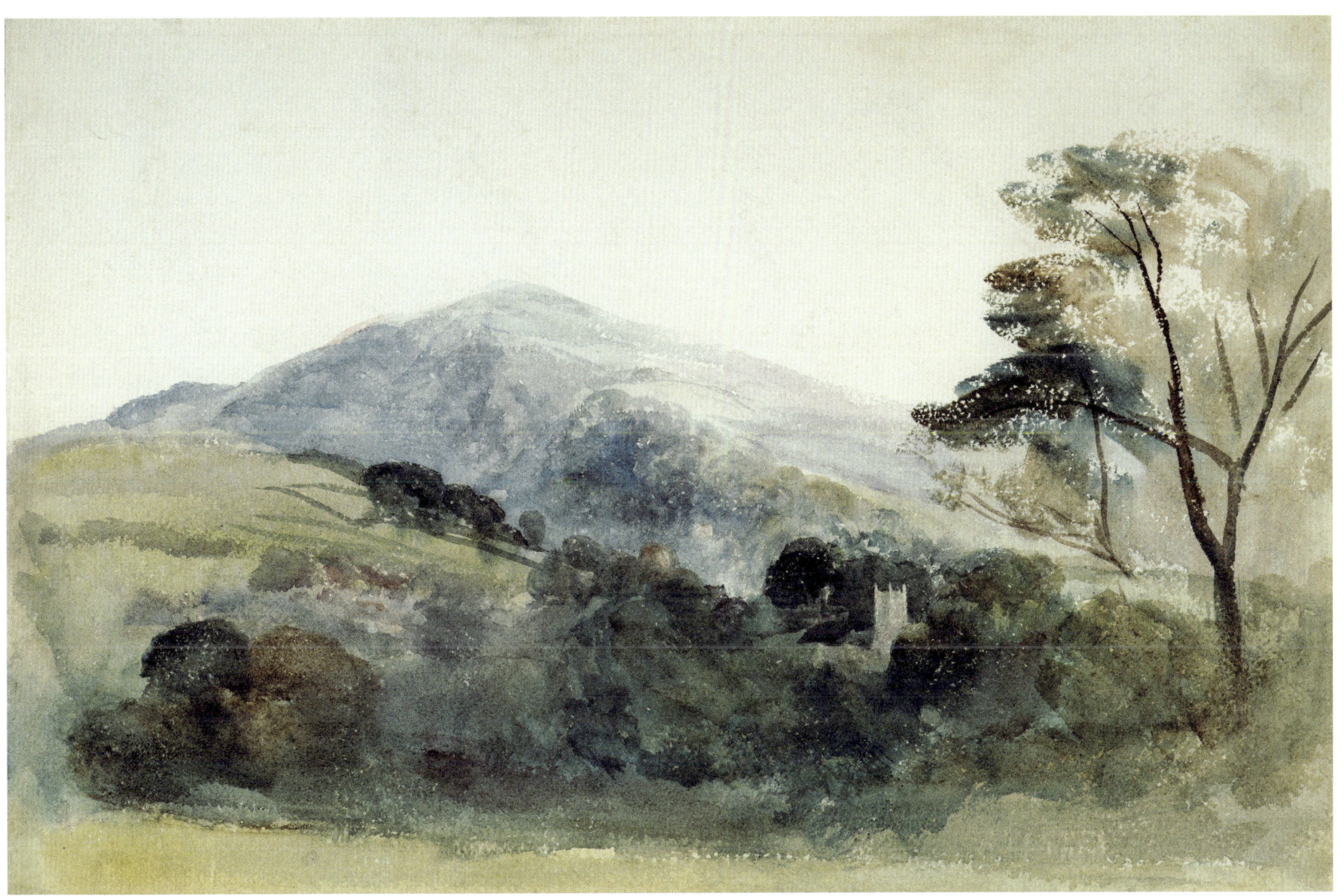

49. Peter De Wint
Glastonbury, early 1840s
watercolour on paper
42.5 x 61.5 cm

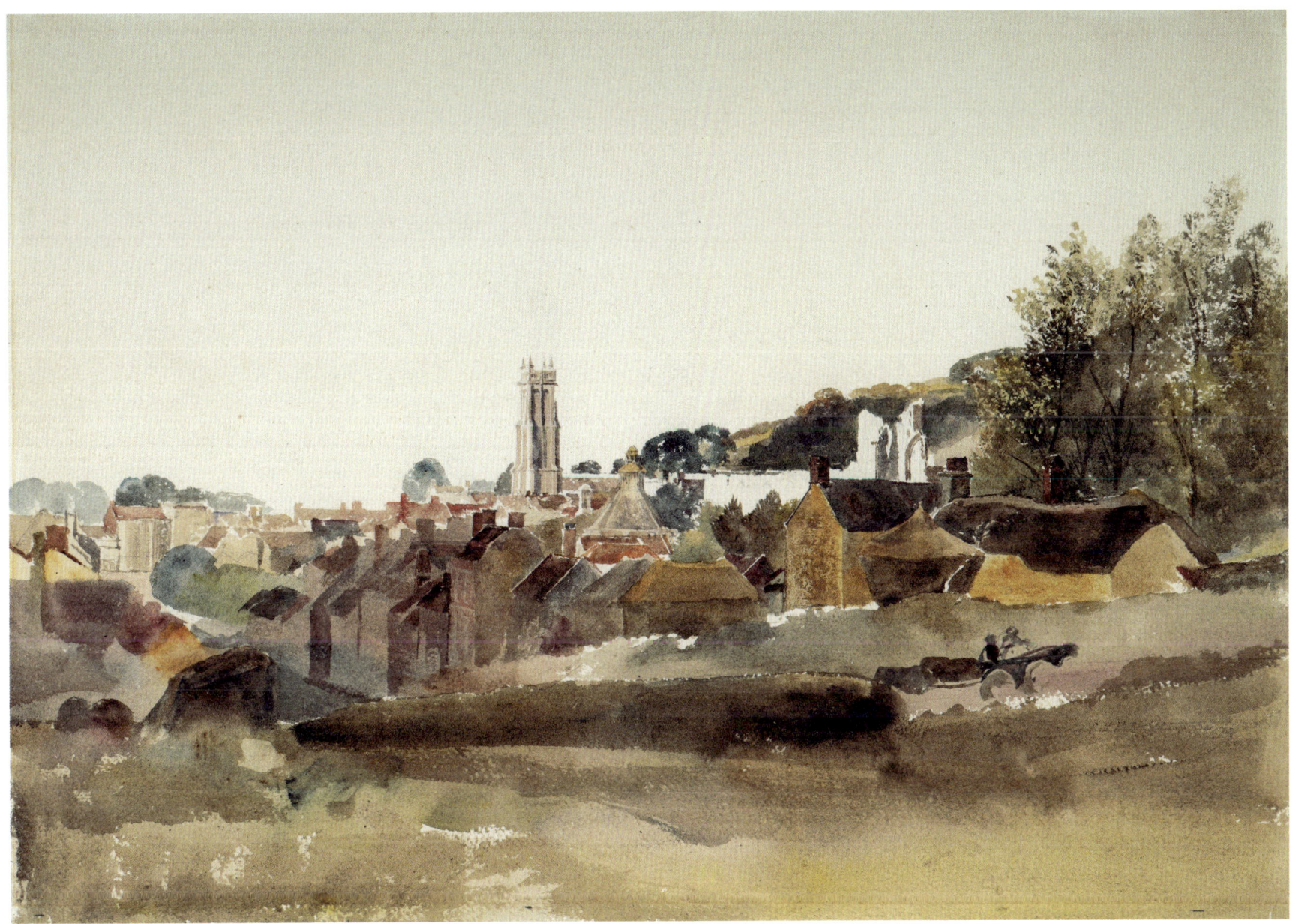

50. Peter De Wint
Bolton Castle, Wensleydale (formerly titled 'Clee Hills Shropshire'), c. 1840
watercolour on paper
38.1 x 52.7 cm

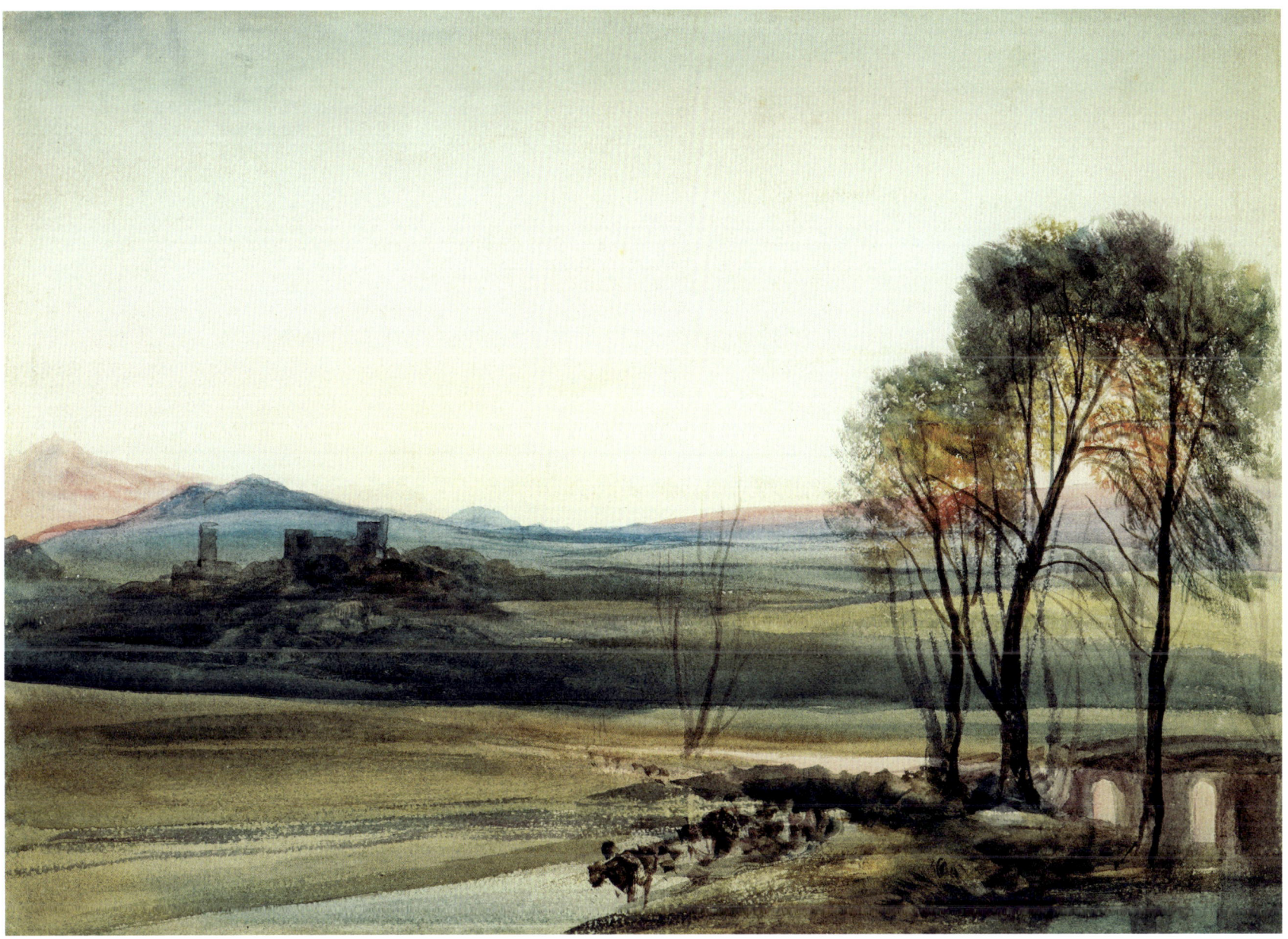

51. Peter De Wint
The Vale of Neath, South Wales, late 1840s
watercolour on paper
29.5 x 46.5 cm

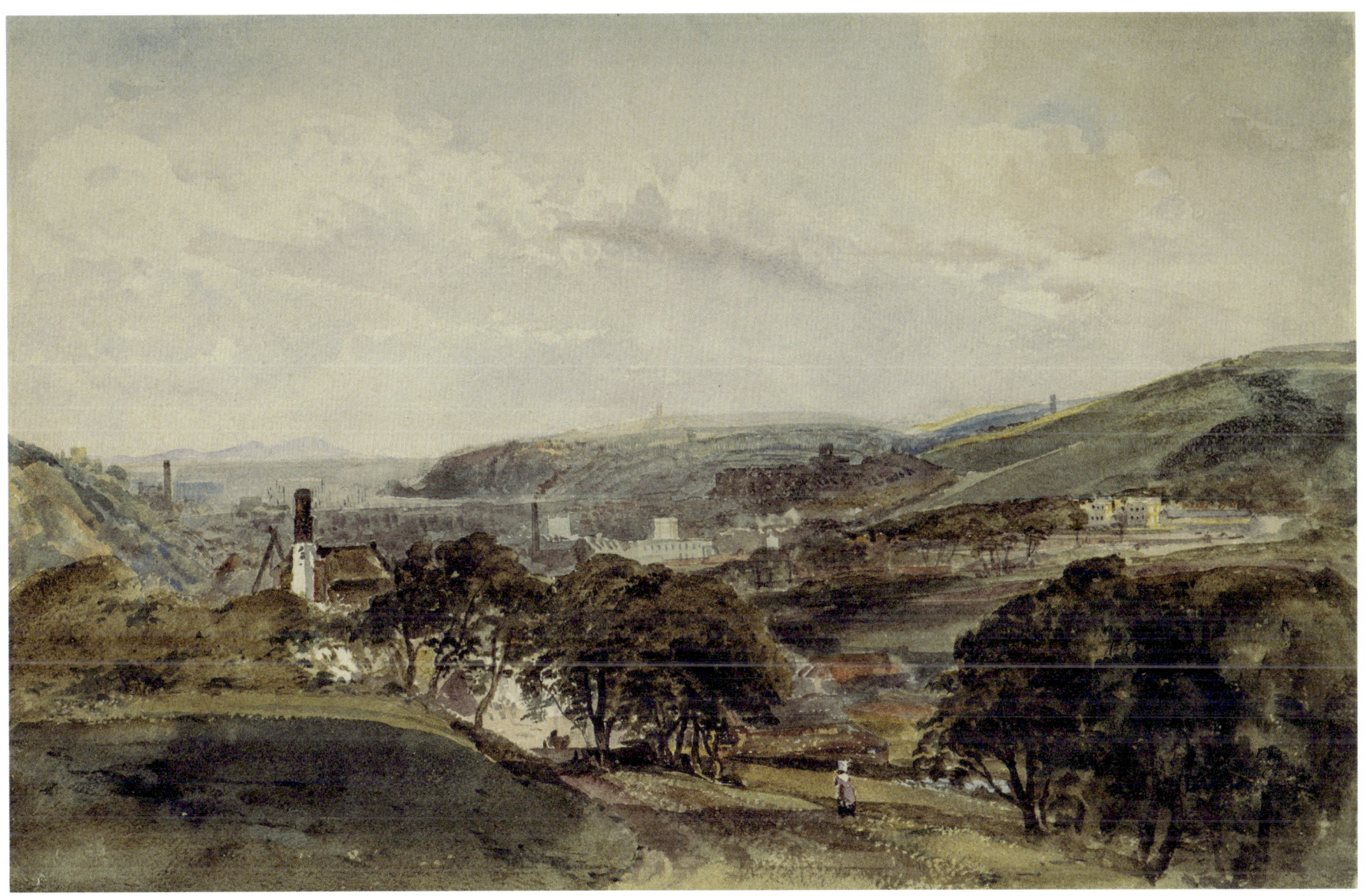

52. Joseph Mallord William Turner
Genoa from the North-East, c. 1838
pencil, watercolour and gouache with pen and red ink on blue paper
14 x 19.1 cm

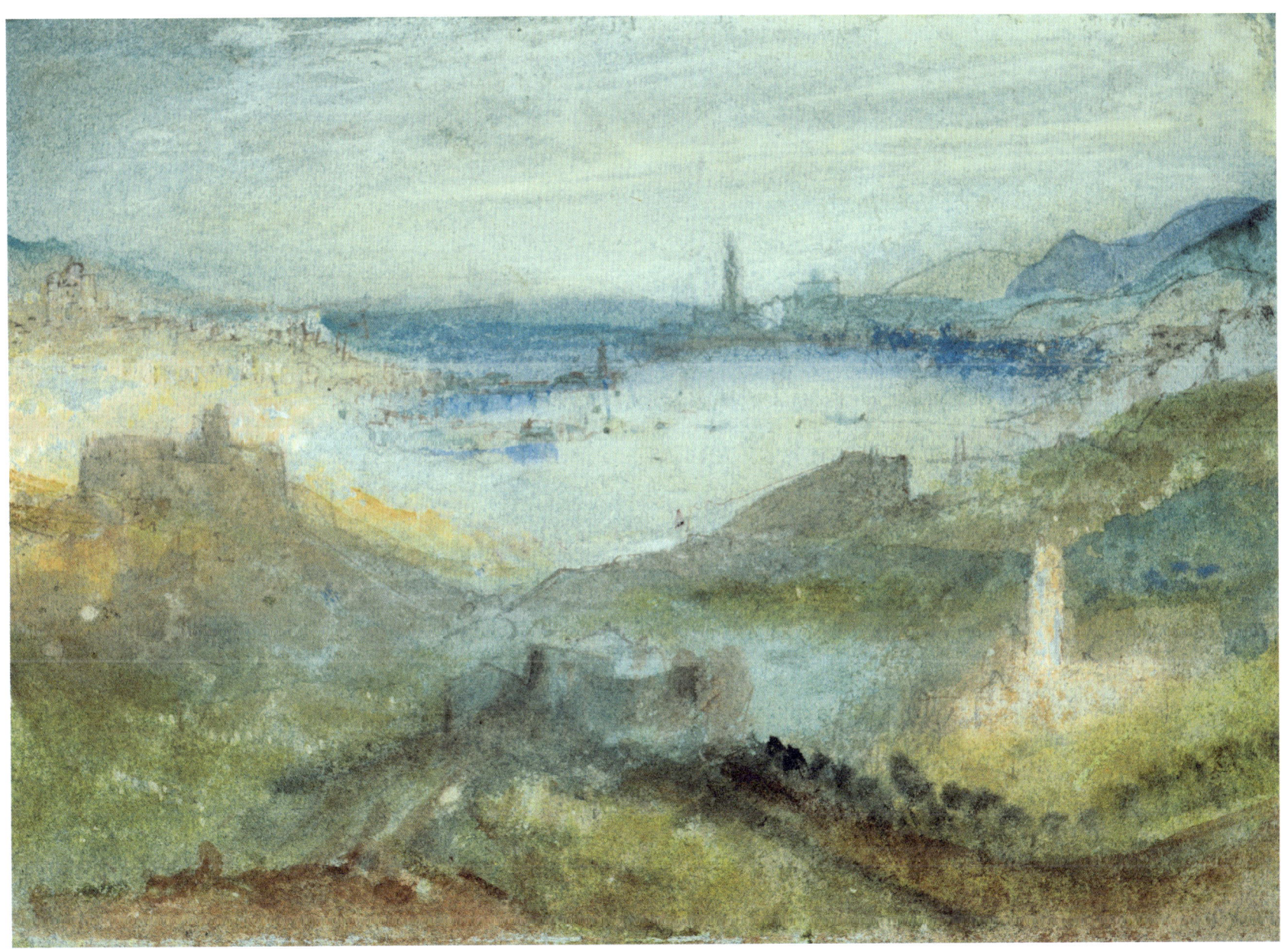

53. Joseph Mallord William Turner
Distant View of Cochem on the Mosel, c. 1841
pencil, watercolour and sepia ink on white paper prepared with a grey wash
15.5 x 22.8 cm

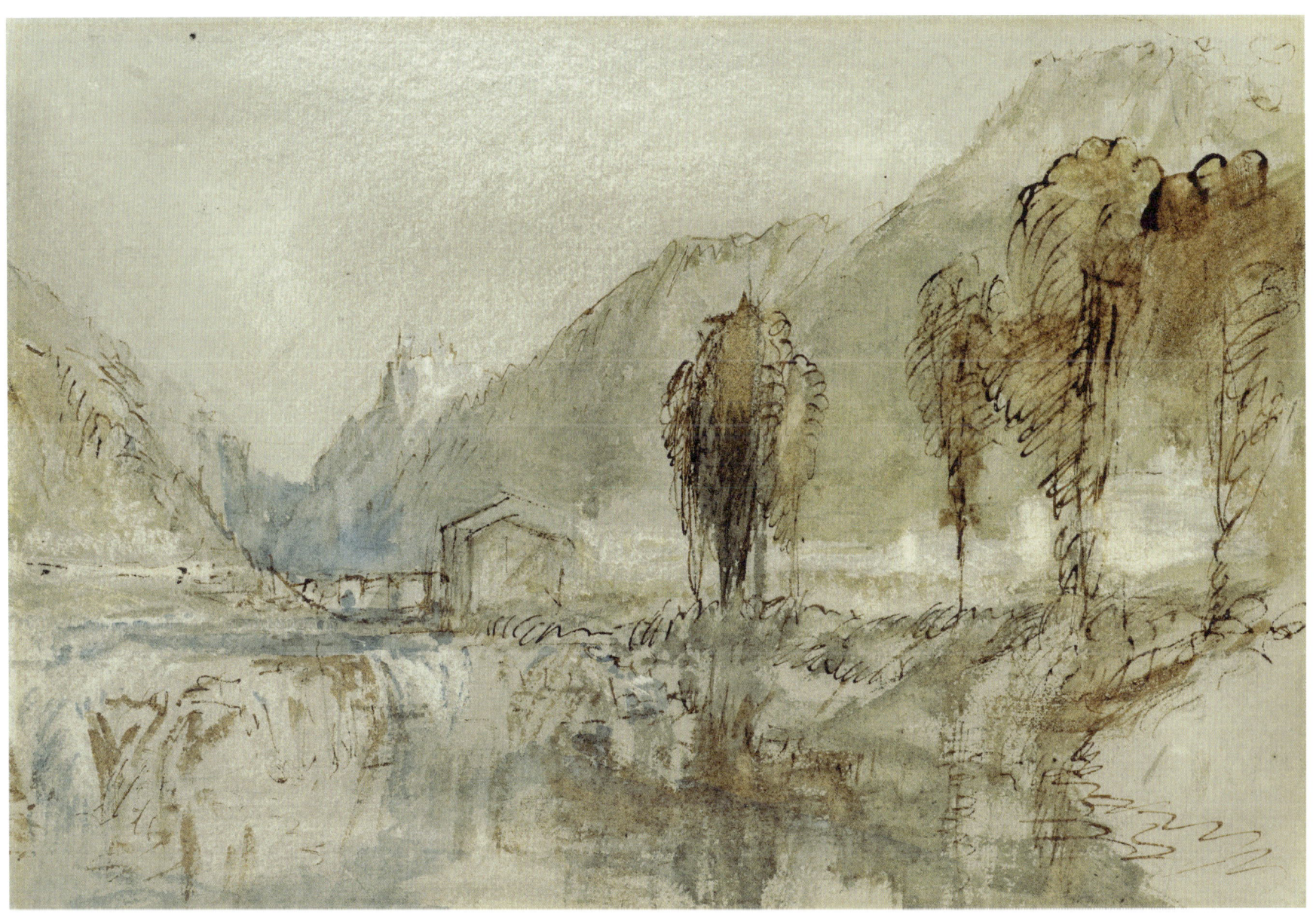

54. Joseph Mallord William Turner
Trutzeltz and Burg Eltz with the Eltzbach, c. 1841
watercolour and gouache on paper
15.5 x 22.9 cm

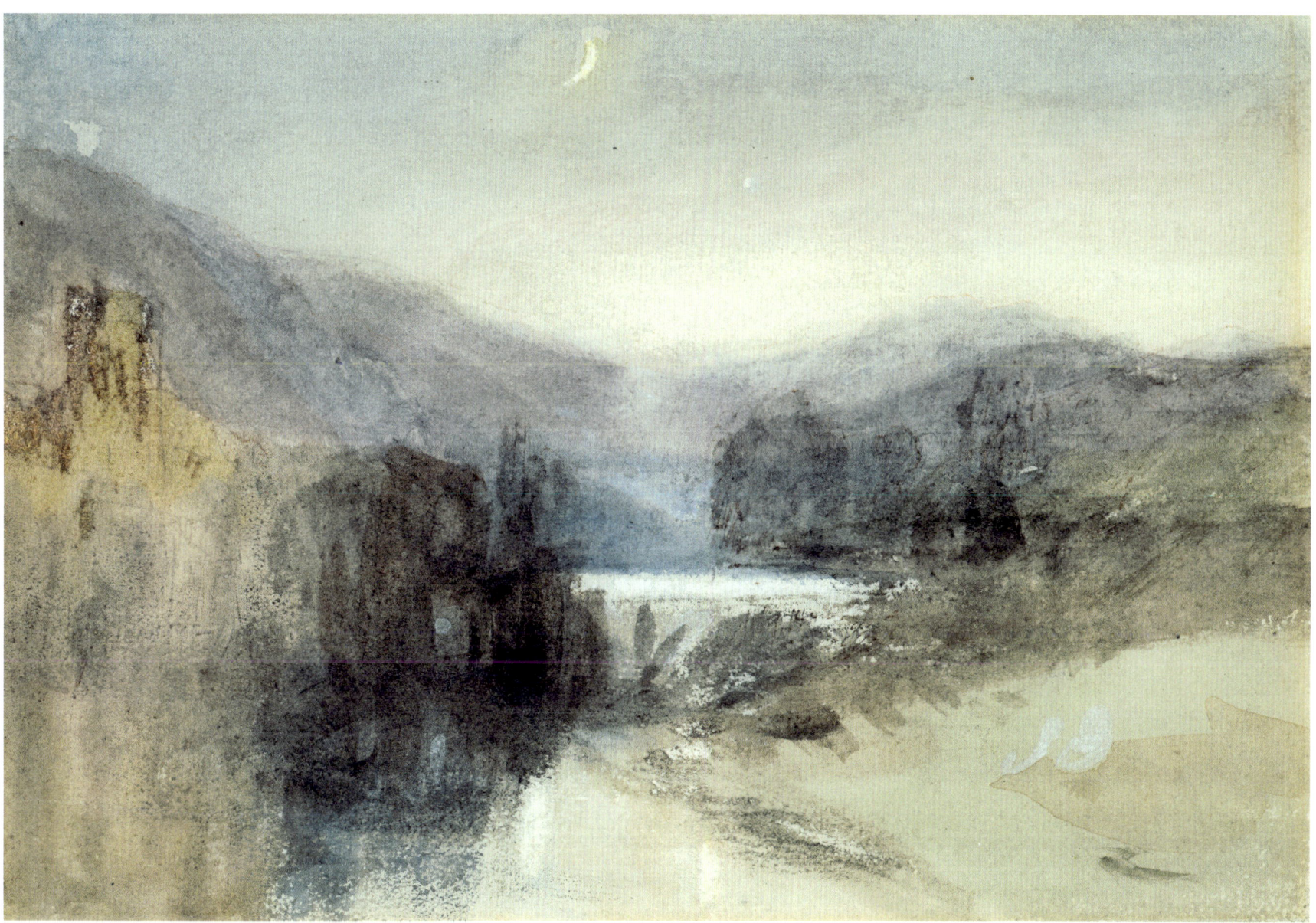

55. Joseph Mallord William Turner
Burg Rheinfels on the Rhine, c. 1841-44
pencil and watercolour with scratching-out on paper
18.5 x 24.1 cm

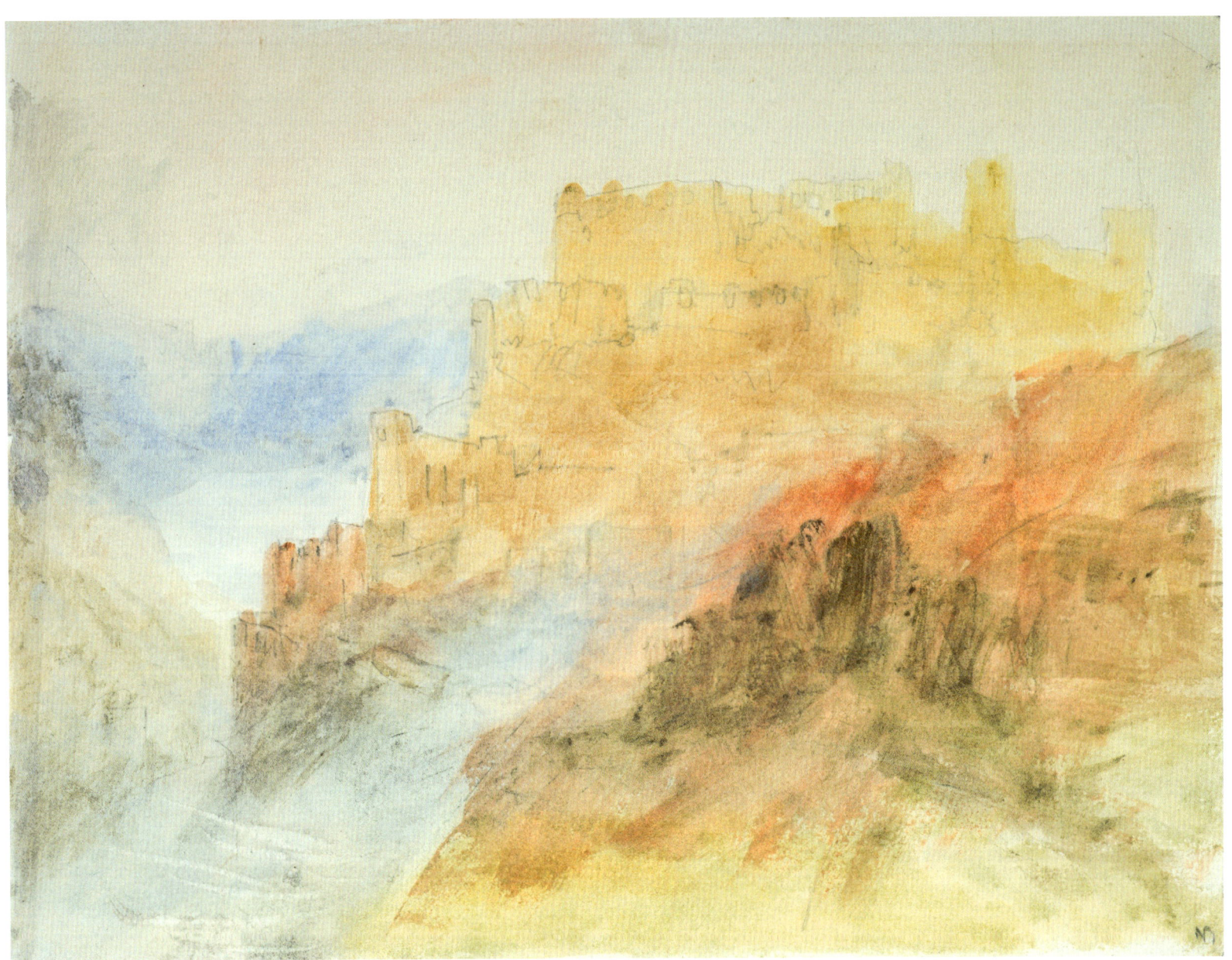

56. Joseph Mallord William Turner
Koblenz and the Fortress of Ehrenbreitstein, 1840s
pencil and watercolour on paper
23.1 x 29.2 cm

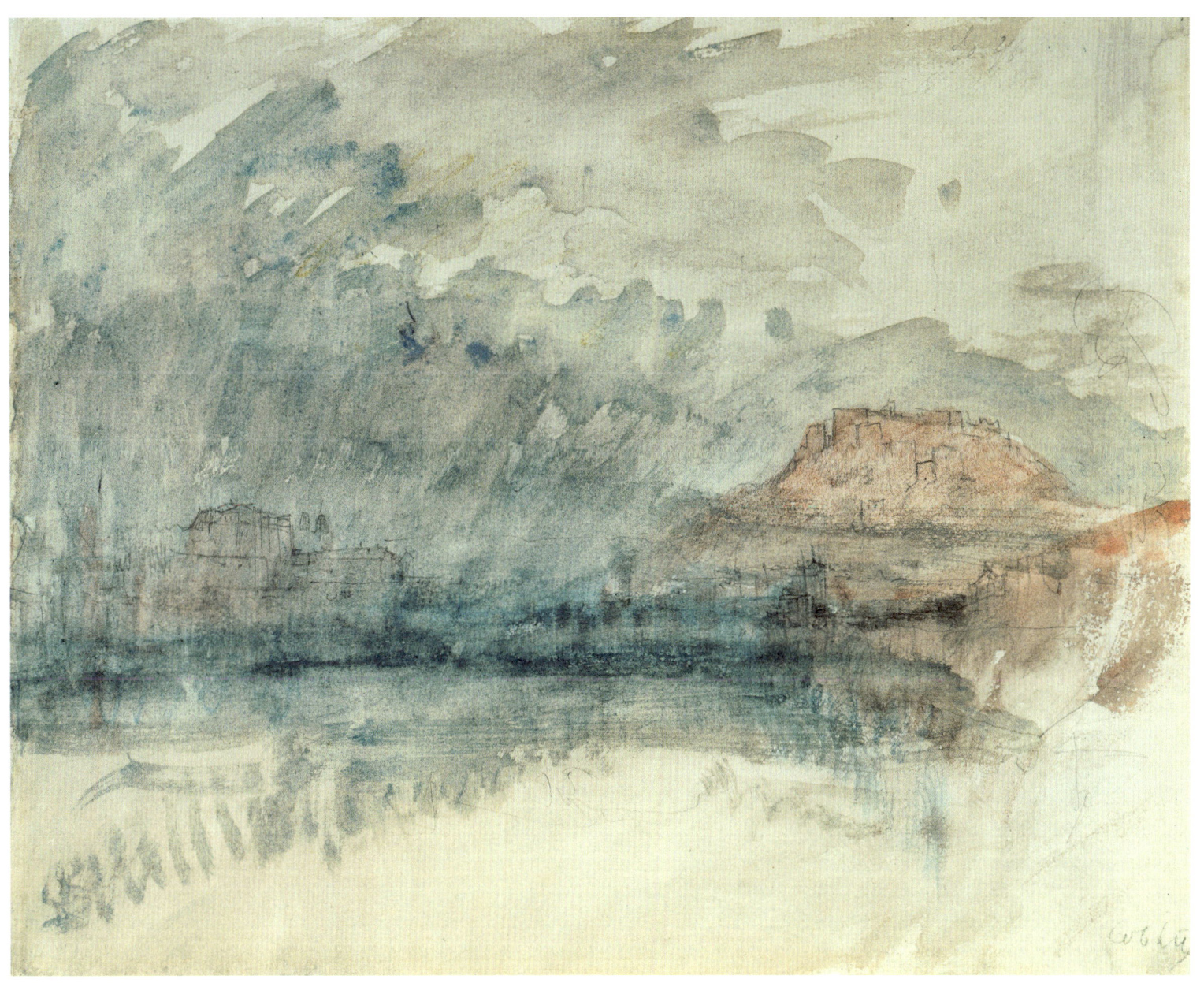

57. Joseph Mallord William Turner
Mount Pilatus, with a Steamboat on Lake Lucerne, c. 1842-44
watercolour on paper
21.6 x 26.9 cm

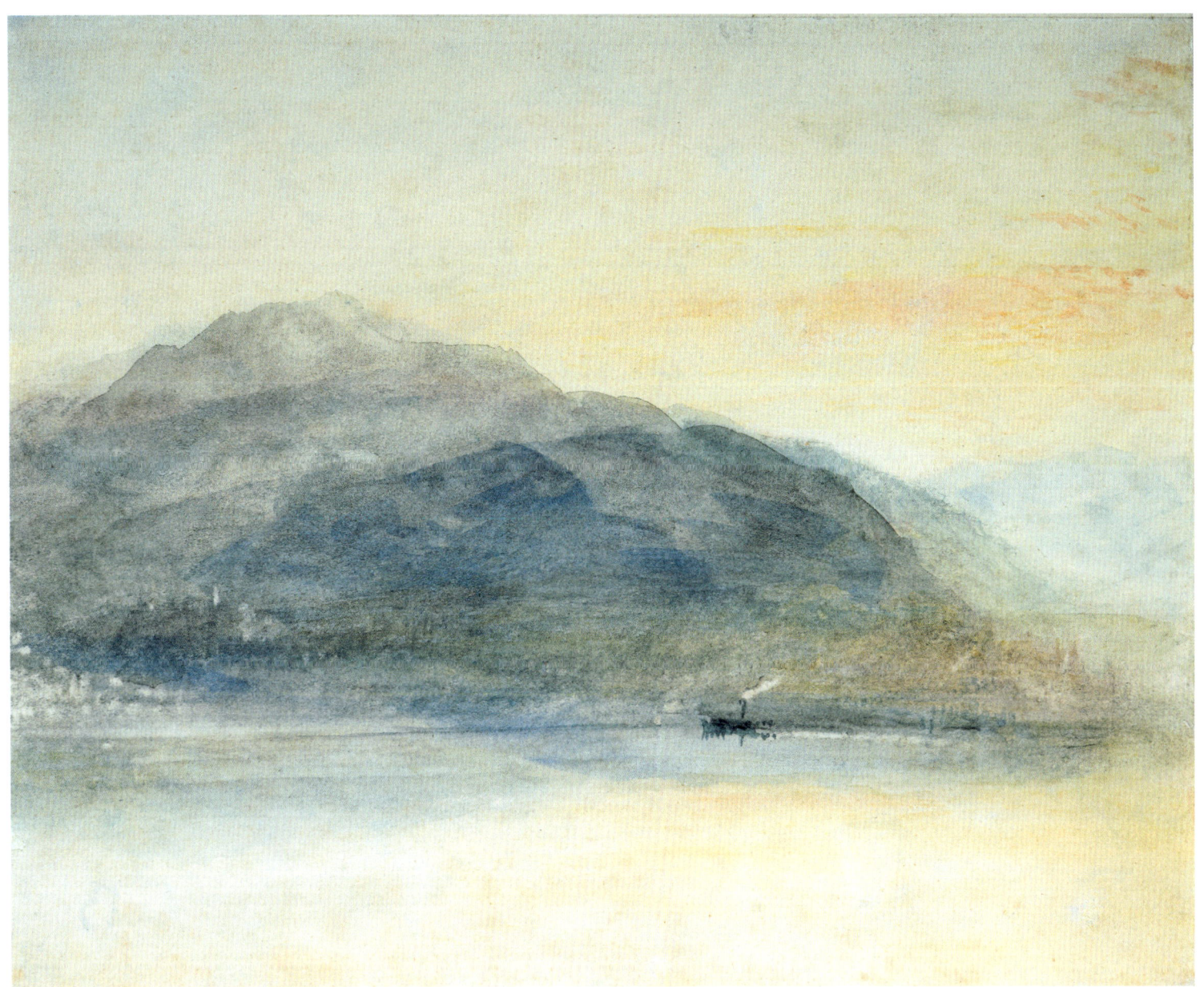

58. Joseph Mallord William Turner
Rainbow over a Swiss Lake (possibly on Lake Lucerne with the Rigi) c. 1842-44
pencil and watercolour on paper
22.6 x 28.7 cm

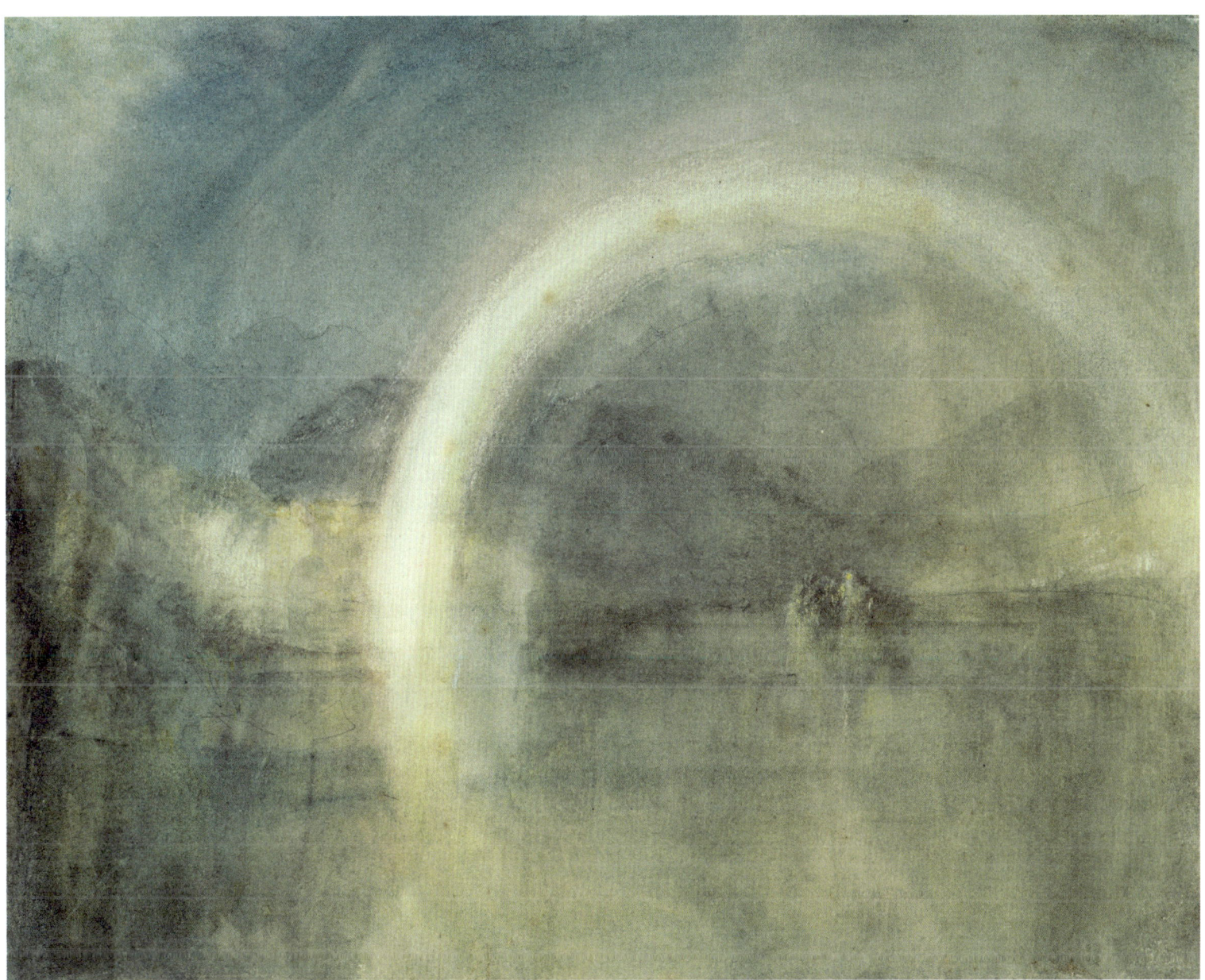

59. Joseph Mallord William Turner
A Swiss Lake (possibly Lake Thun with the Stockhorn), c. 1842-44
pen and brown ink, watercolour and gouache on paper
23.1 x 28.8 cm

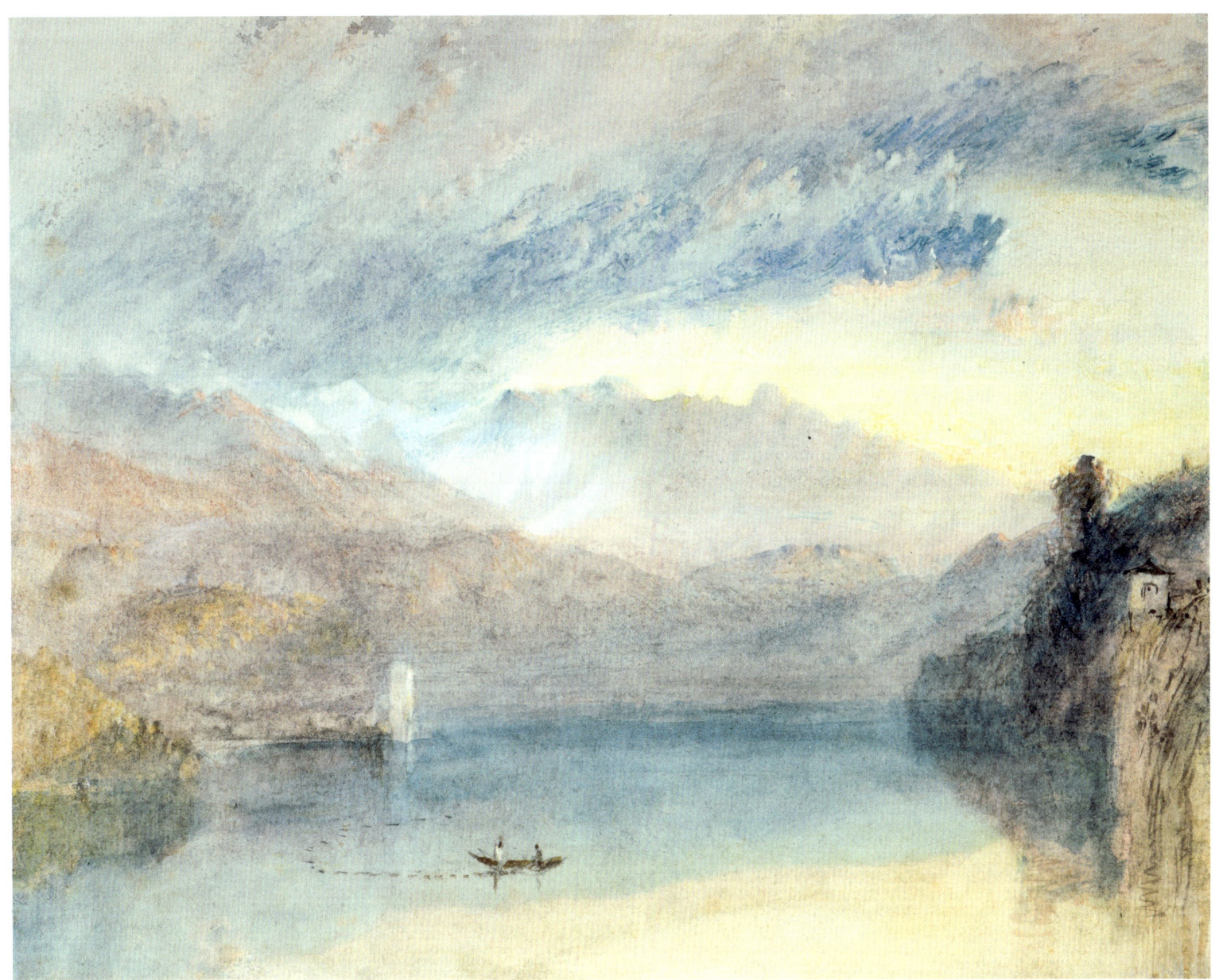

60. John Sell Cotman
Draining Mill, c. 1830-31
pencil, pen, brown ink and watercolour on paper
52.7 x 38.1 cm

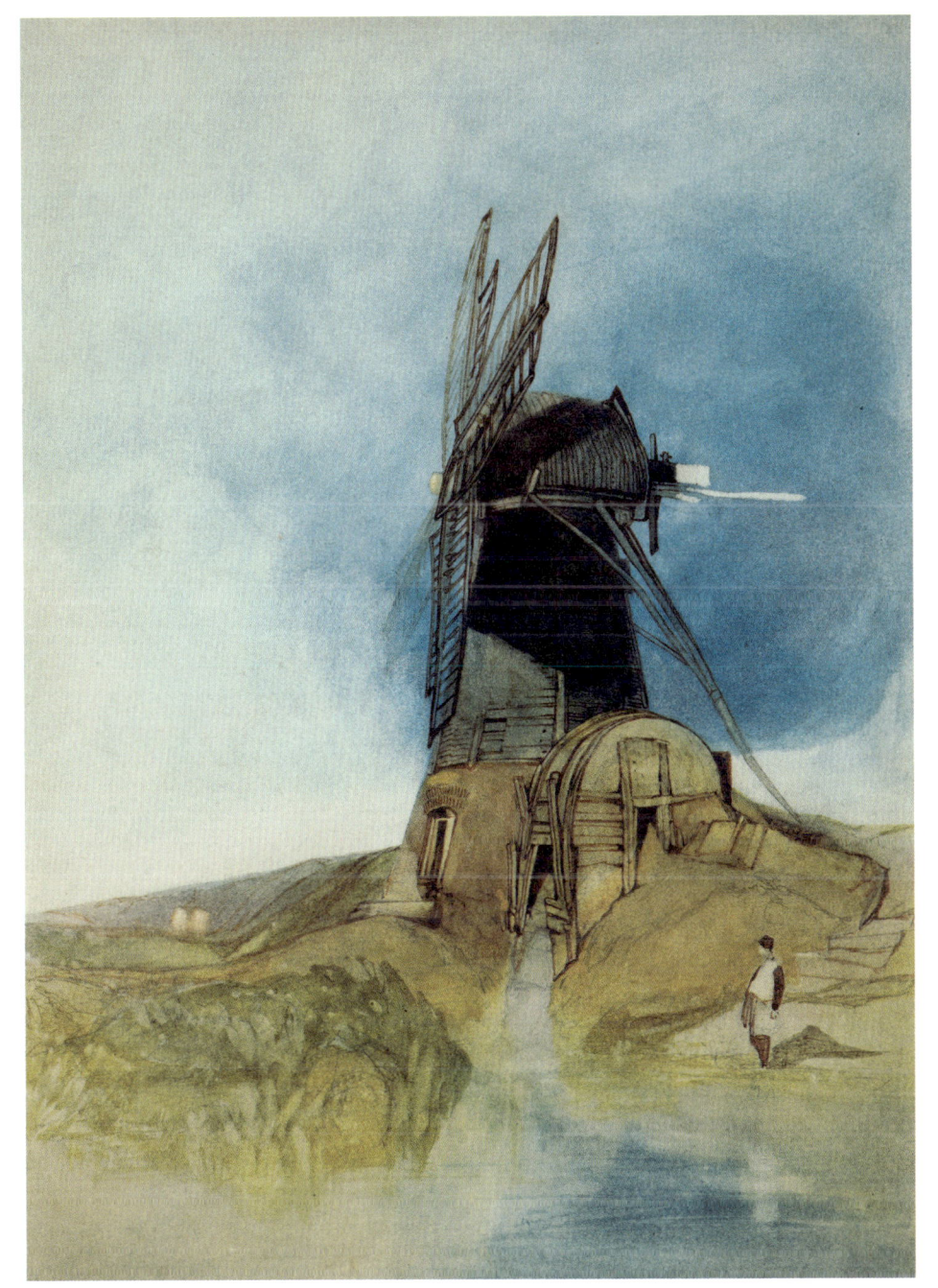

61. John Sell Cotman
Cader Idris, c. 1835
watercolour and gouache on paper
23.5 x 39 cm

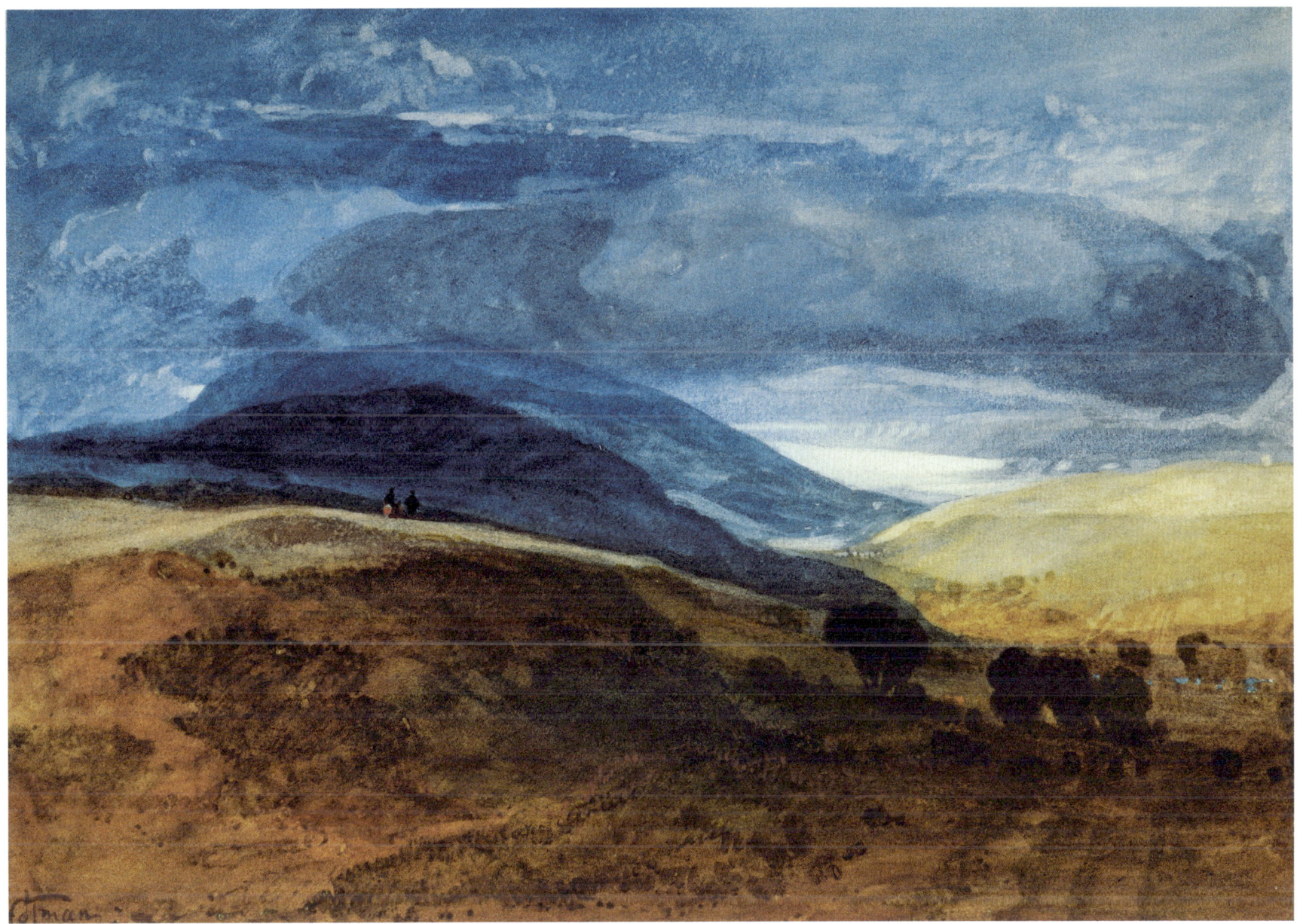

62. John Sell Cotman
A Figure in a Boat on a River, late 1830s
watercolour and gouache on paper
17.8 x 27.9 cm

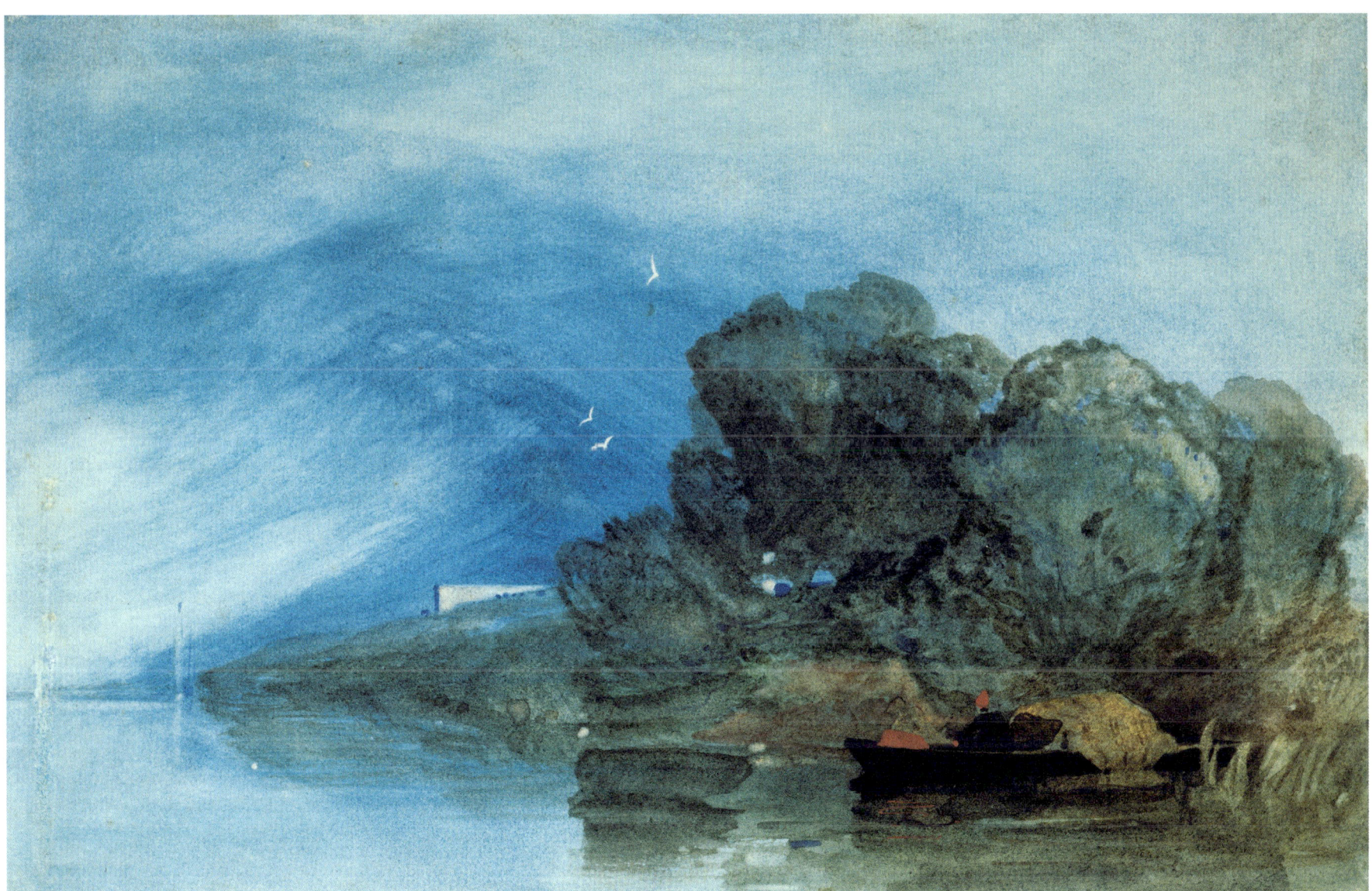

63. John Sell Cotman
An Open Landscape with a Figure in a Blue Coat, c. 1838-41
pencil, watercolour mixed with paste, and gouache on paper
20.3 x 28.8 cm

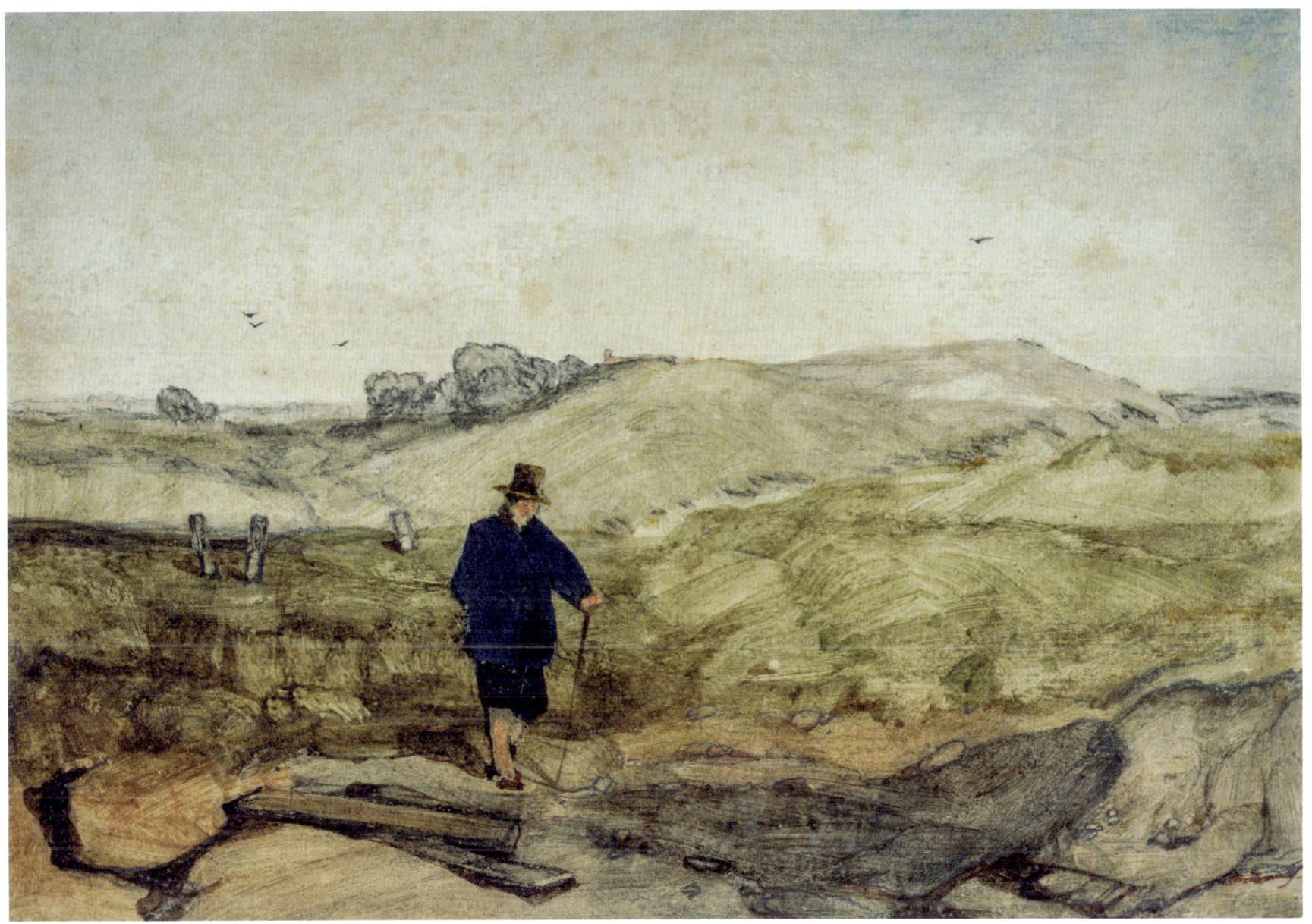

64. John Sell Cotman
A River Bank with Trees, c. 1840-42
pencil, watercolour mixed with paste, and gouache on paper
18.7 x 26.9 cm

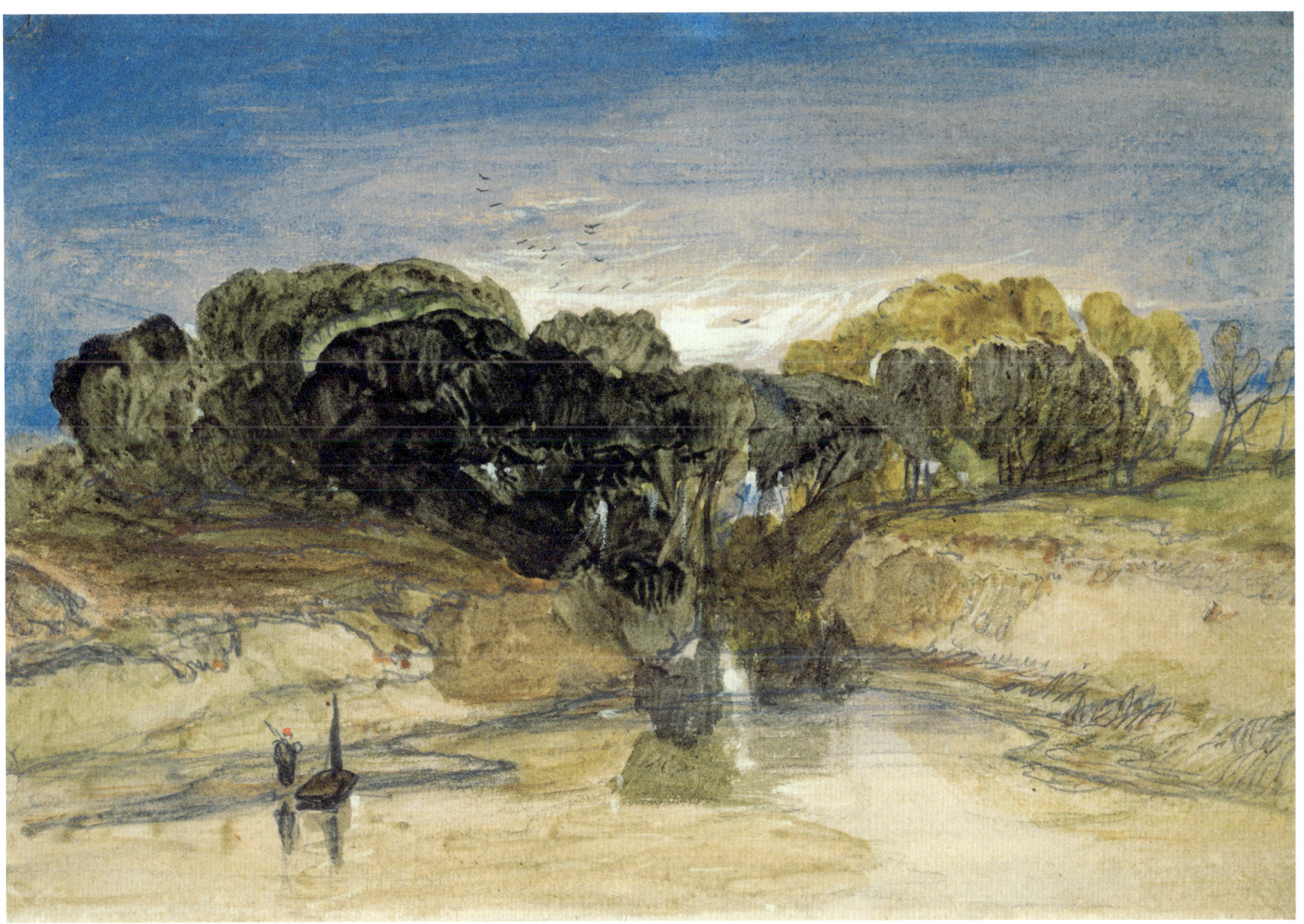

Index of artists

Half title: Detail of John Sell Cotman, A Figure in a Boat on a River (no. 62)
Pp. 2-3: Detail of J. M. W. Turner, Evening: Figures on a Beach (no. 31)

Published to accompany the exhibition
Impressions in Watercolour: Turner and his Contemporaries
at the Holburne Museum, Bath, 23 May–31 August 2025
and the Towner, Eastbourne, 22 October 2025–12 April 2026

This exhibition has been made possible by the provision of Government Indemnity. The Holburne Museum and the Towner would like to thank HM Government for providing Government Indemnity and the Department of Culture, Media and Sport and Arts Council England for arranging the indemnity.

Published by The Holburne Museum,
Great Pulteney Street, Bath BA2 4DB
in association with Pallas Athene (Publishers) Ltd,
2 Birch Close, London N19 5XD

© The Holburne Museum, Bath 2025
'Nature Raw or Cooked: Approaches to Sketching in British Landscape Watercolours' © Ian Warrell 2025
'Perception, taste and judgement: Sir Hickman Bacon and his watercolour collection' © Timothy Wilcox 2025
Design and layout by Alexander Fyjis-Walker
© Pallas Athene (Publishers) Ltd 2025
Photographs by Fisheye Images
Copy editing by Lisa Adams
With special thanks to David May and Philip Yarranton
at Empress London

All rights reserved

ISBN 978 1 84368 264 6

Printed in England by Empress London
on Munken Kristall Rough

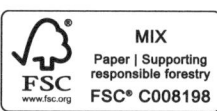